JACK THE
RIPPER'S
SECRET CONFESSION

Jack the Ripper's Secret Confession

Secret Confession

The Hidden Testimony of Britain's First Serial Killer

David Monaghan & Nigel Cawthorne

A Herman Graf Book
Skyhorse Publishing

Skyhorse Publishing books may be purchased in bulk at special discounts for sales promotion, corporate gifts, fund-raising, or educational purposes. Special editions can also be created to specifications. For details, contact the Special Sales Department, Skyhorse Publishing, 555 Eighth Avenue, Suite 903, New York, NY 10018 or info@skyhorsepublishing.com.

www.skyhorsepublishing.com

10 9 8 7 6 5 4 3 2 1

Library of Congress Cataloging-in-Publication Data

Monaghan, David.
  Jack the Ripper's secret confession : the hidden testimony of the world's first serial killer / David Monaghan and Nigel Cawthorne.
     p. cm.
  Includes bibliographical references.
  ISBN 978-1-60239-799-6
  1. Jack, the Ripper. 2. Serial murders--England--London--History--19th century. 3. Serial murderers--England--London--History--19th century.
4. Whitechapel (London, England)--History--19th century.
5. London (England)--History--19th century. I. Cawthorne, Nigel, 1951- II. Title.
  HV6535.G6L6565 2010
  364.152'32092--dc22
                                                            2009035656

Printed in the EU

CONTENTS

PREFACE

The pain a murderer inflicts can last 100 years. It stabs through generations like a knife through flesh.

I saw such pain in a Philadelphia hotel room in 2005. I was there to make a film about two lovely sisters, Beth and Brenda Pietzel. Their great-great-grandfather, Ben, had been one of the 200 or so victims murdered by Herman Webster Mudgett, a Chicago insurance scamster and corpse seller who went by the name H.H. Holmes. Mudgett was like Walter. His last two victims were girls, found naked. He had cashed in on his crimes with two book-length confessions before he was hanged in 1895. I did not know Beth and Brenda had not read Mudgett's frank confession of how he had tied Ben to a chair and burned him alive. I asked them to read aloud Mudgett's 110-year-old words about their great-great-grandfather. I watched horrified when the sisters flinched, then cried on camera over the suffering of a man they had loved, but who had been killed so long ago. I felt as if Mudgett had reached across a century and had me inflict wounds for his pleasure.

The tears of Brenda and Beth made me wary about writing a book about Jack the Ripper. His killings tore branches from many family trees. People alive today still suffer. Airing the words of a killer must be done with caution, for a murderer confesses for his own motives – and a sadist's impulse is to inflict pain. I had no intention of being the tool for Walter's sadism to inflict more pain on this generation. But now is the time to set the record straight.

A century of state bans and underground hype elevated Walter's 1888 sex memoir to near-mythical status. Literary types praised him as an erotic genius, a tell-it-straight liberal out to pop the hypocrisy of the corseted moralists of his age. By 2009, my home city's hippest magazine, *Time Out*, voted Walter to be London's most erotic writer, ahead of Shakespeare. I felt sick.

I had fed this hype. I'd first read *My Secret Life* to make a documentary about Walter. The film saluted him as a racy pornographer and a saucy cad. But after seeing the tears of the Pietzel sisters in Philadelphia, I reread the book. For the first time, I was able to read the bits still banned in Britain at the time I made my film. This time, I wasn't falling for Walter's tales of pleasure. The uncensored memoirs reeked of his victims' pain. My nerves jangled. The smug text chimed with what I knew about killers, particularly the jumbled chronology that marked Mudgett's 1894 confessions. I sat bolt upright when I got to the end of Volume 4, Chapter 1. At the heart of a memoir about lovemaking, the diarist dropped in the identity of a murdered corpse floating in the Thames. Why would a man want to boast of his connection to a corpse?

By then, I had been studying serial killers' confessions for years. I'd travelled to Florida to see the so-called 'Charm Killer' Glen Edward Rogers convicted. He had confessed to some heavy-metal kids that he had killed Nicole Simpson before going on a cross-country spree. I had gone to Cambodia to see Pol Pot's torture chamber, Tuol Sleng, a factory for false confessions. I wanted to get to the bottom of the tale told by a tortured soldier, of shooting British academic Malcolm Caldwell in the last days of the Khmer Rouge.

Gloucester builder Fred West had killed thirteen women and girls with his prostitute wife, Rose, before confessing in 1994. To make a film series, I had combed every word of his mammoth admission. The grubby handyman fancied himself a Lothario, was obsessed with sex and had a stab at a biography, too. And, like Walter, Fred West killed to cover up the fact that he had sex with children. West killed his teenage daughter Heather when she threatened to leave home and tell of his incest. West's first wife and childminder had been killed and cut up before they had a chance to expose his paedophilia. Here was a powerful motive for multiple violent murder, with no need to reference Masonic rituals or royal affairs, such distractions as which had given the unknown killer of Whitechapel with the veneer of sophistication. A killer of prostitutes would be more likely found by looking for the perverted, than by looking into a palace.

By chance, my life in London has dogged the Whitechapel killer's footsteps. I lived in the old Commercial Street police station building. It was where my investigations into Walter began and where many detectives on the trail of the Ripper were based in 1888. If those bobbies had got their hands on *My Secret Life*, with its ramblings of blood, rape and virgin-buying in 1888, Walter would have been considered a very likely candidate for arrest indeed.

David Monaghan
London 2009

INTRODUCTION

Locked in the closed cupboard at the British Library is an extraordinary work. Deposited there with a huge collection of pornography, it has lain virtually undisturbed for more than fifty years. It is called *My Secret Life* by Walter and, when various abridged and facsimile editions were produced, it was billed as a classic of Victorian pornography. Indeed, it was once referred to as the 'Koh-i-noor of English erotica'.

The original edition under lock and key in the British Library's Private Case – the nation's repository of obscene and other banned material – comes in eleven volumes. They were printed secretly in Amsterdam between 1888 and 1894. No one knows how many sets were produced. A preface to the index says: 'six copies only having been struck off and the type then broken up'. But this claim, like much in the book, is disingenuous. The author may have been trying to boost its rarity value, for at least twenty sets have been identified in private collections over the last century. However, it is generally assumed that the printer, thought to have been the Belgian publisher of erotica, Auguste Brancart, would have run off a few extra for himself. Charles Carrington, a British publisher of erotica working in Paris, produced a limited run of 200 copies of the first six chapters of the first volume under the title *The Dawn of Sensuality* in 1900. Carrington is thought to have been the go-between who carried the manuscript between Walter and Brancart. In 1902, he was selling the complete eleven-volume set (twelve volumes if you include the separate and extensive index added in around 1897 or 1898).

On the title page of the original it says: 'Not for publication.' The book was never meant for general distribution. Instead, the original volumes circulated among a close coterie of subscribers. Only five or perhaps seven sets are thought to survive today. They are now so rare and valuable that one set recently sold at auction for $47,839 – more than $5,000 above the reserve price.

Over the years, publication of the book has been repeatedly banned. In 1932, a New York publisher was arrested for publishing three volumes. It was only in 1966 that Grove Press in New York managed to publish *My Secret Life*, bound in two volumes. The following year a facsimile copy was produced by Pendulum Press of Atlanta, Georgia. However, when a printer in Bradford, named Arthur Dobson, tried to produce a British version of the Grove edition in 1969, he was sentenced to two years' imprisonment as a 'professional purveyor of filth' by Mr Justice Veale. The British had to put up with various abridged and bowdlerized versions until 2004, when the full eleven volumes became available on the internet – 110 years after they were completed and forty-four years after the *Lady Chatterley* trial. So what's all the fuss about?

It has to be said that the author, who identifies himself only as Walter, was a secretive chap. The introduction constructs the fiction that the book is the work of the 'oldest friend' of the man now purveying the work to the world, or at least to a handful of trusted friends. This was a common device employed by Victorian pornographers. This 'friend' had entrusted the manuscript to the author of the introduction. Three years after his friend died, the trustee came across the manuscript again and read it. 'The more I read it, the more marvellous it seemed,' he wrote. But still he did not know what to do with it.

At length I came to the conclusion, knowing his idiosyncrasy well, that his fear was only lest any one should know who the writer was; and feeling that it would be sinful to destroy such a history, I copied the manuscript and destroyed the original. He died relationless. No one now can trace the author; no names are mentioned in the book, though they were given freely in the margin of his manuscript, and I alone know to whom the initials refer. If I have done harm in printing it, I have done none to him, have indeed only carried out his evident intention, and given to a few a secret history, which bears the impress of truth on every page, a contribution to psychology.

There follow two prefaces, purportedly written by the 'friend', that is, the author of the book itself. In the first, he explains how and why he has covered his tracks.

I have one fear about publicity, it is that of having done a few things by curiosity and impulse (temporary aberrations) which even professed libertines may cry fie on. There are plenty who will cry fie who have done all and worse than I have and habitually, but crying out at the sins of others was always a way of hiding one's own iniquity. Yet from that cause perhaps no mortal eye but mine will see this history.

The Christian names of the servants mentioned are generally the true ones, the other names mostly false, tho phonetically resembling the true ones. Initials nearly always the true ones. In most cases the women they represent are dead or lost to me. Streets and baudy houses named are nearly always correct. Most of the houses named are now closed or pulled down; but any middle-aged man about town would recognize them. Where a road, house, room, or garden is described, the description is exactly true, even to the situation of a tree, chair, bed, sofa, pisspot. The district is sometimes given wrongly; but it matters little whether Brompton be substituted for Hackney, or Camden Town for

Walworth. Where however, owing to the incidents, it is needful, the places of amusement are given correctly. The Tower, and Argyle rooms, for example. All this is done to prevent giving pain to some, perhaps still living, for I have no malice to gratify.

In the second preface he debates whether, having reread the manuscript some years after its competition, he would burn it or print it. He concludes: 'Shall it be burnt or printed? How many years have passed in this indecision? Why fear? It is for others good and not my own if preserved.'

By Volume 3, he drops all pretence, writing: 'I have read through the two volumes in print.' As the work then continues for another eight volumes, the author can scarcely be dead. 'These details also gave studies of character, and specially of my own character, and as I now read the narratives in print after the lapse of so many years they seem to me to be needed to explain myself, even to myself.'

Over the years, there has been a great deal of speculation about the identity of Walter. Many theories have been floated, but Walter has succeeded in keeping the literary detectives guessing. Gordon Grimley, the editor of an abridged edition published in Britain in 1972, noted that the author had constructed a series of defences and screens to conceal forever his true identity.

In this he never tripped nor faltered; even with the appropriate maps of the time at one's side it is impossible to re-create even one of his shorter journeys to or from any of his successive London homes. The seeker finds himself left in the middle of the street with, as it were, a Victorian fog descending and Walter's cab disappearing around the corner.

He is as elusive as Jack the Ripper.

The author succeeds in hiding his identity in over a million words of what has been described as the 'the most famous and the longest sexual autobiography written in the nineteenth century'. This is a remarkable achievement.

The critic Mara Mirsky, writing about the Wordsworth Editions abridged version published in 1995, described *My Secret Life* as 'a parade of genitalia, pornographic writing of the most explicit and lascivious kind, often banal and repetitive'. However, that is to miss the point.

What had been left out of the abridged version was the author's cruel and criminal activities. The man reveals himself to be a calculating sadist with an uncontrollable temper. He was paranoid about being blackmailed. The book is full of the most violent images. He compares a woman's vulva to 'a split gaping like a dog with its throat cut'. A keen hunter, he constantly makes connections between sex and blood sports.

'Once I recollect shooting at a rabbit with my prick out of my trowsers,' he writes. He would wear his hunting clothes when he was trawling streets for sex.

Walter was obsessed with prostitutes – or gay women, in the parlance of the time. He boasted all manner of sexual perversion and a vast range of fetishes, from the sight of blood to child rape. Yes, among other things, Walter was a paedophile. The prosecution in the 1969 obscenity trial described Walter's repeated rape of a ten-year-old ballet girl from Vauxhall Gardens as 'the most evil thing you have ever read'.

These are excellent reasons for Walter wanting to hide his identity. But there is more. From the descriptions of the women in the book, it is quite possible to identify some of the victims of Jack the Ripper and the victims of the Thames Torso Murders that took place in the environs of the river. Indeed, Walter hazards a guess that a female torso found floating in the Thames is a prostitute who had betrayed him. At the time, many people thought that Jack the Ripper was responsible for the Thames Torso Murders, as the victims – other women of the street – were dismembered in a similarly vicious fashion. However, London was wracked with panic over Jack, so the police were insistent that he had stopped after just five murders – small beer for a serial killer these days. It is interesting to note that while nearly every woman in *My Secret Life* is a prostitute and had good reason to fear Jack the Ripper, he is never mentioned by them in their conversations. At the time, they would have talked of little else.

So why would a murderer paranoid about being black-mailed write about his victims? Plainly, Walter was showing off. Although the author of *My Secret Life* did not dare con-fess openly – or even identify himself – while he was still alive, he was, in fact, boasting that he was the world's first serial killer. The small coterie who bought his book were men of a similar taste. They were, in days long before the Internet, a paedophile ring, if you will, but he did not kill the young girls for whom he had a particular craving. With the exception of his last victim, Mary Jane Kelly, who was twenty-five, Jack the Ripper's victims were all in their mid-forties. It was not the young girls he craved that he killed, but the older women who procured the children for him. There was little danger that the children were going to blackmail him. The danger came from the older women who provided them. Killing them not only rid himself of a danger, he was also providing a valuable service for his readers as they would have used the same panders.

It is clear from the book that Walter had little feeling for other people. The few men he mentioned were up to the same thing as he is. His wife was someone to be tricked, abused and avoided. Like most middle-class men of his day, he had little feeling for the working class at all. The lower orders were people to be despised. He did not mind short-changing any of the prostitutes he went with. He did not mind threatening them and positively enjoyed hurting them. To him they were just a collection of orifices. They were, to use his own word, cunts.

Perhaps Walter knew, over a century after his death, that researchers would come across this testimony deep inside the bowels of the British Library, unscramble his coded confession and at last identify the real Jack the Ripper and give him the recognition he long craved.

1

A Maniac on the Loose

As Constable John Neil was walking down Bucks-row,
Thomas-street, Whitechapel, about a quarter to four
o'clock this morning, he discovered a woman between
thirty-five and forty years of age lying at the side of the
street with her throat cut right open from ear to ear, the
instrument with which the deed was done tracing the
throat from left to right. The wound was an inch wide,
and blood was flowing profusely. She was immediately
conveyed to the Whitechapel mortuary, when it was
found that besides the wound in the throat the lower
part of the abdomen was completely ripped open, with
the bowels protruding. The wound extends nearly to her
breast and must have been effected with a large knife. As
the corpse lies in the mortuary it presents a ghastly sight.

That was the gruesome story reported by the *Pall Mall Gazette*
in its fourth edition on Friday, 31 August 1888 under the
headline: 'Horrible Murder in East London'.

Although the murder had taken place only hours before,
that evening's paper reported more grisly details. The woman's
hands were bruised, showing that she had been involved in a
ferocious struggle for her life. The impression of a ring was
left on one of the deceased's fingers. She had once been married, although there was nothing to show that the ring had
been wrenched from her during the struggle. Some of her front

teeth were missing and her face was bruised and discoloured. Her clothes were torn and cut in several places, again bearing testimony to the ferocity of the attack. By the time the body reached the mortuary at half-past four in the morning, it was still quite warm so she had been murdered not long before she was found. It was not much to go on.

'The affair up to the present is enveloped in complete mystery, and the police have as yet no evidence to trace the perpetrators of the horrible deed,' said the paper.

The *Pall Mall Gazette* was no scandal sheet. It was founded as a daily evening paper in 1865. For one penny, it aimed to provide a digest of the news that had appeared in the morning papers, as well as substantial articles on the political and social questions of the day. Originally a supporter of the Conservative Party, it changed hands in 1880 and aligned itself with the Liberals. The great crusading journalist William Thomas Stead took over as editor in 1883 and contributors included George Bernard Shaw, Anthony Trollope, Frederick Engels, Oscar Wilde, Robert Louis Stevenson, John Ruskin, Rudyard Kipling and H.G. Wells.

The offices were at 2 Northumberland Street, next to the newly built Charing Cross railway station, the London terminal of the South Eastern Railway company. 'There may have been less convenient, dark and dirtier daily paper offices in London than our building, but I have never heard of them,' wrote *PMG* journalist John William Robertson Scott, recalling the time the machine room flooded before the Victoria Embankment was built. For Stead, journalism was a moral crusade and the journalist the 'Sandalphon of humanity' – Sandalphon was an archangel, alternately the 'Angel of Glory' or the 'Angel of Prayer', according to the poet Longfellow. Stead was the pioneer of modern investigative journalism and introduced the newspaper interview as a literary form.

Stead was most famous for his campaign against child prostitution in a series of articles called 'The Maiden Tribute of Modern Babylon'. These resulted in both Stead being jailed for three months and the passing of the Criminal Law Amendment

Act of 1885, which raised the age of consent for girls from thirteen to sixteen years. An amendment to the bill also outlawed acts of 'gross indecency' between males whether in 'public or private'. Oscar Wilde fell foul of this ten years later.

Something of Stead's character, it was said, could be seen in his handwriting. 'There was such grit, vigour and industry in it that his nibs have had but a short life,' said Scott. Stead was one of the first people to use a fountain pen. His character also showed in his dress. He was once seen in the office in a shirt 'tied with a tassel at the neck, that looked like a pyjama jacket'. However, his vigour had a downside.

'Few editions got out on time if Stead was in the office,' said Scott. 'But the PMG, in spite of coming out late, and in spite of its worn type and antiquated machines, was read and quoted.'

However, its glory days were gone. After the Bloody Sunday riot of 13 November 1887, where the police and troops violently suppressed a socialist rally in Trafalgar Square, Stead and the *Gazette* had lent support to the demonstrators and the paper's circulation was on the decline. Stead showed little interest in the finances of publishing.

'The business side was a meagre, minor department somewhere upstairs, for which there was now and then heard a blast over the trains we missed,' said Scott.

The newspaper's owner, Henry Yates Thompson, was not best pleased. The decline in circulation was hitting him in the pocket and, on 24 September 1888, Stead had to accept a pay cut from £1,200 to £1,000 a year. But at the time of the 'Horrible Murder in East London', Stead was still riding high, having recently returned from Russia where he had interviewed the tsar and Leo Tolstoy.

The day after the first murder, Stead published a follow-up story naming the victim. The Saturday paper carried the headline: 'The Terrible Murder in Whitechapel – Identification of the Deceased'. The story read:

The woman who was murdered under circumstances of a most revolting character in Bucks-row, Whitechapel,

> *yesterday morning, has been identified as Mary Ann, or Polly, Nichols, by several of the women with whom the deceased lived in a common lodging-house at 18 Trawl-street, Spitalfields. Women from that place were fetched, and they identified the deceased as 'Polly', who had shared a room with three other women in the place on the usual terms of such houses – nightly payment of 4d. [2p] each, each woman having a separate bed. The deceased had lodged in the house only for about three weeks. Nothing more was known of her but that when she presented herself for her lodging on Thursday night she was turned away by the deputy because she had not the money. She was then the worse for drink, but not drunk, and turned away laughing, saying 'I'll soon get my "doss" money; see what a jolly bonnet I've got now.' She was wearing a bonnet which she had not been seen with before, and left the lodging-house door.'*

Where had she got the bonnet? She did not have enough money for a bed for the night in a dosshouse, so it seems likely that a man had given it to her.

The answer may lie in the volumes of *My Secret Life*. Walter would buy bonnets for his paramours. 'If you'll let me fuck you I'll make your dress up, and give you a bonnet and parasol,' he told a girl he called Sarah, whom he had met for the first time five days before. Walter also gave a bonnet and a parasol to Sarah's 'niece' Lizzie – a virgin she procured for him – who was then involved in a threesome.

'I'll give you a bonnet, and we will go to Vauxhall – don't let your sister know,' said Walter, when seducing Ester, the sister of Matilda, whom he had raped earlier. 'It's my fate to have sisters,' lamented Walter.

Buying a bonnet for a young girl named Louise caused problems with Walter's regular mistress, Camille, who had procured Louise for him. Again, Walter thought they were sisters, although Camille denied it.

But the bonnets had deeper sexual significance for Walter. In Switzerland, he was staying in a hotel when he heard a young woman's laugh. He went to the keyhole and looked through it to see a naked eighteen-year-old American woman. After examining her from all sides, he had a siesta.

> *When I looked again, there was the young lady sitting still naked at the table examining a bonnet. She put the bonnet on, and went to a looking glass, and I had the pleasure for the second time in my life as well as I can recollect, of seeing a naked woman with a bonnet on. It started a letch in me which I satisfied at a future day – and the sight now made my cock stand suddenly. It had not done so before at seeing the slim American lass naked.*

After PC Neil discovered the body of Mary Ann Nichols in Buck's Row, close by a number of slaughterhouses, Dr Rees Ralph Llewellyn, the medical officer for the East and East Central districts, arrived from his surgery at 152 Whitechapel Road. He issued a statement, saying that he had been called to Buck's Row at about five minutes to four by PC Thane, who said a woman had been murdered. The *Pall Mall Gazette* continued:

> *He found the deceased lying on the ground in front of the stable-yard door. She was lying on her back, with her legs out straight, as though she had been laid down. Police-constable Neil told him that the body had not been touched. The throat was cut from ear to ear and the woman was quite dead. The extremities of the body were still warm, showing that death had not long ensued. There was a very small pool of blood on the pathway, which had trickled from the wound in the throat, not more than half a pint at the outside. This fact, and the way in which the deceased was lying, made him think at the time that it was at least probable*

> *that the murder was committed elsewhere, and the*
> *body conveyed to Buck's-row.*

This was later discounted. The blood had, in fact, been
absorbed by her clothing.

> *At half-past five he was summoned to the mortuary*
> *by the police, and was astonished at finding the other*
> *wounds. He had seen many horrible cases, but never*
> *such a brutal affair as this. There is a gash under the*
> *left ear reaching nearly to the centre of the throat, and*
> *another cut, apparently starting from the right ear. The*
> *neck is severed back to the vertebra, which is also slightly*
> *injured. The abdominal wounds are extraordinary for*
> *their length and the severity with which they have been*
> *inflicted. One cut extends from the base of the abdomen*
> *to the breast bone. Deceased's clothes were loose, and*
> *the wounds could have been inflicted while she was*
> *dressed.*

On Monday, 3 September 1888, the *Pall Mall Gazette* continued the story under the headline: 'The Brutal Murder in
Whitechapel – What the Police Think About the Crime'.

> *The murder committed in the early hours of Friday*
> *morning of Mary Ann Nichols has so many points of*
> *similarity with the murders of the two other women*
> *in the same neighbourhood – one, Martha Turner, as*
> *recently as August 7, and the other less than twelve*
> *months previously – that the police admit their belief*
> *that the three crimes are the work of one individual.*
> *All three women were of the same class, and each of*
> *them was so poor that robbery could have formed no*
> *motive for the crime. The three murders were com-*
> *mitted within a distance of two hundred yards of each*
> *other. The husband visited the mortuary on Saturday*
> *and on viewing the corpse, identified it as that of his*

wife, from whom he had been separated eight years.
He stated that she was nearly forty years of age. The
husband, who was greatly affected, exclaimed on rec-
ognizing the body: 'I forgive you, as you are, for what
you have been to me.'

The first of the victims the *PMG* referred to was forty-five-year-old Emma Elizabeth Smith. She had been attacked on 3 April, the night of Easter bank holiday, immediately before Stead's trip to Russia. A resident of a lodging house at 18 George Street, Spitalfields, she was attacked in Osborn Street. However, she was almost certainly not a Ripper victim. She had been raped and robbed in the early hours, but had made it back to her lodging house where she told the deputy keeper, Mary Russell, that she had been attacked by at least three youths, the youngest no older than eighteen. Friends took her to the London Hospital where she fell into a coma and died the next day at 9 a.m. A post-mortem revealed that a blunt object had been inserted into her vagina, rupturing her peritoneum. The police assumed she had been attacked by members of a local Old Nichol gang, but no one was arrested. However, the case was filed alongside the 'Whitechapel Murders' and in September 1888 the press began describing her as the Ripper's first victim. She did share some similarities to other victims. According to Walter Dew, a CID officer attached to H Division – or the Whitechapel Division – of the Metropolitan Police: 'There was something about Emma Smith which suggested that there had been a time when the comforts of life had not been denied her. There was a touch of culture in her speech, unusual in her class.'

Martha Turner, who was murdered on 7 August, was more commonly known as Martha Tabram. She was born Martha White in Southwark in 1849. Her parents separated when she was sixteen and her father died soon after. On Christmas Day 1869, she married Henry Samuel Tabram, the foreman at a furniture factory, at Trinity Church in St Mary's Parish, Newington. They had two sons, but in 1875 Henry left due to her heavy drinking. However, he continued to support her until she moved in with Henry Turner, a carpenter. She continued her drinking and would stay out late, if not all night.

By 1888, Turner was out of regular employment and was scraping a living hawking cheap trinkets, pins, needles and menthol cones. The couple lodged at 4 Star Place, Commercial Road. A few weeks before the murder, they were behind with the rent and moved out. Turner found accommodation in the Victoria working men's home on Commercial Street. Martha's last known address was 19 George Street, Spitalfields. By then she was supplementing her income with prostitution.

On bank holiday Monday, 6 August, she went drinking with Mary Ann Connelly, who was known as 'Pearly Poll'. They picked up two soldiers. According to Pearly Poll, they were guardsmen – a corporal and a private. They were seen drinking with them in several pubs, including the Two Brewers and the White Swan on Whitechapel High Street. At 11.45 p.m., they split up. Pearly Poll took her corporal into Angel Alley to have intercourse with him against a wall; Emma (as Poll called Martha) and the private went into George Yard, now Gunthorpe Street, presumably for the same purpose.

At 2 a.m., PC Thomas Barrett saw a young Grenadier Guard in Wentworth Street, the north end of George Yard. When PC Barrett asked him why he was there, the guardsman said that he was waiting for a chum who went off with a girl. At 3.30 a.m., licensed cab driver Alfred Crow returned to his lodgings in George Yard Buildings, a tenement converted from an old weaving factory on the north-east side of George Yard. He noticed what he thought was a tramp sleeping on the first-floor landing. This was not an uncommon occurrence, so he went on to bed.

At 4.45 a.m., the light was improving when John Reeves, another tenant of George Yard Buildings, came downstairs and noticed the body on the first floor. But he also noticed that it was lying in a pool of blood. Her legs were open as if she had just had sexual intercourse. He went off to find a policeman, and returned with PC Barrett. Dr Timothy Killeen, who had a surgery at 68 Brick Lane, was called. He arrived at 5.30 a.m. and estimated that death had occurred some two hours earlier.

Dr Killeen also carried out the post-mortem. He counted thirty-nine stab wounds in all and noted that the breasts, belly and genitals were the principal targets, although there were nine stab wounds to the throat, which would have prevented her crying out. One cut to the lower part of her body was three inches long and one inch deep. Killeen also noted that all but one had been made with an ordinary penknife. The exception was a wound on the sternum which, he thought, had been made with a dagger or a bayonet.

'The wound over the heart was alone sufficient to kill,' said the *Illustrated Police News* of 18 August 1888, 'and death must have occurred as soon as that was inflicted. Unless the perpetrator was a madman, or suffering to an unusual extent from drink delirium, no tangible explanation can be given of the reason for inflicting the other thirty-eight injuries, some of which almost seem as if they were due to thrusts and cuts from a penknife.'

It is interesting to note that, as a young man, Walter was destined for the army, but when his godfather died, leaving him an inheritance, he gave up his commission. He could not touch the money until he was twenty-one, so he took a job in the 'W--- Office'. Like most men in Victorian England, Walter carried a penknife. But unlike most men, Walter's knife was firmly linked to sex. It was a vital tool in his voyeurism. At a railway station in the south of France, he used his penknife to open a peephole so he could watch women relieving themselves in the adjoining compartment. He used it to bore holes through doors to see his aunt and cousins undressing. Hiding under the bed when his lover's sister called unexpectedly, he used his penknife to cut a slit in the valance so he could watch when the sister undressed, a sight that moved him to masturbate twice. While at a family get-together, he and his cousin Fred used a knife to cut a slit in wallpaper that had been pasted over cracked boards so they could watch his young cousins bathing. But Walter expressed qualms:

> *Had it been servants, I should have been delighted at a peep; but to rip a hole to spy on young ladies, and one of those his sister, revolted me. 'Damn it Fred, it's not the thing, one is your own sister.' 'Pough! you have seen their cunts.' . . . 'Ah! those were children.' 'Well ** and ** are only larger, and have hair on their cunts, and you need not look.'*

In the end, of course, Walter could not resist ogling.

Walter also carried a gimlet for making holes to peep through. When he checked into a hotel, he waited to see which rooms were occupied by young women or young married couples and tried to get a room next to theirs. If there was no communicating door he could make a peephole in, he would come up with some objection and refuse it. In *My Secret Life* Walter recorded using his gimlet this way dozens of times. 'Thus I got many opportunities, and had some very pleasant, and at times, chastely voluptuous sights.' He even called his penis a 'piercer' – a term he used eight times in *My Secret Life*.

A gimlet is a narrow, sharp tool that could have easily been used to kill Martha Tabram. Indeed, it had only been assumed that the fatal wound in Martha Tabram's chest had been caused by a bayonet because she had been seen with a soldier. A handwritten note in the Home Office files says, 'some of the wounds are so narrow that a bayonet was first suspected as the weapon. But bayonet wounds are quite unmistakable'. This casts doubt on the idea that she was killed using a bayonet.

A curious witness on the streets of Whitechapel the night Martha Tabram was killed was the disgraced MP, Colonel Francis Hughes-Hallett. In 1887, he had been caught committing adultery with his twenty-two-year-old stepdaughter, from whom he had also extorted £5,000. He was shunned by his parliamentary colleagues and hounded by the press, especially the *Pall Mall Gazette* – the previous year Stead had trashed the career of Sir Charles Wentworth Dilke, whom many had tipped as a future prime minister, after he was cited in a sensational divorce scandal. Hughes-Hallett was also an amateur actor and handled press relations for Buffalo Bill. Walter hung out in the Café Europe, the actor's haunt in the Haymarket. They may also have run across each other at the United Service Club where Hughes-Hallett was a member. Hughes-Hallett was also a special investigator for the army.

Soon after the murder, Hughes-Hallett headed for America. He arrived in New York on 30 September 1888, the night the Ripper is thought to have claimed his third and fourth victims. Interest was at fever pitch and on 6 October he told the American press that the 'perpetrator of these atrocities is a West End man, a gentleman, a person of wealth and culture perhaps, but certainly of intellectual qualities, finesse and keen discrimination'. Then he told a remarkable story. On the night of Martha Tabram's murder, he said he was 'convinced that my man had left his club . . . and disguised himself for his nocturnal revel'. Hughes-Hallett also left his club, went home, changed out of his evening dress and donned a disguise, then took a cab to the East End, arriving at George Yard soon after Martha Tabram was murdered.

'This brings one to my theory of who the thug is,' said Hughes-Hallett. 'I believe him to be an army doctor retired, perhaps, or a medical student, or a gentleman who has read medicine as amusement, or as a part of a liberal education. He is a man of the world, a gentleman, a club man, perhaps, who pursues his customary action during the day, and at night sallies out with his knife and dagger to feast a homicidal mania bred in him by disease, most likely contracted from some of the unfortunate women to whom he confines his horrible revenge. By the organs he has cut out and carried away, he proves himself a sexual pervert, that is the victim of a brain bias superinduced by the disease alluded to, and driving him to frenzy at stated intervals.'

From *My Secret Life* we know that Walter regularly suffered from sexually transmitted diseases that he caught from prostitutes. He had his penis pierced with a metal rod to cure his first dose of venereal disease, which he got from a prostitute as a teenager.

'My clap brought on a stricture,' he wrote, 'obliging me to have a bougie passed every other day to stretch the pipe often, and causing me to piss clots of gruelly blood, about an hour afterwards. I dared not fuck, but once frigged, and it brought on the inflammatory stage again. At length I got better, but with a gleet which wetted the tail of my shirt through daily . . .'

The curious thing about Hughes-Hallett's story is how did he know to go out that day? The murder of Emma Smith had taken place four months before. The police thought it was a gangland killing. There was no indication that a maniac was on the loose. Did he know the Ripper, or at least have his suspicions? Was the suspect a member of his own club whom he had seen leaving early that evening? Walter, with his military connections, was almost certainly a member of the United Services Club. One night, he was on his way to his club and mentions walking 'down to the colonnade of the Opera House'. The United Service was at 116–17 Pall Mall, on the corner of Waterloo Place, across the road from the colonnade of Her Majesty's Opera House, until it was razed in 1893.

At the inquest, the deputy coroner George Collier concluded that the murder of Martha Tabram was 'one of the most brutal [crimes] that had occurred for some years . . . almost beyond belief . . . the person who had inflicted such injuries could have been nothing less than a fiend'.

PC Barrett was taken to the Tower of London to attend an identity parade of Grenadier Guards. The man he picked out had an alibi. Two days after the murder, Pearly Poll turned up at Commercial Street police station. She, too, was taken to the Tower, but could not identify anyone there. However, she disclosed that the men she and Martha had been with on the bank holiday had had white bands around their caps, indicating that they were Coldstream Guards. Another identity parade was set up at the Wellington Barrack in Birdcage Walk.

This time she picked out two men. Both had unshakeable alibis.

It was the one wound made by what could have been a bayonet that led the police to believe that Martha's murderer had been a soldier – probably the guardsman she had been with that evening. However, they were last seen together at 11.45 p.m. At 1.50 a.m., a tenant of George Yard Buildings, Mary Mahoney, had returned. When she climbed the stairs to her flat there was no one on the landing. The body had been there at 3.30 a.m., around Dr Killeen's estimated time of death. Martha would have had plenty of time to bid adieu to her guardsman and pick up another client, or two.

On the night Mary Ann Nichols died, she bumped into her roommate at Thrawl Street, the elderly Ellen Holland, who knew her only as Polly and had not seen her for a week. Mrs Holland gathered that Polly had been staying at the White House, a common lodging house in Flower and Dean Street, one block from Thrawl Street, where men and women could sleep together. Seeing that Polly was drunk, Mrs Holland begged her to come back to Thrawl Street with her. 'I have had my lodging money three times today and I have spent it,' she said. 'It won't be long before I'll be back.' As they talked, St Mary's clock struck 2.30 a.m. They were at the corner of Osborn Street and Whitechapel. At that time, the services of a destitute prostitute like Mary Ann Nichols could be bought for tuppence or thruppence – the price of a large glass of gin. The doss was fourpence, so Mary would need to find two clients. Mrs Holland then watched as her friend Polly staggered eastwards up Whitechapel Road to her death.

Because of the murders of Emma Elizabeth Smith and Martha Tabram – and other violent assaults on women – Whitechapel was heavily patrolled the night Mary Ann Nichols died. Hundreds of policemen were on the streets each night. PC Neil passed down Buck's Row every thirty minutes. His beat had taken him far from the scene of the crime.

'The farthest I had been that night was just through the Whitechapel Road and up Baker's Row,' PC Neil told the inquest. 'I was never far from the spot.'

Whitechapel Road ran parallel to Buck's Row, one block south, while Baker's Row ran north and south at the western end of Buck's Row. Nor was he the only copper on the beat. PC John Thain passed down Buck's Row on his beat around 3.15 a.m. and reported seeing nothing unusual. Around the same time, Sergeant Kerby also passed down Buck's Row and he, too, saw nothing untoward.

Other people were about at that time in the morning. Before PC Neil discovered the body, carman – the driver of a streetcar or horse-drawn carriage – Charles Cross was walking down Buck's Row in the direction of Baker's Row on his way to work. On the south side, outside the gates of a stable yard, he saw what he took to be a tarpaulin. He was halfway across the street when he realized that he was mistaken. It was then that he heard footsteps. Another carman, named Robert Paul, was coming down the street in the same direction.

'Come look over here,' said Cross. 'There's a woman lying on the pavement.'

They crossed the road to examine her. In the gloom they could see that her skirt was raised almost to her waist, but not the gash across her throat that had almost severed her head.

'I believe she is dead,' said Cross.

He touched her face, which was still warm. Paul crouched down and touched her breast.

'I think she's breathing,' he said, 'but very little if she is.'

Paul suggested that they prop her up, but Cross would not touch her beyond helping to pull her skirts down. They were both late for work and agreed they would head off and report what they had found to the first policeman they saw. They had only turned the corner into Baker's Row and reached the first junction with Hanbury and Old Montague Street when they met PC Jonas Mizen. They told him that they had seen a woman lying in Buck's Row.

'She looks to me to be either dead or drunk,' Cross said, 'but for my part I think she is dead.'

By that time, PC Neil had found the body of Mary Ann Nichols. It was still warm and her new straw bonnet trimmed with black velvet lay beside the mutilated corpse. PC Thain turned up and was sent to fetch Dr Llewellyn. Meanwhile, PC Mizen turned up and was sent to fetch an ambulance and further assistance from Bethnal Green Police Station. Dr Llewellyn arrived soon after and pronounced that the woman was dead 'but a few minutes'.

Across the street, the nightwatchmen at Schneider's tar factory and Browne & Eagle's wool warehouse had heard nothing, nor had the keeper at the board school immediately to the west of the stable yard. Mrs Emma Green, a widow who lived at New Cottage, Buck's Row, adjoining the stable yard to the east, heard nothing until she was aroused by the police knocking on her door at four in the morning. Mrs Purkis, who lived across the street, had not been able to sleep that night. Consequently, her husband Walter had slept only fitfully. They, too, only learned of the murder from the police.

In nearby Winthrop Street, three slaughtermen working at Harrison, Barber & Co. Ltd and a watchman guarding a sewage works for the Whitechapel District Board of Works could shed no light on the incident. The *Pall Mall Gazette* reported:

> *Several persons living in Brady-street state that early in the morning they heard screams, but this is by no means an uncommon incident in the neighbourhood; and with one exception nobody seems to have paid any particular attention to what was probably the death struggle of an unfortunate woman. The exception was a Mrs Colville, who lives only a short distance from the foot of Buck's-row. She says she was awakened in the morning by a woman screaming "Murder! police!" five or six times. The voice faded away as though the woman was going in the direction of Buck's-row, and all was quiet. She only heard the steps of one person.*

The *Evening News* of 1 September also reported Mrs Cowell's account, but pointed out that if the killer had cut Mary Ann Nichols' throat at the onset of the attack she could not have cried out. This led to the theory that she had been murdered in Brady Street, then carried or dragged into Buck's Row. No evidence was found to support this.

According to the *Evening News*:

> *Shortly after midday some men who were searching the pavement in Buck's-row above the gateway found two spots of blood in the roadway. They were nine feet away from the gate, and they might have dropped from the hands or clothing of the murderer as he fled away.*

This was the only clue the Ripper left. Despite the number of policemen in the area, sleepless local residents, nightwatchmen, night workers and people on their way to work, no one had seen the bloody assassin escaping. He vanished, apparently, into thin air.

'He came, no one knew whence and departed, no one knew whither,' said Detective Constable Dew. This is an enduring mystery.

'Someone, somewhere, shared Jack the Ripper's guilty secret,' said Dew. 'Of this I am tolerably certain. The man lived somewhere. Each time there was a murder, he must have returned home in the early hours of the morning. His clothing must have been besplattered with blood. These facts alone ought to have been sufficient to arouse suspicion, and to cause a statement to the police. Suspicion, I have no doubt, was aroused, but that statement to the police was never made.'

This posed another puzzling question.

'Why should anyone seek to shield such a monster?' asked Dew.

The killer – a 'sexual maniac' according to Dew – had simply gone to ground.

2

THE RIPPER'S LAIR

In 1888, there was a self-confessed maniac on the streets of Whitechapel. It was Walter. The author of *My Secret Life* had a friend whom he called Henry who provided the perfect lair, as Walter explained:

> I had a friend who like me was intended for the army, his father was a gun manufacturer. The eldest son died, and the old man saying that five thousand a year should not be lost to the family, made his other son – my friend – go into the business. He resisted, but had no alternative but to consent. Their dwelling-house was just by ours, but the old man now insisted on his son residing largely at the manufactory where he invited me to stay at times with him, which I did.
>
> Several houses adjoining belonged to the old man, at the East-End of London, where the manufactory was. Some faced an important thoroughfare, the rest faced two other streets, and at the back, a place without a thoroughfare, on one side of which was the manufactory and workmen's entrance; on the other side stables. The whole property formed a large block.

Walter is mistaken, or being deliberately misleading. No gun factory in the East End matched this description. However, there was a gun-proofing house where guns were tested. It belonged to the Worshipful Company of Gunmakers. James Purdey, the patriarch of the famous gun-making company, had been born in Whitechapel and became Master of the Worshipful Company of Gunmakers in 1843. His son, James Purdey Jr, took over the company in 1858. The proofing house was at 48–50 Commercial Road, right in the middle of the area where the Ripper murders took place, on the other side of the London Hospital from Buck's Row where Mary Ann Nichols was slain.

The place was a maze. A private staircase led from a sitting room into the 'manufactory'. From there, you could go unnoticed into the warehouse, or the backstreet, or out of the front door of the house. The basement was used as a storeroom for muskets, put into wooden boxes that stood in long rows upon each other like coffins. Where there were muskets, there were probably bayonets.

The keys had been entrusted to Walter's friend, whom he called 'Henry'. Food and wine were laid on. This was welcome as the young Walter's mother kept him almost without money. Together, they would go down into the basement from where they could peer up gratings in the sidewalks.

> *At one end and on the principal street was a row of windows, beneath what was then a first class linen-draper's shop – first class I mean for the East-End – a large place for those days, and always full. Women used to stand by dozens at a time, looking into the shop windows which were of large plate-glass – a great novelty in those days – people waiting for omnibuses used also to stand up against the shop.*

Fortunately, the young Henry shared Walter's sexual interests.

> *Henry and I were old school friends, I had seen and felt his cock, he mine; I had not been with him an hour before he said, 'When the workmen go to dinner, I will show your more legs than your ever saw in your life.'*

'Girls?' said I. 'Yea, I saw up above the garters of a couple of dozen yesterday in an hour.' 'Could you see their cunts?' 'I did not quite, but nearly of one,' said he. I thought he was bragging, and was glad when twelve o'clock came.

At that hour down we went, through the basement stored with muskets; it seemed dark as we entered, but soon we saw streams of light coming through the windows at the end; they had not been cleaned for years. We rubbed the glass and looked up. Above us was a flock of women's legs of all sizes and shapes flashing before us, thick and thin in wonderful variety. We could see them by looking up, it being bright above; but dark and dusty below, they could not by looking down see us through the half cleaned windows; or notice round clean spots on the glass, through which two pairs of young eyes almost devoured the limbs of those who stood over them . . . for several days did we go into the place, gloating over such of the women's charms as we could discern; legs we saw by the hundreds, garters and parts of the thighs we saw by scores: quite enough to make young blood randy to madness, but the shadowy mass between the thighs we could not get a glimpse of.

But Walter would not be disappointed.

'There are vaults,' said I, 'if there, we could see right up, and be at the back of the women.' We tried unused keys to find one to open the door, and at length to our intense delight it unclosed. We stepped across the little open space under the gratings into the empty vaults, and there arranging to take our turns of looking up at the most likely spots, we put out our heads and took our fill at gazing. We were right under the women, who as they looked into the shop windows, jutting out their bums in stooping, tilted their petticoats exactly over our heads . . .

In those days even ladies wore no drawers. Their dresses rarely came below their ankles, they wore bustles, and standing over a grating, anyone below them saw much more, and more easily, than they can in these days of draggling dresses and cunt-swabbing breeches, which the commonest girl wears round her rump. For all that, so close to the thighs do chemise and petticoats cling, it was difficult to see the hairy slits, which it was our great desire to look at. Garters and thighs well above the knees, we saw by scores. Every now and then either by reason of scanty clothing, or short dresses, or by a woman's stooping and opening her legs to look more easily low down at the window, we had a glimpse of the cunt; and great was our randiness and delight when we did . . .

One day, quite at the end of the gratings, two women, neat, clean, plump, and of the poorer classes (for we could soon tell the poorer classes from their legs and under-clothings), stood close together. It was my five minutes. Henry was at my back. They had been standing talking, close together, not seeming to be looking at the shop, in fact they were at the spot where the shop window finished. One put her leg up against a ledge, keeping the other on the grating; it was a bright day, and I saw the dark hair of her cunt as plainly as if she were standing to show it me. The next minute she gathered up her clothes a little high, and squatted down on her heels as if to piddle, her bum came down within four or five inches of the grating and I saw, through the bars, her cunt open just as a woman does when she pisses. I thought she was going to do so, when a plaintive cry explained it all; she had a baby, and all the movements were to enable her to do something to it conveniently. At the same time her companion dropped on one knee, pulling her clothes a little up, and arranging them so as to prevent soiling them, she put the other leg out in front, and sat back on the heel of the kneeling leg. Then was another split, younger and lighter-haired, partly visible from below, but not so plainly as the dark-haired one; and they did something in that position for five minutes to the squalling child.

I lost all prudence, whispered to Henry; and together we stood looking, till they moved away. 'My prick will burst', said I. 'So will mine', said he. The next instant both our pricks were out, and looking up at the legs, stood we two young men, frigging till two jets of spunk spurted across the area. It would have been a fine sight for the women had they looked down, but women rarely did. They stood over the gratings usually with the greatest unconcern, looking at the shop windows, or only glanced below for an instant, at the dark, uninhabited looking area.

For Walter, this became an unhealthy obsession.

Henry had business to attend to, I none. I ceased to think about what might be said of our being so much in the store-house and used to go by myself, and stay there two or three hours at a time. Then I gave way to erotic excesses. My prick would stand as I went down the stairs. I used to wait prick in hand, playing with it, looking up and longing for a poke until I saw a pair of thighs plainly, then able to stand it no longer, frigged; hating myself even whilst I did it, and longing to put my spunk in the right place. I used to catch it in one hand, whilst I frigged with the other, then fling the spunk up towards the girls' legs. It was madness; for although the feet of the women were not three feet above my head, yet the smallness of the quantity thrown (after what stuck to my fingers), and the iron bars above, seemed to make it impossible that any of it should reach its intended destination; but I think it did one day. A youngish female was stooping, and showing part of her thighs. I flung up what I had just discharged; suddenly

*her legs closed, she stepped quickly aside, looked down
and went away. I am still under the impression that a
drop of my sperm must have hit her naked legs.*

Henry and Walter's circle then grew wider.

*We both also grew more lascivious, having frigged
before each other, we took to frigging each other. I went
to my home, on going back, found he had taken other
young men to see the legs. One night five of us had
dinner, we smoked and drank, our talk grew baudier;
we had mostly been schoolfellows, and dare say we had
all seen each other's doodles, but I cannot assert that
positively. We finished by showing them to each other
now, betting on their length and size, and finished up
by a frigging sweep-stakes for him who spent first.*

*At a signal, five young men (none I am sure nineteen
years old) seated on chairs in the middle of the room
began frigging themselves, amidst noise and laughter.
The noise soon subsided, the voices grew quiet, then
ceased, and was succeeded by convulsive breathing
sighs and long-drawn breaths, the legs of some writhed,
and stretched out, their backsides wriggled on the
chairs, one suddenly stood up. Five hands were frigging as fast as they could, the prick-knobs standing
out of a bright vermillion tint looking as if they must
burst away from the hands which held them. Suddenly
one cried 'f-fi-fir-first', as some drops of gruelly fluid
flew across the room, and the frigger sunk back in the
chair. At the same instant almost the other jets spurted,
and all five men were directly sitting down, some with
eyes closed, others with eyes wide open, all quiet and
palpitating, gently frigging, squeezing, and titillating
their pricks until pleasure had ceased.*

*Afterwards we were quiet, then came more grog,
more allusion to the legs of women, their cunts and
pleasures, more baudiness, more showing of pricks*

and ballocks, another sweep-stakes, another frigging match, and then we separated.

I do not think that excepting to Henry, that baudy evening ever was referred to by me.

I got up, I recollect, next day ashamed of myself, and felt worse, when he remarked, 'What beasts we made ourselves last night.' What changes since then. Two of the five found graves in the Crimea, the third is dead also; Henry and I alone alive. He with a big family, with sons nearly as old as he was at the time of the frigging matches. I wonder if he ever thinks of them, wonder if he ever has told his wife.

But Walter's self-loathing proved no obstacle.

I spent much time now in this leg inspection and frigging myself, till I could scarcely get semen out of me. I hated myself for it, yet went on doing it, when luckily I lost the exciting sights. Some women happened to look down and saw us. A man without a hat came several times and looked down the gratings. Henry's father came to the manufactory, as he often did, went into the stores, asked who had opened the area-door, locked it up, had a new lock put on, and forbade anyone to go into the stores excepting to get out the guns, and so we lost our game. We never asked a question, nor made a remark on the matter; and came to the conclusion that someone had complained to the linen draper that persons were looking up the women's legs, and that he had written to Henry's father on the matter. I went home used up, and in a state of indescribable disgust with myself, entirely ceased masturbation, and in a month went again to visit my friend, – he had found another grating.

The back of the manufactory as said was in a cul-de-sac. There were but the manufactory and stables in it. The workmen entered that side. There were

*gratings, and coal-vaults beneath the street similar
to those beneath the linen-draper's shop. Workmen's
wives bringing their husbands' dinners, used to stand
and sometimes sit down over the gratings, but their legs
when seen were rarely worth the seeing; it was usually
but a sight of dingy petticoats, and dirty stockings.
We were however content to look up at them, for they
belonged to women, but soon tired of doing so.*

However, Walter and Henry did not stop and found themselves
introduced to a number of unpleasant perversions.

*One night (we had never been there at night before),
for some reason or the other which I don't recollect,
we went down and found two women pissing down
the grating, then a man and woman together, and discovered it to be the pissing-place of the gay women, in
the main thoroughfare; and where if the nights were
dark, couples used to come for a grope, a frig, or even
for a fuck at times. The pissing often took place over a
grating, we could hear, and feel, but not see.*

They simply got a lamp and, whenever they fancied it, they
took the private staircase down to the grating.

*When we heard feet, or a rustle of petticoats over the
grating, taking up the light we sometimes saw a white
bum, a split gaping like a dog with its throat cut, and a
stream of water splashing from it.*

Given the proximity of the cellar to Buck's Row where Mary
Ann Nichols had her throat cut – and the sites of the other
Ripper murders – the image of "a split gaping like a dog with
its throat cut" used by Walter here is chilling.

*We never used to move, but sooner than not see it all
and as well as possible, let the stream come over us.*

Sometimes two women came together; sometimes we could hear to our mortification that they were pissing on the pavement close by, without coming over the grating. We could often hear their conversation. Now and then a woman shit down the grating; we used to watch the turds squeeze out with a fart or two, with great amusement. Once a man did the same; we saw prick, balls, and turd, all hanging down together. We could not help laughing, and off he shuffled as if he had been shot. He must have heard us.

There was one woman whose face we never saw, but who came and pissed over a grating so regularly every evening, and sometimes twice; that we knew her arse perfectly. We lost sight of her and used to wonder if she had found us out, for she finished one night with such a loud fart, that we laughed out, and she must have heard us.

Although this sounds like two young men just having fun, there was a darker side to it.

One night half a dozen ladies came, we knew they were ladies by their manner and conversation, which we could hear perfectly, there being no carriage traffic in the street. 'Can anyone see?' said one. 'No,' said another, 'make haste.' We heard the usual leafy rustle, and immediately a tremendous stream was heard; then two more sat down close together. I turned on the light at all risks, there were two pretty white little bums above us, with the gaping cunts, they were of quite young girls, without a hair on them; the women then were scared, I suppose, for they moved. One said, 'Make haste, don't be foolish, nobody is coming.' A rustle again, off went the slide, up went the light; what a big round bum, what a great black-haired open cunt did we see, and a stream of water as if from a fire-engine. 'Oh! there is a light down there,' said one. Up

> *went the bum, piss still straining down, down went the*
> *clothes, and all were off like lightning.*

Walter got a thrill from seeing the genitals of young girls and began to enjoy frightening women. Soon the voyeurism moved up a notch.

> *Another night we heard two pairs of feet above us, one*
> *was the heavy footstep of a man. 'Don't be foolish,*
> *he won't know,' said a man in a very low tone. 'Oh!*
> *no, no, I dare not,' said a female voice, and the feet*
> *with a little rustling moved to another grating. Henry*
> *and I moved on also. 'You shall, no one comes here,*
> *no one can see us,' said the man in a still lower tone.*
> *'Oh! I am so frightened,' said the female. A little gentle*
> *scuffling now took place, and then all seemed quiet but*
> *a slight movement of the feet. 'Are they there?' whis-*
> *pered Henry from the vault. I nudged him to quiet, and*
> *putting the light as high up as I could, pushed aside the*
> *slide a little only.*
>
> *We were well rewarded. Just above our heads were*
> *two pairs of feet, one pair wide apart; and hanging*
> *only partly at her back the garments of a female; in*
> *front the trousers of a man with the knees projecting*
> *slightly forward between the female's legs, and higher*
> *up a bag of balls were hanging down hiding nearly the*
> *belly and channel, which the prick was taking. The*
> *distended legs between which the balls moved, enabled*
> *us however to get a glimpse of the arse-hole and of a*
> *cunt. The movement of the ballocks showed the vigour*
> *with which the man was fucking, but there must have*
> *been some inequality in height; and either he was very*
> *tall, or she very short; for his knees and feet moved*
> *out at times into different positions. He then ceased*
> *for an instant his shoving, as if to arrange himself in a*
> *fresh and more convenient posture, and then the lunges*
> *recommenced. He must have had his hands on her*

naked rump, from the way her clothes hung, showing her legs up to her belly, or to where his breeches hid it, or where the clothes fell down which were over his arm.

Once, I imagine, the lady's clothes were in his way for there was a pause, his prick came quite out, her feet moved, her legs opened wider. He did not need his fingers to find his mark again, his long, stiff, red-tipped article had slidden in the direction of her bumhole; but no sooner had they readjusted their legs, than it moved backwards, and again it was hidden from sight in her cunt. The balls wagged more vigorously than ever, quicker, quicker; the lady's legs seemed to shake, we heard a sort of mixed cry, like a short groan and cry together, and a female voice say, 'Oh! don't make such a noise,' then a quiver and a shiver of the legs, and all seemed quiet.

When I first had removed the slide, I did so in a small degree, fearing they might look below and see it; but if the sun had shone from below, I believe now they must have been in that state of excitement, that they would not have noticed it. To see better I opened the slide more, and gradually held the lantern higher and higher, until the chimney through which the light issued was near to the grating. I was holding it by the bottom at arms length; and naturally, so as to best see myself. Henry could not see as well, although standing close to me, and our heads nearly touching. 'Hold it more this way,' said he in an excited whisper. I did not. Just then the lady said, 'Oh! make haste now, I am so frightened.' Out slipped the prick, I saw it. At that very instant, Henry pulled my hand, to get the lantern placed so as to enable him to see better. I was holding it between the very tips of my fingers, just below the feet of the copulating couple. His jerk pulled it over, and down it went with a smash, just as the lady said, 'Make haste, I am so frightened.' A huge prick as it seemed to me drew out, and flopped down, a hand grasped it, the petticoats were falling round the legs, when the crash of the lantern came. With a loud shriek from the lady, off the couple moved, and I dare say it was many a day before she had her privates moistened up against a wall again, and over a grating.

The sight of two people having sex excited Walter hugely.

Henry and I, laughing, picked up the lantern and got back to the house; I went to my bedroom in a state of indescribable randiness. I had for some time broken myself of frigging, and now resisted the desire, tried to read but could not, undressed and went to bed. My prick would stand. If it went down for a minute and my thoughts were diverted, the very instant my mind recurred to those balls wagging above my head, up it went again. I tried to piss, the piss would not run. At that time when my prick was stiff, I used to pull the prepuce back, so as to loosen it. I laid down on the bed, prick stiff. If it could have spoken, it would have said, 'Frig or fuck, you shall, before I give you rest.' So I pulled the prepuce slowly back, only once, and as the knob came handsomely into view, out shot my spunk all over the bed-clothes.

Getting up to wipe and make things clean, I saw something on the brim of my cap which I had worn; the cap was on the table. I took it up and found a large spot of sperm which had come from the happy couple, it must have followed the withdrawal of the prick; and had my head been a little more turned up, it must have tumbled on my face. I did not mind wiping up my own sperm, but doing so to theirs seemed beastly. Yet what was the difference?

Looking up through the grating provided Walter with a comprehensive sexual education.

We heard one night someone squat down, and turned up the light; there were petticoats, legs and an arse, but instead of the usual slit, we saw to our astonishment a prick and balls hanging down between the legs, it was a man in woman's clothes, and he was shitting. The sight alarmed us; we talked over it for many a day afterwards, for we did not then know that some men are fond of amusing themselves with other men.

I never saw but that one couple fucking, but we could hear groping and frigging going on close by. We heard women say, 'Oh! don't!' Gay women we heard say, 'Here is a good place,' but they did not often select the gratings. Why? I cannot tell, for they were partly in recesses in the wall which enabled people to get more hidden. The bars were wide apart, and I suppose the regulars did not like that, yet they often used the gratings for pissing down.

These sights did not occur all at once. I went home, stopped, returned, and so on; in the meanwhile not having women, I then frigged, left off, then took to it again, and so time went on. Fewer women came at last up the street, we imagined that with all our care, they had found out that people were beneath the gratings, and avoided them. The favourite place was the recess at the workmen's door to the factory at which were two steps; we could hear but not see when a couple was there, we used then to go up into the factory and listen at the door. Generally, feeling and frigging was only going on, bargaining for money first. 'Give me another shilling. Oh! your nails hurt. What a lot of hair you have. What a big one! Oh! I am coming! Don't spend over my clothes,' and so on, we heard at times.

The basement of the manufactory also led Walter to the first victim in his career as a rapist, though he was not yet nineteen. While Henry attended to the business, Walter would wander into the back street just as the men's wives brought them their lunch. They loitered over the gratings that Henry and Walter used to look up at night.

'I had once or twice looked up their clothes,' said Walter, 'but found little inviting, with the exception of a plump little pair of legs that belonged to a Mrs Smith.'

She looked about twenty-six; her husband twenty years older. He was a good workman but a brute to his wife. Some said his wife drank. They often rowed at lunch time. If she moved over the grating, Walter would dodge downstairs to look up her skirt, 'and then had a desire to fuck her'. 'Our eyes had often met, I had even got out of her way when passing her, a courtesy not often then shown by gentlemen to work-people. I used to stare at her so, that she began to look confused when I did.'

Sometimes Walter spoke to her husband about gun-making, but thought of nothing but having sex with his wife. Having been brought up religiously, Walter was still shocked at the idea of adultery.

One day, Walter heard a furious row and Mr Smith hit his wife.

'I would not stand for it,' said one of the women.

'He ought to be proud of such a wife, the old beast,' said another.

Walter heard Mrs Smith sobbing.

'I have had a little drink,' said she, 'I told him so. He makes me so unhappy . . . he is not a man,' she went on, 'not in bed, not anywhere . . . I put up with everything, it's full six months since he's been a husband to me, although we sleeps in the same bed.'

Walter was between eighteen and nineteen and did not have the remotest idea of getting Mrs Smith, although 'I longed for her lewdly when my cock stood'. He was timid with women until he knew them well, and had little idea of married life, although 'I imagined then that married people were always doing it, that women were randier than men, a common belief of young people.'

Nevertheless, Walter followed Mrs Smith about. One by one her sympathizers dropped off and he saw her go into a public house, then another. She came out wiping her eyes. After another couple of pubs, he accosted her. Even as a youth, Walter had no qualms about taking advantage of a drunken woman.

Without any definite intention as far as I can remember, but simply for lewd gratification, I went up to, and addressed her. She recognized me and stood stock still. She had a small bottle of what I found afterwards to be gin in her hand, which she put into her husband's dinner can. I told her I was sorry for her, having heard the row and all she had said. The reference to her wrongs roused her, and she said vehemently, 'He is not a man anyhow or anywhere,' and then was silent. I did not know what to say more, and walked on by her side. After a time she said, 'Why are you walking with me sir?' The only reply I made was that I liked it, and was sorry she had such a bad husband. She said she would rather be alone, but I walked on with her, she carrying the little tin can with a cover. I, not knowing what to do, offered to carry it for her, but she would not let me.

She then told him that he could not come any further as the neighbours would talk if they saw her walking with a 'gentleman'. They shook hands and she walked off, but Walter followed her at a distance. After a while he thought better of it. Then he saw the top of her husband's lunch pail on the path. It was the excuse he needed.

I walked about for half an hour before I mustered up courage to go to the house. She opened her eyes wide when she saw me. 'What do you want?' 'Here is the top of the dinner-can,' said I innocently. 'Oh!' said she, 'I am so glad, he would have hit me if I had lost it.' As she took it I entered and closed the door.

She had finished the gin; the empty bottle was on the table.

Walter thought she may have been more than 'fuddled'. He 'told her he had heard . . . that for months [her husband] had not been a husband to her.' That set her off. She said she was sure he was spending his money on some dolly, and cried. Then she said, 'Well, that is no business of yours, I am a fool for talking to a young gentleman like you, I don't know what you are doing here.'

> *'Let me do it to you,' said I, 'I have seen up your clothes, let me, you are so nice, and I want you so badly; why should you not, he is no husband to you, and you such a nice woman.' That was my artless beginning, or something like it. Fright at my impudence was struggling against my cock-stand. For a second she seemed speechless, then replied, 'Well sir, you ought to be ashamed, a married woman like me.' 'He is no husband to you, he never does it to you, you know, I heard you tell the women so; they laughed, and said he had some hussy whom he did it to.' 'That's no business of yours, but he is a bad one,' and she began crying again. 'Now go, sir, go. If he came home, he would murder me, if he found you here.*

Then it got unpleasant.

> *I don't know how the next came off, but I know I was kissing her, that I got my hand up her clothes, on to her cunt, that I pulled out my prick, that the struggling ceased, that I edged her to the bedroom, and that up against the bed she made a stand. 'Oh! my God sir, I am a married woman, pray don't.' Paying no heed, I got her clothes up and as she stood, was bending and trying to get my cock up her; but she was little, and I could not; it shoved up against her navel, and motte. That, I suppose, stirring her lust, overcame her, for she got on the bed. I got on her, and up her in a second.*

I was in a bursting state of randiness, and she must have been the same. I was ready to spend, she readier; for I had no sooner entered her than her breath shortened, she clasped me tight, quivered and wriggled, and we both spent. I lay up her, cock ready for further work.

He had sex with her again without pulling out his penis.

The quiet dreamy enjoyment had barely began, when she pushed me off and sat up saying, 'What have I done? What have I done? I am a married woman!' Then comes tears, then a kiss from me, then talk, then tears, and at intervals she told me a story of a bad, brutal, morose husband, who had not fucked her for months. Half frightened, half hysterical, it seemed as much pleasure to her to tell me her misery, as it had been to have me doing her husband's work. We moved off the bed. 'Oh! my God,' said she, 'look at the bed.' I saw one wet patch as large as a tea-cup, and another as large as a crown at the spot where her bum had laid on the counterpane. 'What shall I do?' 'Wash it.' 'But I have no other.' It was a bore no doubt. I left without being able to get permission to see her again, but only tears, and an expression of her conviction that she was a wicked woman.

Mrs Smith asked him not to tell anyone and he did not even mention it to Henry. For three or four days afterwards she did not come to the factory. So he went to her cottage, but she was out. When she did turn up again, he followed her home once more.

She opened the door, nearly fell back with surprise, and before she could recover herself I was indoors. I had an altercation, a refusal, almost a fight, but I conquered. Again she was fucked on the bed . . .

She kept exclaiming, 'Oh! if he should come home!'
I fell to work again with vigour, and soon again spent.

Walter did not take no for an answer.

In about a week I had her again at her cottage. Then
she said if I came any more she would have trouble,
for neighbours had already remarked a gentlemen at
the house. I disregarded this, went and knocked. She
opened the door cautiously with the chain up and,
seeing me, shut it in my face. I was then about going to
my own home, and feared I should not have her again,
but found out that the husband spent his evenings at
a tavern (I had a strange pleasure in looking at him
after I had had his wife), that he was to be at some
workman's carousal, watched him to the public-house,
then ran to his cottage, gave a single loud knock at the
door, which was this time opened unsuspiciously, and
in I pushed before she could scarcely see who it was.

The next sentences are the first in Walter's memoir that link
him to murder. And like many even more shocking crimes he
recounts later, Walter veils his violence and creates a potential
fall guy for his own crime. Walter, the well-bred friend of the
factory owner's son, is stalking the abused young wife of a
factory worker. He has used force to have her once, almost
fights to have her the second time. He pushes his way into
her cottage for a third. The young wife is resisting. Walter
continues:

I had difficulty in persuading her to let me, she was
more timid than ever, but promised that I would never
come again. Then she got on to the bed. The crisis was
just over when we heard a knock. With a shriek, she
pushed me off and got up. 'He will murder me, he will
murder me,' said she. I stood blank with bewilderment,
relieved by another knock and a voice crying 'beer'.

> *She fell on the floor fainting, and so alarmed me that*
> *I nearly called in the neighbours.*

After Mrs Smith shrieks 'he will murder me', she ends up unconscious on the kitchen floor. Now Walter completes his rape of the comatose wife.

> *I put a pillow under her head. I don't know what*
> *induced me, for not three minutes before I was fright-*
> *ened out of my life, but as she laid there close by the*
> *fire (at the knock we had rushed into the kitchen),*
> *I pulled up her clothes. The flickering of the fire showed*
> *her thighs and cunt in a strange light to me. As I pulled*
> *her legs asunder, I felt ashamed, but lust was strong.*
> *I looked at the cunt, the novelty of an insensible woman*
> *on the floor excited me. The next instant, in spite of her,*
> *for she recovered just as I laid on her, my prick was up*
> *her, and my knuckles on the hard bit of dingy carpet,*
> *and as I grasped her bum, it seemed that my poke was*
> *most delicious. So much for novelty and imagination.*
> *I left immediately afterwards.*

That a teenage stalker should have sex with an insensate woman is bad enough. What Walter writes next is that he is responsible for the 'half murder' of Mrs Smith.

> *In about three weeks, I went to see Henry again as*
> *I said, but really to get to Mrs Smith, and found her*
> *husband had been discharged. I went off to the cottage;*
> *it was empty. They had gone no one knew where, and*
> *he had half murdered his wife. I wondered if it had*
> *been about me. Then my conscience upbraided me with*
> *having committed adultery. I took to going to church*
> *more regularly, and repeated the commandments*
> *emphatically.*

It is the first vanishing of a sex partner in Walter's memoir of his secret life. And it is a double event. Tellingly, Walter recited all the imperatives authored by God and given to Moses; his conscience scolded him for more than the Seventh Commandment on adultery. Walter shared with us a deeper secret of his secret life. At the age of nineteen, Walter told us that, under a cross, he mouthed again and again the commandment 'Thou shalt not kill'.

In the Mortuary

It was only when they got Mary Ann Nichols' body to the mortuary and stripped her that they discovered she had been disembowelled. According to Dr Llewellyn, this had been 'performed with anatomical knowledge'. Ellen Holland was brought from Thrawl Street and identified the dead woman as 'Polly'. Her two petticoats both bore the stencil of Lambeth Workhouse. Mary Ann Monk was brought from Prince's Road. She gave the deceased a name, Mary Ann Nichols, whom she had last seen at seven o'clock entering a public house on New Kent Road. The police then traced her father, Edward Walker, who identified her from a small scar on her forehead, sustained as a child, and her estranged husband, William Nichols, who had stopped paying his wife maintenance in 1882 when he learned she was making her living by prostitution.

No money was found on her body, but PC Neil noted that 'an unmarked white handkerchief was found in her pocket'. He mentioned this at the inquest as if it were unusual and noteworthy. The implication is that a woman of her class would rarely have access to fresh linen.

Walter liked to give handkerchiefs to prostitutes. This started when he was quite young. One evening, he was taking a walk when he was accosted by a woman who asked him for a sovereign. He said he only had a shilling.

> *'Make it two,' said she. 'I have not got more.' 'Give it me then.' I stopped in astonishment at the idea of her*

*taking such a trifle. 'She is going to take it and go off,'
thought I, for I had known such a thing, but I gave
her the shilling and then stood still. 'Well, are you not
going to have it?' said she, 'make haste.'*

They had sex quickly up against a fence.

*Scarcely recovered from my pleasure and still won-
dering how I had such pleasure with so poor a woman,
I suppose I must have said something of the sort, for
she remarked, 'Why not? We are all made the same
way, and if some of us had more cheek, we might have
as good clothes as the best, but there are plenty of real
gents glad enough to have us.'*

Walter was wiping his penis with his silk handkerchief when
he wanted some more.

'Let me feel you, and do it again,' he said, 'and I will give
you this silk handkerchief, for I have no more money.'

'I suppose it is silk,' she said, taking it and accepting it.

Walter's mind was still turning to the delight of the sex he
paid for with a handkerchief when he compiled his memoirs in
the lead-up to 1888.

*I think now of the exquisite delight with which I felt
the thighs and bum of that poor woman, who might for
all I could see, have had the great, or the small pox, or
have been as ugly as the devil; but I stroked her belly,
twiddled her wet cunt-hair (she had pissed), plunged
my fingers into her wet cunt, and at length spent again
in it, with more delight than I have had with some of
the most dashing women since that time.*

Later, he made a practice of this.

*When with but little money, I used to take out my
best silk handkerchiefs, and give them with money,*

and once or twice I gave nothing else. One night to
a nice-looking girl I said I could give her nothing but a
handkerchief. 'All right,' said she without a murmur.
When I had fucked her, she laid still on the bed and
before she washed her cunt examined the handkerchief
very carefully. 'It's a rare good new one, it will pop for
half-a-crown where I am known, where did you prig it?'

'Prig' was slang for steal.

At Mary Ann Nichols' inquest, PC Neil also said: 'On the
body was found a piece of comb and a bit of looking-glass.'

Plainly, a comb would have been important to a prostitute.
Walter noted that 'cheap women' often stole combs and soap
from a bawdy house he frequented in J***s Street. He also
used them in love play. He recalled having a black woman
in a brothel in Paris. It was the first time he had been with a
'Negress' and spent some time examining her.

The hair interested me . . . I asked her for a comb, and
when she had fetched one, I combed, with the finely
toothed part, the hair on her mons. Immediately it
had passed thro the comb, it curled up and laid flat as
before. The Negress laughed her funny laugh, loud and
long – never had a man combed it before, she said.

The fragment of looking glass was also a prized possession.
Mirrors had played a part in Walter's sex life since he was
young.

He liked looking at himself in the mirror naked when he
had an erection and placed the mirror so that servant women
could see him if they looked through the keyhole, which he
knew they did. He even masturbated to put on a show for
them. Sometimes he just used the mirror for erotic purposes
on his own.

There was a good fire in my room. I stripped naked
and my prick stood rigidly, I could think of nothing

> *but the unknown lady, and resisted a desire to frig but walked about with my stiff prick, admiring myself in a cheval glass, and put myself into various eccentric attitudes, looking at it all the time. Then all constraint left me, I stood up against the glass and wetting my right hand, the tip of my prick with my spittle, I enclosed its whole length with both hands, but instead of moving them and frigging the usual way, I pushed my prick thro them as if they were a cunt, oscillating my bum, and thinking of the unknown lady's backside and thick clitoris, and spent my sperm on to the looking glass. Then mad with myself for doing so, went to bed.*

Later in life, he took his lover, Big Sarah, 'to J***s Street, which I liked better than T***f***d Street, for that though the quietest, and only frequented by swells of middle-age, was old-fashioned, dingy, and dull; whereas J***s Street had looking glasses, gildings, red satin hangings and gas-lights'.

Again, the mirror played an important part in Walter's interactions with prostitutes inside his favourite bawdy house.

> *There was a large glass against the wall, so placed that those on the bed could see every movement. I drew the curtain aside. We fucked enjoying the sight of our thrustings, heavings and backside wrigglings, and passed the night in every baudiness which then I practised. 'Do you like looking?' 'Yes I like it, but it makes me do it all of a sudden.' It was true, for I found that when fucking her, if I said, 'Look at us, look at me shoving,' directly she looked it fetched her; her big arse quivered . . . I placed the cheval-glass at the side of the bed. The sudden squeeze and jerk of her arse as she looked amused me, and I always arranged for the spectacle with her. I did not usually do this with women.*

That is not true. He used one with a woman he identified only as H.

> *One day I wished we had a looking-glass to see our-*
> *selves in when fucking. I had told her of the glasses*
> *at French houses. She, excepting in a cheval glass, had*
> *never seen herself reflected in copulation, and wished*
> *she could . . . I paid for a looking-glass which she got.*
> *It was nearly as long as her bed.*

On another occasion, he met a woman named Victoria beside Nelson's Column and took her to a house in Kensington. Walter doubled his interest in mirrors.

> *I stirred the fire, and moved the cheval glass, so that*
> *in two glasses we could see ourselves reflected . . .*
> *Restlessly, her eyes first turned to the chimney glass,*
> *then to the cheval glass, and I saw she was delighted*
> *at seeing herself with me naked in the reflection of the*
> *glasses.*
> *'Did you never see yourself reflected in a glass naked*
> *with a man like this before?' 'Never,' said she, emphati-*
> *cally. 'Do you like it?' 'We look very beautiful, don't*
> *we,' she replied.*

Walter usually took ex-ballet dancer, Sarah F**z**r, to a house in L**t*e P***l**d Street, but it did not have any looking glasses of any size. So instead he took her to a well-known house, the A*ma, where "there were glasses in profusion".

> *In the various ways which I amused myself with her,*
> *one very large cheval glass increased my pleasure.*
> *I mostly managed to get the room in which that par-*
> *ticular glass was, for I soon became known. They gave*
> *me what I wanted and never disturbed me however long*
> *I stayed.*

After that, he took her regularly to the A*ma, where he could 'look at the reflection of our naked bodies in the glasses'.

> *We used to attitudinize before the looking glass, laugh at our postures, and say what money men would give to see us two naked together. I dare say rich men have induced ballet girls to do as much, but more they could not; and I was fortunate to have had such voluptuous entertainments so cheaply. Then I fucked her wheelbarrow fashion.*

On another occasion, he and his lover watched in a mirror as he had sex in her armpit. Mirrors were a vital component in his voyeurism and he used them in homosexual encounters too. However, there was another incident involving a mirror that was even more sinister. Within Walter's story is a clue as to how a shard of mirror could end up in the hands of a low prostitute, provoking murderous feelings in a man like Walter.

> *One muddy night in the Strand there was an exceedingly well-dressed and very short-petticoated (they all wore them then) girl of about seventeen years of age; her legs especially pleased me, they were so plump and neat, and her feet so well shod. After my offer had been accepted, we went to a house in a court just by Drury-lane Theatre, and to a top-floor front-room very handsomely furnished. She lived there, and was a dress-lodger as I found afterwards.*

A dress-lodger is a woman who accepts a fine dress from a madam and pays her back by prostituting herself. If she ran off with the dress, she would be charged with theft.

> *She was beautifully clean, had fine linen, and was no sham in any way; a fresh, strong, plump, well-made young girl with lovely firm breasts, and a small quantity of brown hair on her cunt. Cunt and breasts looked*

only seventeen years; backside, thighs, arms, calves looked twenty. She stripped, and with but one feel and a stretch of her pretty cunt-lips, and a moment's glance I plugged her, and recollect now my enjoyment of her. Then I dressed, and so did she. Though so young, she was a well-trained whore, had much pleased me by her freedom in manner, even to the way in which she washed her cunt and pissed after her fuck. I was not with her I should say twenty minutes if so long; my lust for her had been so strong.

'What's this?' said she disdainfully as I gave her half-a-sovereign. 'What I promised you.' 'Oh! no you did not, I expect five pounds.' I expostulated. 'Look at this room, look at my dress, do you expect me to let a man come here with me for ten shillings?' 'It's all I promised, had you refused I should not have come with you.' Then I put on my hat, and moved towards the door; she placed her back against it. 'You don't go out of here till you give me three sovereigns.' It must be added that I had paid for the room what appeared to me then a large sum.

I was in for a row, had not as much as two pounds about me, and was fearful of exposure. Just then a row in a baudy house would have injured me, if known.

I gave her ten shillings more, she took it, but refused to let me go, she did not believe I had so little money, – I was a gentleman, let me behave as such, – no I should not go till I gave her what she asked. I tried to pull her from the door, but could not, then sat down on the chair, saying that if I must wait, why so I must.

She tried coaxing; I told her I was entitled to another fuck for my other ten shillings. Well I might if I gave her another twenty shillings. I put hands up her petti-coats, and fingers up her quim, thinking she was giving way, but no. I had forgotten my fears in my randiness which came on again by fumbling about her rump and cunt, and pulled out my prick stiff again. She bent

over me, and gave it two or three frigs. That so excited
me, that verily I believe I should have given her the
money if I had had it, for the pleasure of having her
again; but putting my hand into my trowsers, found
silver only to something like a pound in value, and
told her that. Then losing her gentility she said, 'I'm
damned if you do go, you bugger, till you have paid me
properly.'

Fear of exposure came over me, but I hid it, and
sitting down looked at her as she stood against the door
in her petticoats, her handsome limbs showing bright
in their silks, and her plump breasts just squeezing the
bubbies over the top of the stays. Laying hold of my
tool I pulled it out. 'Stand there as long as you like,
you look lovely, as you won't let me fuck you, I'll frig
myself.' Suiting the action to the word I began fist-
fucking, not meaning however to finish so. It was but
chaff, for indeed I was funky.

She stood looking till I said, 'I'm coming, I'm
spending, lift up your petticoats, and let me see your
cunt.' Then unlocking the door and opening it quickly,
she bawled out, 'Mrs. Smith, Mrs. Smith, come up,
here's a bilk, come up quickly.'

I was now near spending as may be guessed, but
buttoning up, went towards the door. She heard me,
turned round, came in, shut the door, and stood with
her back to it till a woman came in; and then she told
her I had given her ten shillings.

The woman was incensed. Was I a gent? She was sure
I was, why not pay properly then? A beautiful young
girl like that, just out, – look at her shape, and her
face, – she had written to a dozen gents who knew
her house, and they had all come to see this beauty, – all
had given her five pounds, some ten pounds, they were
so delighted with her, – and much of the same talk. The
girl began to whimper, saying she never had been so
insulted in her life before.

I told her that I had only promised ten shillings, but had given more; that the girl was certainly beautiful, and the room elegant; but I was poor, and would not have come at all had I known the cost. I had not the money, and therefore could not pay. Then the bawd's tone changed. She was not going to have the poor girl insulted in that manner, she knew better about my means of paying, and I should not go till I paid more. We went on wrangling until the bawd said, 'Well if you have not money give us your watch and chain, we will pawn it and give you the ticket, and you can get it out of pawn.'

I had hidden my watch, nearly always did so then when I went with whores whom I did not know, but saw in this a threat, and was getting more funky, yet determined to resist whatever came of it; so said I had no watch, and if I had, that I would see her damned first, before I gave it up. 'Oh! won't you,' said she, 'we will see if you won't, we don't allow a poor girl to be robbed by chaps like you in our house. Call up Bill,' said she to the girl. I saw that a bully was about to be let on me, and my heart beat hard and fast; but give up my watch I made up my mind I would not unless they murdered me. I had an undefined suspicion that they would ill-treat and rob me, and prepared for the worst, my pluck got up then.

But fear of exposure was before me. 'Look,' said I, 'I have no watch, I have given her twenty shillings, here is every farthing I have about me', and emptied my purse (there was but a shilling or two in it) before them, and put all the money I had loose in my pocket on to the chimney-piece. There was I think about seventeen shillings in all. 'Look it is every farthing I have, you may have that you damned thieves, take it and let me go, see my pockets are empty', and I turned them inside out.

'You've got more,' said she, 'be a gent, give her three pounds, she never has less, look at her, poor thing!'

The girl stood whimpering, she and the woman stood with their backs to the door, I with my back to the two windows of the room which looked out on to the public court; the fire-place was between us, the foot of the bed towards it; the fire was burning brightly, the room was quite light. There they stood, the clean, fresh, wholesome-looking lass, and besides her a shortish, thick, hooked-nosed, tawney-coloured, evil-looking woman, – the bawd, she looked like a bilious Jewess.

The woman kept repeating this for a minute or two. I refused to give any more, and grew collected. 'Come now, what are you going to do?' said the woman, 'you are wasting all her evening.' I took up half-a-crown off the mantle-shelf, and pushing the rest along it. 'I must keep this,' said I, 'but take all the rest, I have no more, I have no watch, let me go.' The woman laughed sneeringly, and did not touch the money, turned round, opened the door, and called out 'Bill, Bill, come up.' 'Halloh!' said a loud male voice from below.

I turned round, and with a violent pull, tore aside the red window-curtains, and throwing up the window, and putting my head out beneath the white blind, I screamed out, 'Police! – police! – murder! – murder! – police! – police!'

Beneath the very window stalked a policeman: heard me he must, the whole alley must have heard me, but the policeman took no notice, and stalking on turned round the corner out of sight. Then the fear came over me that he was bribed, I feared they might be coming behind me, and turned round; the woman was close to me, the girl at her back. 'What are you doing?' yelled the woman, 'what are you kicking up a row for? Shut the window, go if you want, who is keeping you? This is a respectable house, this is.'

A tumult of ideas and fears rushed through my mind, I feared Bill was close at hand, and pushing the woman back with one hand, I seized the poker with the right

one. 'Keep back, or I will smash you,' said I, flourishing
it, and again I shouted out, 'Police! – police!' but not
with my head out of the window this time.

The old woman backed and shut the door again, the
young one came forwards speaking in a hurried tone,
the old one dropped her voice to a whine; she did not
want to keep me if I wanted to go. 'Shut the window,
let her shut it, give the poor girl two pounds then, and
go.' Her house was a respectable house, the police knew
it, why did I come to such a house if I had no money?
The girl cried; I blustered, swore, and all three were
speaking at the same time for two or three minutes.

'Let me go.' 'Who stops you?' said the old woman,
'give me the money.' 'Open the door, and go out first
then.' 'I shan't,' said the woman with a snap and a look
like a demon. I turned round, and with the poker made
a smash at the window. The curtains had swung, the
white blind was down, but I heard the glass shiver and
crash, a shout of 'Hulloh!' from someone in the court.
I raised the poker again against the looking glass. 'Get
out, or I'll smash this, and you, and everything else in
the room,' striking a chair violently, and breaking it . . .

Walter's syntax is not very clear here, but it does seem that it
is the mirror he smashes, given that is what he first threatens
to break.

I now did not care what I did, but was determined to
fight Bill, or anyone else, and not be robbed.

The women were cowed, they cried out, 'Pray drop
the poker'. They meant no harm, the girl always had
three pounds at least, if I would not – why I would
not – they never have had such a row in the house
before. To have her twice, and give her ten shillings
was shameful. 'A lie, you bloody bawd, I have only
had her once, and she has had twenty shillings.' 'Well,
there's a good gentleman, go, and don't make a noise

as you go downstairs. Look at her, poor thing, how you have frightened her. She will let you have her again, if you like – won't you Lucy? Well come along then, but don't make a row. Leave the poker, what do you want that for?' whined the woman.

I would not relinquish the poker; they should go out first. The woman went, the girl waited behind to put on her frock. As she did so the little bitch lifted her petticoats to her thighs, showed her cunt, jerked her belly, winked and nodded her head in the direction of the old woman. I did not know nor heed what she meant by her nod and wink. 'Get out, get on, get out, I won't have you behind me.' She made a farting noise with her mouth and, dropping her clothes, went out. I followed her, looked at the doors on each landing as I passed, fearing someone might come out behind me, and edged downstairs sideways, looking both up and down. One door slightly opened and closed again; at the street door the old woman said she was so sorry, it was all a mistake, and hoped to see me again. My blood was roused, I would have smashed woman or man who stood in my way and, eyeing the girl, said, 'Look at me well, if you meet me in the Strand again, cut away at once, get out of my sight, or I'll give you in charge for annoying me, or robbing me, you bloody bitch, look out for yourself.' Then dropping the poker on the mat I went out, glad enough to be away from the den.

About a fortnight afterwards I saw the girl in the Strand, followed her for a quarter of an hour, saw her speak to various men, saw that an old, common, low servant followed her at a distance, occasionally stopping to speak with her, and turning up a street for that purpose. There was a fascination about looking at the girl; she was showily but handsomely dressed, her legs looked lovely. I longed to fuck her again, but without any intention of gratifying my lust, for I loathed her whilst lusting for her. She turned up C. t. a. Street,

> *stood over the gutter and pissed standing, the old woman talking to her and partly hiding her whilst she emptied her bladder. I waited till she had done. It was only about half-past nine o'clock.*

Walter was describing his stalking pattern. He had been a practised rapist since his teens. Now middle-aged, he was sexually frustrated by a bout of poverty that had shamed him in front of a young woman. Walter's solution was to tail the target of his lust and hate without being seen. What is telling is that Walter waited until the women entered what for him was a fetish place – a secluded pissing spot – before he struck.

> *She came towards me thinking I wanted her. I moved back close to a lamp, and raised my hat. 'Look at me, you damned whore, you attempted to rob me the other night, go out of the Strand, or I'll tell the next policeman you have picked my pocket.' She turned on her heels and bolted without uttering a word, the old woman after her, cursing.*

There was no street murder in Walter's encounter. His damned whore was simply threatened with the police. But the young dress-lodger went on to suffer a distinctive fate in Walter's text.

> *A month or two afterwards I saw her again, she was speaking to a group of gay women. Said I, 'That bitch attempted to rob me the other night at Court.' 'It's a lie,' said she, but again turned round, and ran up a side-street as fast as she could. I don't recollect seeing her afterwards.*

The prostitute Walter threatened to smash with the poker disappeared, last seen running up an alley in fear. Walter now used a stock phrase that reads like an alibi: 'I don't recollect seeing her afterwards.' He did not say that he pursued the girl into the darkness and cut her throat. The author has already told us many pages of his secret history had been consigned to the flames, but what Walter said in his next sentence relates to murder.

> *I often used to go and look at the house when that way, it was such a needy-looking house outside with a narrow steep staircase starting close to the street door. No one would have imagined it was so handsomely furnished inside (although I only saw the top-room). Two or three years afterwards there was a row there, a man tumbled down the stairs (or was pitched down), and was picked up dead. The owner of the house was transported. I don't know if it was the same man who was called Bill, but suspect it was, and that many a visitor had been bullied out of his money in that house.*

Walter ends his tale with a killing. Murder was on his mind when he wrote of the 'bloody bitch' dress-lodger he longed to fuck.

4

THE DEVIL AT LARGE

On Saturday, 8 September 1888, the Pall Mall Gazette said:

> *Something like a panic will be occasioned in London today by the announcement that another horrible murder has taken place in densely populated Whitechapel. This makes the fourth murder of the same kind, the perpetrator of which has succeeded in escaping the vigilance of the police. The triumphant success with which the Metropolitan Police have suppressed all political meetings in Trafalgar-square contrasts strangely with their absolute failure to prevent the most brutal kind of murder in Whitechapel.*

This was the murder of forty-seven-year-old Annie Chapman, also known as Dark Annie. Her body was found in the backyard of 29 Hanbury Street, a dwelling house frequented by prostitutes and their clients. It was discovered a little before 6 a.m. by John Davis, a carman who lived with his family on the third floor of no. 29. He was on his way to work. When he spotted the body of a woman lying on the ground with her skirts raised to the crotch, he ran to get help. Outside 23a Hanbury Street, he met James Green and James Kent waiting outside the workshops of Joseph and Thomas Bayley, where they worked. They followed Davis back into the yard to no. 29 to see the body, which had already been discovered by boxmaker Henry John Holland. They set off to find a policeman.

Inspector Joseph Chandler of H Division was on duty in Commercial Street near the corner of Hanbury Street. Several men rushed up to him.

'Another woman has been murdered,' said one of them.

Chandler recorded in his report:

> *I at once proceeded to 29 Hanbury Street and in the backyard found a woman lying on her back, dead, left arm resting on her left breast, legs drawn up, abducted, small intestines and flap of the abdomen lying on the right side, above the right shoulder, attached by a cord with the rest of the intestines inside the body; two flaps of skin from the lower part of the abdomen lying in a large quantity of blood above the left shoulder; throat cut deeply from left and back in a jagged manner right around the throat.*

According to the *Pall Mall Gazette*:

> *Her throat was cut open in a fearful manner, so deep, in fact, that the murderer, evidently thinking he had severed the head from the body, tied a handkerchief round it so as to keep it on.*

This was discounted by the police surgeon, Dr George Bagster Phillips, who concluded that the handkerchief could not have been tied around the neck after the throat had been cut.

Dr Phillips conducted a post-mortem. The *Lancet* quoted Dr Phillips saying

> *that the mutilation of the body was of such a character as could only have been effected by a practised hand . . . the abdomen had been entirely laid open; that the intestines, severed from their mesenteric attachments, had been lifted out of the body and placed on the shoulder of the corpse; whilst from the pelvis the uterus and its appendages, with the upper portion of the*

*vagina and the posterior two-thirds of the bladder, had
been entirely removed. No trace of these parts could be
found, and the incisions were cleanly cut, avoiding the
rectum, and dividing the vagina low enough to avoid
injury to the cervix uteri. Obviously the work was that
of an expert – of one, at least, who had such knowledge
of anatomical or pathological examinations as to be
enabled to secure the pelvic organs with one sweep of
a knife . . .*

Dr Phillips told the inquest: 'The mode in which the knife had
been used seem to indicate great anatomical knowledge.' The
wounds had been inflicted by a very sharp knife at least five
or six inches long and Dr Phillips was in awe of the skill of the
perpetrator:

*I myself could not have performed all the injuries I
saw on that woman, and effect them, even without a
struggle, under a quarter of an hour. If I had done it in
a deliberate way, such as would fall to the duties of a
surgeon, it would probably have taken me the best part
of an hour.*

Walter had something of a medical background. His godfather
was a surgeon-major in the Army and he had a friend who was
a 'surgeon with a crack regiment'. On one occasion, he offered
a prostitute named Camille ten pounds to arrange for him to
see the vulva of a supposed virgin named Louise. 'Then I had
a suspicious fit. All the old Major had told me about fellows
being sold, and taken in by women who were not virgins came
to my mind.' So he sought professional advice.

*I thought still I was to be fooled, so I called upon
my old schoolfellow, who used to say, 'Snatch at her
cunt, and show her your cucumber.' He had been one
at the frigging match, and had just been appointed
assistant-surgeon at a hospital; he was a bachelor and*

baudy-minded as ever. 'M . . . ,' said I, 'have you ever seen a virginity?' 'Many,' he replied, 'I have dissected them, and if girls have anything the matter with their wombs, or cunts, we get a look, they don't mind a doctor. If a girl has piles, I make her turn up, and have opened several fine women's virgin cunts, asking questions all the while, if they feel this or feel that. They say yes or no, which of course I knew they would say, but they think I am very clever for asking. Some like a young doctor's fingers on their privates, though they say they object. Assistants only get the chance with the poor, the better classes have older married men.'

I asked him to explain one to me on a woman, and he did. We went home with the same women; they were astonished, for instead of pulling our pricks out, we both merely felt and looked at them, and he gave me a full lecture. It was an odd sight to see him explaining the situation of a virginity, I holding a candle to see better . . .

From reading, his descriptions, his sketches and what he pointed out on three different cunts, I felt satisfied that I should know a virgin . . .

Walter frequently masqueraded as a surgeon or a doctor, so that he could make intimate examinations of young girls. The women who procured virgins for him frequently introduced him as a doctor. He even bought medical books and carried a bag. He used the doctor ruse on a young virgin named Winifred. Initially, she resisted his blandishments, but he persuaded her.

'I shouldn't hurt you, you are so handsome that I wanted to look at you naked. Doctors know how to get pleasure and give pleasure to girls, without doing them injury.' 'You a doctor? Why didn't you say so before?' 'Why should I?' The girl began to think and agreed to meet me the next afternoon . . .

Pretty soon, he got her to come to a bagnio with him and strip off. Then he deflowered her. After a brief affair, she went away and they corresponded.

> *I sent her five pounds to help her to go with. She wrote to thank me, and I thought I had heard the last of her, but I met her again four years afterwards by chance. She never knew my real name and address, and I always wrote in a feigned hand.*

He often disguised his identity and used this 'feigned hand' on another occasion, arranging an assignation with a married woman. The Ripper was thought to have disguised his hand in letters and postcards to the press, police and president of the Whitechapel Vigilance Committee. On 6 October 1888, the *St James Gazette*, reported:

> *The police authorities of Whitehall have had reproduced in facsimile and published on the walls of London the letter and postcard sent to the Central News Agency. The language of the card and letter is of a brutal character, and is full of Americanisms. The handwriting, which is clear and plain, and disguised in part, is that of a person accustomed to write a round hand like that employed by clerks in offices.*

But what immediately derailed the investigation of the murder of Annie Chapman was a leather apron that was found near the standpipe in the yard. This immediately struck a chord with the public. Just three days before, on 5 September, *The Star* had run a story under the headline: '"Leather Apron" – The Only Name Linked with the Whitechapel Murders. A Noiseless Midnight Terror.'

A man wearing a leather apron had been harassing prostitutes in the Whitechapel area. He carried a sharp knife. Two weeks before, he had drawn it on a woman called 'Widow Annie' near the London Hospital and threatened to 'rip her up'.

Some fifty women interviewed by a reporter between midnight and 3 a.m. that morning gave a description of 'Leather Apron'.

'What he wears on his feet the women do not know,' said the paper, 'but they all agree that he moves noiselessly. His uncanny peculiarity to them is that they never see him or know of his presence until he is close by them . . . The noiselessness of 'Leather Apron's' movements recalls the statement of Mrs Colwell, of Brady-street. She said that about the time the murder was said to have been committed she heard a woman running up the street shrieking "Murder; Police." "She was running away from somebody," said Mrs. Colwell, "who, from the way she screamed, was hurting her as she ran. And it struck me as very strange that I did not hear the sounds of any footsteps whatever except hers."'

The Star concluded: 'The strangest thing about the whole case is that in view of public opinion in Whitechapel, the man has not been arrested on suspicion, and his whereabouts on the night of the murder inquired into.'

It was widely believed that 'Leather Apron' was a Jew and, when word spread of the leather apron being found near the body of Annie Chapman, Jews were attacked. On 10 September, John Pizer, a Polish Jewish boot-finisher from Mulberry Street, was identified as 'Leather Apron' and arrested. However, the following day, he was cleared of the murders of both Mary Ann Nichols and Annie Chapman. Mrs Amelia Richardson, who lived at 29 Hanbury Street, told the inquest that the apron belonged to her son. She had washed it and left it out to dry. There were no traces of blood on it and none in the pans beneath the standpipe.

There were some chilling parallels between the murders of Mary Ann Nichols and Annie Chapman. Both had gone missing from their regular lodgings a week before they were murdered. Annie Chapman said she had been in 'the infirmary', though no woman matching her description was admitted to the Whitechapel or Spitalfields Workhouse Infirmaries at the time. Both women had been supported by their estranged husbands until they turned to prostitution, although Annie Chapman's maintenance had been terminated by her husband's death. Both had children, notably daughters who might follow them into their trade. Mary Ann Nichols had Alice Esther, born in 1870, and Eliza Sarah, born in 1877, along with three sons. Annie Chapman had Emily Ruth, born in 1870, and Annie Georgina, born in 1873. Her one son John was a cripple and sent to a home. Emily Ruth died of meningitis at the age of twelve.

Both had been drinking and neither had the money for a bed that night. Annie Chapman had been to see one of her sisters in Vauxhall who had given her five pence, although it seems she spent it on drink. John Evans, the watchman at Crossingham's Lodging House, 35 Dorset Street, where she had been staying, said that she had sent out one of the lodgers for a pint of beer. Soon after, she told Tim Donovan, the deputy at the lodging house: 'I haven't sufficient money for my bed, but don't let it. I shall not be long before I am in.'

Donovan was less than sympathetic. 'You can find money for your beer,' he said. 'You can't find money for your bed.' As she left the premises, she said: 'Never mind Tim, I'll be back soon. Don't let the bed.'

Both Mary Ann Nichols and Annie Chapman had the marks of rings left on their fingers. However, there were abrasions on Chapman's fingers indicating that her rings may have been torn off during the attack, although they may have been taken by the mortuary attendants. Newspaper reports said that she also had two brightly polished farthings – worth a quarter of a penny – that were sometimes passed off as half-sovereigns, old farthings as sixpences.

Near Annie Chapman's feet were found a small piece of muslin and two combs – a small-toothed comb and a pocket comb in a paper case. Dr Phillips did not think that they had been simply thrown on the ground.

'They had apparently been placed there in order,' he told the inquest, 'that is to say, arranged there.'

By her head was part of an envelope containing two pills. The back of the envelope bore a seal and the words 'Sussex Regiment' embossed in blue. On the other side, in handwriting, were the letters 'M' and 'Sp', possibly the beginning of the word 'Spitalfields'. However, no member of the Sussex Regiment admitted to writing to anyone in Spitalfields and the handwriting did not match any of the signatures in their paybooks. However, a postmaster also stocked the regiment's envelopes and sold them to the general public. Another lodger at Crossingham's told the police that he had seen Annie Chapman with a box of pills on the morning before her death. The box had broken apart and Annie had wrapped the remaining two pills inside a piece of paper, possibly torn from an old envelope she had found on the kitchen floor.

Pills feature in *My Secret Life*, too. They were used in Walter's plan to deflower an underage girl named Emma, who was deaf, while he once again pretended to be a doctor:

> *The desire for a youthful virginity seems to have been strong on me. Sarah said she'd try and find one. Then I became exacting, and wanted one without any hair on her cunt, and I would see her virginity also before I broke it. I told her of the lovely little lass Betsy Johnson had got me, what I paid her, of the little virgin I got at the L*c**t*r S****e brothel, that I'd had both at brothels, and I must now have the girl whom Sarah got, at her lodgings, or at some quiet place, not a brothel . . .*
>
> *Once or twice after, it was mentioned casually, when my prick was stiff and a good dinner was in me, for the letch was still on me occasionally, tho I had ceased to expect to gratify it.*

Soon after Sarah invited him to her lodgings; 'Two rooms on the second floor in G***k Street, Soho.' She had found him a virgin.

> *She let me in herself. 'I have a new little maid, and don't want her to see that you are strange here. I have told her I expect a friend, a doctor. If you like her, I will see*

what can be done. She'll be in, in a quarter of an hour.
Her name is Emma.'

The girl who had been sent on an errand was about
fifteen, or barely so, short and thickset and had large
earnest eyes but not a handsome face. She was rather
deaf. The idea of having her pleased me, I began
thinking how I should like to please her, hurt her vir-
ginity, frig, lick, fuck, and generally teach her the art of
love, in a snug private room like Sarah's.

Sarah told him that the girl was of German extraction.
She had no mother and her father was a drunken tailor. The
girl had kept his rooms, but she had a younger sister who
could do this, so he told Emma to get a job in service. Sarah
had taken her on and dismissed her other maid. The first step
was to get the girl drunk.

I sent the girl out for gin, brandy, etc., etc., giving her
always the change, my custom of ingratiating myself.
Her face brightened at the gifts. She sat at needlework
whilst we talked. 'This is my friend Dr H**m**d, he
has often attended to me. Now he shall see to you,
if you don't get better,' said Sarah, telling me that
she had indications of her first poorliness, and that she
had advised her to let a doctor look at her when alone.
Then to me when alone, 'And as you are the doctor,
you can satisfy yourself.'

The question uppermost in Walter's mind was: was she a
virgin? Sarah believed so. When Sarah's common-law husband
was away, she got her servants to sleep with her, so she had
seen the girl undress and wash.

She always made her servants do that every week, or
they would not be in the same bed with her. The girl
had the slightest sign of dark hair on the motte, but not
a bit on the lips.

When the girl was asleep, Sarah had examined her more closely, both visually and manually. Sarah also got the girl drunk and played with her sexually. Then Walter and Sarah disappeared into the bedroom.

> *'I mean to let her know I am gay,' said she, 'get her lewed and it will all go right. Your being a doctor will do it. My poorliness is coming on, and I have told her I have shown you my cunt. That doctors often see the cunts of women who want advice about poorliness' – only Sarah usually said 'my thing' when she spoke of her cunt.*

Two days later, Walter met up with Sarah. By this time, she had satisfied herself that Emma was a virgin.

> *'She is all right, no one has been up her, you can come tonight and see for yourself. I have seen her thing, and if you say you must look at it, she'll let you. I have told her that she must have no nonsense with a doctor.'*
> *'But she'll expect medicine.' 'Well, you must give her something which will open her bowels. She'll never think you are going to do her good unless you make her belly ache.'*

For the next two evenings, Walter examined the girl 'as nearly as I could in a cool, medical sort of way' and asked her medical questions about her bowels, her urine and her 'poorliness' (her period). She had not yet menstruated. Touching the young girl and her 'nascent bubbies' had got him unbearably aroused.

> *I could feel no hair, or scarcely any. It is strange, that altho Sarah thought I had better proceed to look at her at once, that I put it off – I can understand why I did it.*

Next time he plied her with 'shrub' – rum mixed with sugar and orange or lemon juice. This, he believed, made young girls feel randy and he renewed his determination to have the virgin Emma. Meanwhile, Sarah talked to her constantly about sex to soften her up.

> *Sarah strove to fill her mind with desire to be fucked, told of the ease and secrecy with which it could be accomplished, and the benefits accruing. Any woman I am certain can persuade a girl to let herself be fucked, if she stimulates rising passions, and incites her to compliance both for sexual gratification and interest, and women like teaching them.*

Today, we would call this grooming. Sarah said she did not like doing this, but some man was going to have her and it might as well be Walter. 'I shall get my new dress,' said Sarah. 'It will do me good and do her no harm.'

> *To this I quite agreed. It is quite true, and what every gay woman has told me, and is my philosophy.*

And if there were any problems, Sarah would deny all knowledge. 'I'll chance it,' she said. 'How am I to know anything about it, she might have done it anywhere, when she goes out. I should swear all was a lie, I should say I never had seen you in my life, and no one shall see you if you come at dark, and only when I tell you.'

A girl Emma knew told her that sex hurt the first time. Sarah told her that it did not – if the girl let the man do what he like and did not resist. She told Walter that Emma thought he was a nice, kind man.

> *'Shall I get into her tonight?' 'I would rather be out when you do it, I have told her she'd be better if she'd been poked, and she said she supposed she should not be quite well till she married. I said she might get poked before that, and her husband know nothing about it.'*

Again, Walter went through the pretence of being a doctor, asking her all sorts of medical questions and insisting on examining her.

> *'I must see you with your clothes off.' 'Go with the doctor,' said Sarah. 'I have told her you'll want to look at her as you have looked at me.' There was such a lot of palaver about the affair, that it crossed my mind I was going to be done.*

The girl lighted a candle and went to the bedroom. In the room was a fire.

> *I could scarcely now preserve the gravity of a doctor.*

She took off her clothes down to her chemise. I asked all the searching medical questions I could. 'Lie down,' he said, 'don't be ashamed, I am accustomed to see girls naked.' Then he got her to open her legs. He held up the candle and examined her, satisfying himself the she was unmistakably a virgin.

> *I could scarcely tear myself from her cunt, praised its looks, said what a nice-made little lass she was. 'And now my dear, tell me, have you ever put your finger up this?' and I touched it.*

She denied it.

> *'Are you sure? Tell me the truth, it is no good deceiving a doctor.' 'No, sir.' 'Now I know you have,' said I, glorying in my baudy treat. 'You have tried?' 'I tried but it hurts me.' 'I must try – if it hurts you a little don't mind – it's for your good.'*

Then he licked his finger and pushed it up. She winced.

> *'Oh, you hurt me, sir.'*

He turned her over and examined her from every angle. Then he rubbed her clitoris with his finger, and asked if she ever did that.

'I fancy you do what so many girls do.'

He kissed her and told her that 'she would not be better till she had had done to her what her own mother had had done'. Walter told himself that the girl was ready, but began to have qualms. He sent Emma out to get some soda water, but was so aroused he quickly had sex with Sarah.

When the girl came back she drank shrub. I spoke of her nice limbs, told Sarah of her form, took half a sovereign out of my pocket, told Sarah to buy her boots, and that I felt inclined to give her a new dress. Then on pretence of satisfying myself, took her into the bedroom and again looked at the virgin cunt, pulled out my prick (and didn't she look) and pissed before her. 'You will be better when you let some one use this with you.' She turned away. I don't think she quite heard what I said.

On his next visit, he talked to her about the action of the medicine he had given her, and 'familiarised her with talking to me about all the little secrets of her sex'. On the subject of talking about sex, Walter writes:

That freedom on subjects usually hidden from each other, paves the way for fucking.

Again he examined her – internally.

Then I hinted again at giving her a dress, told her she had better not mention about having had a doctor to anyone, and stifling my wants I went into the other room to Sarah.

Walter showed no qualms about hurting Emma. Indeed, in *My Secret Life* he relates his 'seduce' in loving and graphic detail. And, in his version of events, Sarah egged him on.

> *Sarah said, 'Try as soon as you can, for with such a young one now, you never know what will take place. She may be fool enough to tell some one, but she won't if she once gets it done to her. I will then tell her that she will be ruined for life if she mentions it.'*

The next night, Sarah said she would stay out until twelve and advised Walter to get Emma drunk on shrub. She told him that Emma was in love with him and was eager to get the dress he had promised. There had been other gifts and the hint that Walter might take her on as a maid. Emma was also impressed that he knew she had tried to put her finger up her vagina. Sarah told her that doctors knew everything about women, and urged him to go ahead.

> *'You'll have her – she has had such a talking to. If she hollows, push a pillow over her face and they won't hear underneath – but the lodger overhead might be coming upstairs, tho he scarcely ever comes in till twelve o'clock. I'll be in the street for him, and come in when he does, we'll come up the stairs together. If I hear anything I'll make a noise and knock at the door, so don't be frightened – only you'll have had her before then.'*

Sarah had prepared the apartment so that if Emma cried out while she was being raped, the neighbours would not hear it. She had nailed a rug over the door inside and put the chest of drawers against it. Emma had been prepared too.

> *Sarah had given her a pill (I had taken her a box of common aperients). 'She thinks you will soon bring on her poorliness, and that she will be quite a woman*

*then.' I sometimes wonder if all this preliminary was
needful . . . Altho the maiden had not been a fortnight
in the house, she had been as far debauched in mind
as she well could be. To have been told all about
fucking, and by a grown woman, to have confessed to
that woman, and to a doctor, all she had done with
her cunt, to have got money, new boots and stockings
and some other things, see the chance of having a
place in the house of a doctor, who twice had looked
at and felt her cunt, was certainly enough to upset
any girl.*

The moment had come.

*That night she let me in, said her mistress was out and
had left no message. 'Never mind, I will wait.' I sent
out for shrub, and prepared to try my luck, but felt as
nervous as if I were going before a judge for murder.
I can't understand myself being like this . . .*

*She had a little shrub. 'Come here, dear, and tell me
about yourself.' I praised her hair and eyes, which were
very good. Taking her between my legs I began feeling
her breasts and belly, asking her medical questions all
the time, then I lifted her clothes and afterwards said,
'Let me see your stockings.' For an instant only she
resisted as a girl might.*

*'Why? I gave them you – I have seen your little cunt
and your little bum, have I not, and must look at them
now.' Then I again lifted her clothes, put my hand up,
and a finger on her clitoris, and talking all the while,
began rubbing it. 'Oh Doctor, don't,' said she, wriggling her little cunt away from me. 'Ah, it's pleasure,
but nothing like the pleasure you'll have when a man
puts his cock up you,' said I, feeling that the ice must
be broken. My prick was getting so rampageous that I
felt inclined to carry her to the bed and ravish her, but
I went on talking.*

> *In a few minutes more, 'I must look at you.' Into the bedroom we went, she took off her clothes, and again I saw her little virgin cunt at the bedside.*
>
> *However much I may plan an attack on a woman, there always comes a time when I follow my instincts and not my plan.*

He uses the word 'attack' here advisedly and, although he claims to have qualms, he describes every detail with relish.

> *When my prick almost feels bursting, and I am over-powered by voluptuousness, I scarcely know what I do, or what course I take. Then if the woman is not quite ready in her lewdness, and I make a false move, and startle, frighten, or delay, my chance is gone. But if she be lewed, sayings and doings dictated by nature infallibly win her. There is a strength of will, and a moral force that a man has when he is furious with sexual want, over any woman whose body is tingling with desire for a male, which make him sure of having her.*
>
> *Up to this time I know all I did, what followed my excited state only leaves the broad incidents clear – I got on the bed, pulled out my prick and said, kissing her, 'Let me fuck you love, your poorliness will come on then – you'll want no more medicine, and have such pleasure.' 'No-hoh, no, sir – I mustn't til I am married – you'll hurt me. I mustn't, Doctor!'*

Walter was prepared to use both force and bribery to get what he wanted.

> *I cuddled her as she attempted to get up, promising money and a silk dress, that I wouldn't hurt, and that whoever told her it hurt told nonsense. 'No-oh-no,' but she was nestling in my bosom ... Suddenly she said, 'Will you take me to help as a servant?' I promised. In*

another minute she was on her back. She begged me to get off . . . There was only one alloy to this pleasure. Without making a noise, she kept crying, and I spent kissing her, her tears running down her face. But I am not sure that these evidences of pain and nervous shock did not add to my enjoyment.

Her pleading, cries of anguish and tears did not put him off. Walter's use of the double negative appears to indicate these turned him on. What excited Walter more than tears was the sight of blood.

Candle in hand I opened her thighs, and saw the results of my pleasure. A mass of blood-streaked sperm filled the mouth of her prick-hole, smears of blood lay between the cunt lips and on the thighs. On my prick was blood where the stem joins the balls . . .

It aroused him and he was determined to rape her again.

She tried to move but too late. 'No, Doctor H**m**d, you shan't . . . ' She gave a little cry and then was quiet. At length she complained that I was making her 'ache dreadful'.

His response? He had sex with her again. This time, he said, she 'spent'. She was now completely docile. He gave her more shrub. She went to sleep and 'I sat down gloriously contented'. But the child's ordeal was not yet over. While she slept, he examined her naked body and masturbated over her, though he claimed to hate masturbation. Then he awoke and examined her more intimately to see what damage he had done.

I gloried in the jagged opening made of the little hole of three hours previously, but felt sorry at the depression she was in, for I could now scarcely get her to reply.

> *Kissing her, promising much, and begging her never to tell anyone, I left her.*

Her silence was vital. Any breath of it outside those four walls and he faced ruin. Sarah was outside. Walter paid her and boasted that the little girl had come. Sarah doubted it and was now eager to get rid of Emma. But Walter protested that he wanted to 'teach her the art of love' and was determined to have the girl again.

The abuse continued. Walter would come round to have sex with both of them and compare them. Walter grew tired of Emma when it appeared sex was no longer hurting her. Sarah wanted to get rid of her too, even though she got two pounds instead of one every time Walter came round.

> *'The little devil bothers me, she is always asking about you . . . She thinks of nothing but your coming, bothers me to read your baudy books (I had lent some), and would talk of fucking all day. I am frightened to let her go out.'*

Walter stopped coming to visit and the girl, once used, was tossed aside.

> *The girl, I heard afterwards, was in tears when she found I did not come. Sarah told her I had gone abroad – I was sorry for the lass, but Sarah had but little pity. She thought the girl had done very well. 'When she came, she hadn't a rag to her back, now she has more good clothing than me.' I had indeed given the girl lots of good clothes. 'She is set up, and has got a good place as a servant, where she will work hard, but what of that. It's better than stopping at home with a drunken father who half-starved and ill-treated her.'*

She had got a job at a little grocer's shop in W**d**r Street. A month later, Walter loitered near the shop and saw two youths. Sarah said he was wrong to go near. 'The best thing for you is never to see her again,' she said. 'If any row comes, I'll swear you never were at my lodgings in your life. No one has seen you come, it has always been dark.'

Walter said that the two youths probably have sex with her.

'I hope they will, that will shut her mouth,' said Sarah. 'She won't go long without it being up her, and the sooner she fucks the better.'

'I never either saw the girl afterwards, nor heard of her,' Walter wrote.

During the whole episode, Walter had been careful not to put himself in a position where he could be blackmailed.

> *At Sarah F**z**'s I never had anything in my pockets to disclose my name.*

But he claimed not to understand why Sarah had not wanted to be at home when he raped Emma, or why she was so eager to get rid of her. Walter did not think he had done anything wrong. However, the law was closing in.

5

DEFLORATION MANIA

When Walter was first stalking the streets of London, Britain was in the grip of 'defloration mania'. Until the end of the eighteenth century, there was little demand for virgins in London's sex trade. The trend seems to have begun with a pernicious little book called *The Battles of Venus*, originally printed in The Hague in 1760 and ascribed to Voltaire. It was translated and reprinted several times in London, where it lost its attribution.

The author wrote:

> *I hold truly that the enjoyment of a virgin, from the point of view of the mind and body of the seducer, is the highest peak of pleasure. In the first place the man's fancy is inflamed with the prospect of enjoying a woman, after whom he has perhaps long desired and tried to win, who he thinks has never before been in bed with a man, in whose arms no man has yet lain and whose virgin charms he will be the first to see and triumphantly enjoy. This exquisite work of the fancy prepares the body in the highest degree for sensual pleasure.*

He went on to describe the delights of defloration in graphic detail. When, for example, should one pluck a maiden?

'The time of enjoying immature beauty seems to be the year before ringlets deck the pouting mount, but all is like her lily hand, both bare and smooth, before the periodical lustration hath stained her virgin shift, whilst her bosom boasts only a general swell rather than distinct orbs, and whilst her tender mind is ignorant of what man can do unto her . . . '

In the *Index Librorum Prohibitorum* (List of Prohibited Books), Pisanus Fraxi, the pseudonym of the great Victorian collector of pornography, Henry Spencer Ashbee, says of *The Battles of Venus*: 'The various "leches" to which men of pleasure are addicted are reviewed, the gambols of young girls in board schools are peeped at, and indeed, the little treatise is pretty exhaustive on the subject.'

Although the author urges the protagonist to 'pity a tender virgin's sufferings' and entreats him 'not be break fiercely in, but to spare fierce dilaceration and dire pangs', he actually extols rape:

> *I cannot conceive a higher banquet to a man of lustful humour, than to see a modest and beautiful woman forcibly stripped naked: to observe her struggling and, discording her hidden beauties by degree, until she comes to her last shift, and then to lay her down, and notwithstanding her efforts, rifle all her charms, and penetrate even into her honeyed treasure.*

The virgin's resistance and her cries of pain:

> *produce an emission copious, rapid and transporting . . . Part of the delight arises from considering that the lewdest part of your body is fixed in the delicious centre of her body, that you feel the convulsive wrigglings of the chaste nymph you have so long adored, and at last feel her diffuse her warm juice throughout her dewy sheath, and moisten the hot, ruby crest of your firm-fixed instrument.*

In fact, the screams of the victims were part of the pleasure. In 1893, reformer Charlton Edholm wrote:

> *Pain became an essential ingredient for pleasurable sex
> ... and since the defloration of very young virgins can
> be excruciating. The screams of children became indis-
> pensable, shrill torture was the 'essence of delight' and
> many gentlemen would not silence a single note. Such
> a process netted the child into permanent prostitution.
> The result is that in nine cases out of ten, or ninety-
> nine out of a hundred, the child, who is usually under
> fifteen, frightened and friendless, her head aching ...
> and full of pain and horror, gives up all hope, and in
> a week she is one of the attractions of the house.*

The demand for virgins led to an increase in child prostitution.
In Crispin Street, Spitalfields, in 1810, there was a brothel that
specialised in girls under fourteen. By the 1830s, it had competition from Catherine Keeley's in Dock Street, Maxwell's
in Batty Street off the Commercial Road, and numerous
other establishments in Mile End Road and Bedford Square
(East). John Jacobs' place in New Norfolk Street offered girls
of twelve, and one ten-year-old was found on the premises.
William Sheen of Algar Place, Wentworth Street, Spitalfield
ran 'pornological clubs' where men and women had sex with
the children he provided. He always had thirty or forty boys
and girls between the ages of nine and eighteen. When the
Society for the Suppression of Vice succeeded in closing down
these places, the inmates who could not be returned to their
friends or family were sent to an asylum.

As the Victorian era drew on, foreign observers were horrified
to see children selling themselves on the streets of Spitalfields
and Bethnal Green in the daytime. At night they moved west.
A correspondent of *Le Figaro* wrote: 'Every evening towards
midnight more than 500 girls aged from twelve to fifteen
parade between Piccadilly Circus and Waterloo Place, that is
on a stretch of ground no more than 300 yards long.' This was
described by Hector France as the '*marché aux enfants*'.

Social purity campaigner Ellice Hopkins, who ran the
London Female Mission to the Fallen, set up by Lord

Shaftesbury in 1858, saw that young girls were increasingly being recruited into London's sex trade by older men. Viennese sexologist Havelock Ellis quoted her insight into how men pulled off this trick:

> '*Many girls,*' *said Ellice Hopkins,* '*get into mischief merely because they have in them an element of the "black kitten", which must frolic and play, but has no desire to get into danger. Do you not think it a little hard,*' *she added,* '*that men should have dug by the side of her foolish dancing feet a bottomless pit, and that she cannot have her jump and fun in safety, and put on her fine feathers like the silly bird-witted thing she is, without a single false step dashing her over the brink, and leaving her with the very womanhood dashed out of her.*'

Walter kept lookout for black kittens to dash. However, there was a far more pernicious trade going on. In London, there was a lively market for maidenheads.

W.T. Stead, editor of the *Pall Mall Gazette*, set about investigating the trade in virgins. A brothel keeper, who himself had married a fourteen-year-old prostitute, told Stead:

> *Maids, as you call them – fresh girls as we know them in the trade – are constantly in request, and a keeper who knows his business has his eyes open in all directions, his stock of girls is constantly getting used up, and needs replenishing, and he has to be on the alert for likely 'marks' to keep up the reputation of his house. I have been in my time a good deal about the country on these errands. The getting of fresh girls takes time, but it is simple and easy enough when once you are in it. I have gone and courted girls in the country under all kinds of disguises, occasionally assuming the dress of a parson, and made them believe that I intended to marry them, and so got them in my power to please a*

good *customer. How is it done? Why, after courting
my girl for a time, I propose to bring her to London to
see the sights. I bring her up, take her here and there,
giving her plenty to eat and drink – especially drink. I
take her to the theatre, and then I contrive it so that she
loses her last train. By this time she is very tired, a little
dazed with the drink and excitement, and very frightened at being left in town with no friends. I offer her
nice lodgings for the night: she goes to bed in my house,
and then the affair is managed. My client gets his maid,
I get my £10 or £20 commission, and in the morning
the girl, who has lost her character and dare not go
home, in all probability will do as the others do, and
become one of my 'marks' – that is, she will make her
living in the streets, to the advantage of my house. The
brothel keeper's profit is, first, the commission down
for the price of a maid, and secondly, the continuous
profit of the addition of a newly seduced, attractive girl
to his establishment. That is a fair sample case of the
way in which we recruit.*

*Another very simple mode of supplying maids
is by breeding them. Many women who are on the
streets have female children. They are worth keeping.
When they get to be twelve or thirteen they become
merchantable. For a very likely 'mark' of this kind
you may get as much as £20 or £40. I sent my own
daughter out on the streets from my own brothel. I
know a couple of very fine little girls now who will be
sold before very long. They are bred and trained for
the life. They must take the first step some time, and
it is bad business not to make as much out of that as
possible.*

*Drunken parents often sell their children to brothel
keepers. In the East End, you can always pick up as
many fresh girls as you want. In one street in Dalston
you might buy a dozen. Sometimes the supply is in
excess of the demand, and you have to seduce your maid*

yourself, or to employ someone else to do it, which is bad business in a double sense. There is a man called S—— whom a famous house used to employ to seduce young girls and make them fit for service when there was no demand for maids and there was a demand for girls who had been seduced. But as a rule the number seduced ready to hand is ample, especially among very young children.

'Did you ever do anything else in the way of recruiting?' asked Stead.

Yes. I remember one case very well. The girl, a likely 'mark', was a simple country lass living at Horsham. I had heard of her, and I went down to Horsham to see what I could do. Her parents believed that I was in regular business in London, and they were very glad when I proposed to engage their daughter. I brought her to town and made her a servant in our house. We petted her and made a good deal of her, gradually initiated her into the kind of life it was; and then I sold her to a young gentleman for £15. When I say that I sold her, I mean that he gave me the gold and I gave him the girl, to do what he liked with. He took her away and seduced her. I believe he treated her rather well afterwards, but that was not my affair. She was his after he paid for her and took her away. If her parents had inquired, I would have said that she had been a bad girl and run away with a young man. How could I help that?

I once sold a girl twelve years old for £20 to a clergyman, who used to come to my house professedly to distribute tracts. The East is the great market for the children who are imported into West End houses, or taken abroad wholesale when trade is brisk.

During his investigation, Stead also met up with two

procuresses in the virgin trade, whom he called Miss X and Miss Z. Stead wrote:

The difference between the firm of Mesdames X and Z and the ordinary keeper of an introducing house is that the procuring of maids (which in the case of the latter is occasional) is the constant occupation of their lives. They do nothing else. They keep no house of ill-fame. One of the members of this remarkable firm lives in all the odour of propriety if not of sanctity with her parents; the other, who has her own lodgings, nominally holds a position of trust and of influence in the establishment of a well-known firm in Oxford Street. These things, however, are but as blinds. Their real work, to which they devote every day in the week, is the purveying of maidens to an extensive and ever-widening circle of customers ... The business was started by Miss X, a young woman of energy and ability and great natural shrewdness almost immediately after her seduction in 1881. She was at that time in her sixteenth year. A girl who had already fallen introduced her to a gentleman, and pocketed half the price of her virtue as commission. The ease with which her procuress earned a couple of pounds came like a revelation to Miss X, and almost immediately after her seduction she began to look about to find maids for customers and customers for maids. After two years, business had increased to such an extent that she was obliged to take into partnership Miss Z, an older girl, about twenty, of slenderer figure and fairer complexion. At one time, Miss Z gave all her time to the business, but one of their customers suggested that it would look more respectable, and besides increase her opportunities, if she resumed her old position as head of a sewing-room. She accordingly went back to her old quarters and resumed the responsibility of looking after the morals and manners of some score young

> *apprentice girls who come up from the country to learn*
> *the business.*

They did not participate in the white slave traffic – English prostitutes were in great demand on the Continent during the nineteenth century – or sell the girls into brothels once they had lost their virginity.

'Our business is in maidenheads, not in maids,' Miss X told Stead. 'My friends take the girls to be seduced and take them back to their situations after they have been seduced, and that is an end of it so far as we are concerned. We do only with first seductions, a girl passes only once through our hands, and she is done with. Our gentlemen want maids, not damaged articles, and as a rule they only see them once.'

The two women specialized in recruiting 'nurse-girls and shop-girls, although occasionally we get a governess, and sometimes cooks and other servants'. Young girls from the country, 'fresh and rosy', were picked up in the shops or when they were running errands.

'But nurse-girls are the great field,' said Miss X. 'My old friend is always saying to me, "Why don't you pick up nurse-girls, there are any number in Hyde Park every morning, and all virgins."'

The two women scoured the royal parks.

'Hyde Park and the Green Park are the best in the morning; Regent's Park in the afternoon,' they said. 'As we go coasting along, we keep a sharp lookout for any likely girl, and having spotted one we make up to her; and week after week we see her as often as possible, until we are sufficiently in her confidence to suggest how easy it is to earn a few pounds by meeting a man . . . Thus we have always a crop of maids ripening, and at any time we can undertake to deliver a maid if we get due notice.'

Miss X and Miss Z avoided telling the girls any explicit details of what they were in for. Some were very naive and found even undressing an ordeal. There were those who knew what was going to happen; others would grow frightened when confronted with the sex act itself. In that case, Miss X and Miss Z would hold the poor girl down while their client raped her. Other procuresses used a 'drowse' or a 'black draught' of laudanum or chloroform, so the girl was unconscious when she was deflowered. For some men this was not good enough.

'In my house, you can enjoy the screams of the girl with the certainty that no one else hears them but yourself,' a seemingly respectable woman brothel keeper told Stead. Her house stood in its own grounds. Its walls were thick and there was a double carpet on the floor. The only window, which opened onto the back garden, had shutters and heavy curtains.

> *The girl may scream blue murder, but not a sound will be heard. The servants will be far away in the other end of the house. I only will be about seeing that all is snug ... Flogging, both of men and women, goes on regularly in ordinary rooms, but the cry of the bleeding subject never attracts attention from the outside world. What chance is there, then, of the feeble, timid cry of the betrayed child penetrating the shuttered and curtained windows? To some men, however, the shriek of torture is the essence of their delight, and they would not silence by a single note the cry of agony over which they gloat.*

Some madams would go to any lengths to satisfy the whims of a rich client, no matter how vile.

'To oblige a wealthy customer who by riot and excess had impaired his vitality to such an extent that nothing could minister to his jaded senses but very young maidens,' Stead reported, 'an eminently respectable lady undertook that whenever the girl was fourteen or fifteen years of age she should be strapped down hand and foot to the four posts of the bedstead, so that all resistance save that of unavailing screaming would be impossible. Before the strapping down was finally agreed upon, the lady of the house, a stalwart woman and experienced in the trade, had volunteered her services to hold down the virgin by force while her wealthy patron effected his purpose. That was too much even for him, and the alternative of fastening with straps padded on the underside was then agreed upon. Strapping down for violation used to be a common occurrence in Hall-moon-street and at Anna Rosenberg's brothel in Liverpool. Anything can be done for money, if you only know where to take it.'

Panders supplied a certificate of virginity with the girls they procured. It was possible to bribe a doctor to supply bogus certificates, but Miss X and Miss Z saw no reason to do that as the supply of virgins was plentiful. Stead put them to the test, ordering five virgins at £5 (£350 today) per maidenhead. The girl would get half of this. Stead told the women that he was buying these girls wholesale with the intention of selling on their chastity. The going rate for a virgin at that time was £10 in the East End; £20 in the West End.

When the two procuresses arrived with the first batch of three, Stead accompanied them to the doctor where they submitted to examination, one by one, without objection. Some naive girls mistook the examination for the act itself.

'To the unutterable disgust of the girls, two of them were refused a certificate,' wrote Stead. 'The doctor could not say that they were not virgins; but neither of them was technically a *virgo intacta*. I then gave them five shillings per head for their trouble.'

The other girl was given a written certificate, which read:

———— ———— W.,
June 27, 1885.
This is to certify that I have this day examined ———
D———, *aged 16 years, and have found her a virgin.*
——— ———, M.D.

The following Monday, two nursemaids were taken to the doctor's and certified as virgins. The next Friday, taking no chances, Miss X and Miss Z turned up with four more girls – three of them were fourteen years old, the other an eighteen-year-old under-cook. Only the eighteen-year-old was certified.

'It is always the young ones who are unable to stand the doctor's examination,' rued Miss X.

The girls who had been certified were then required to sign a document agreeing to surrender their newly confirmed virginity. It read:

Agreement

I hereby agree to let you have me for £5, and will come
to any address you send me at two days' notice.
Name, —— + (her mark), aged 17.
Address, 318, S —— Street.

If the girls were underage, they would also have to get a certificate signed by one of their parents saying that they consented to her 'seduction'. It was a common way for working-class families to make a bit of money.

Miss X and Miss Z went to all this trouble because of the competition from girls whose virginity had been 'restored'. They were so plentiful that the market for uncertificated virginity was depressed.

The anthropologist Professor Benjamin Tarnowsky wrote in 1890: 'Forty years ago not less than £50 was paid for a *virgo intacta*, now one can be bought for £5. Forty years ago one did not dare demand medical proof of virginity, now one can get this for £1.'

One of the most notorious madams of the day was Mary Jeffries. She had an assistant called Mrs Travers (real name Elizabeth Hobbs) who procured girls at railway stations by offering to watch them while the parents went to gather luggage or buy tickets, then kidnapping them.

Demand was so great that girls had to be recycled. In Ostend, Stead found a midwife who performed abortions and 'patched up' or 'vamped up' the girls brought to her by panders.

'The number of vamped-up virgins that Mrs Jeffries is reported to have procured for her aristocratic clientele in the neighbourhood of the Quadrant is regarded in the profession as one of the most remarkable achievements of the great Chelsea procuress,' wrote Stead.

In an earlier era, the famous prostitute and madam Charlotte Hayes said it was perfectly possible for a woman to lose her virginity 500 times and still continue to pass as a virgin. She boasted that she had had her own virginity restored 1,000 times by a Dr O'Patrick. Doctors turned to medieval Arabian medical texts to discover how to do it. There were two main components to the process. The first was to simulate some blood flow during penetration as if the hymen was being torn. This was achieved by putting a blood-filled fish bladder or a sponge soaked in blood into the vagina before intercourse. Worse, a leech could be inserted so, when an eager lover, dislodged it, blood would run. Worse still – excruciatingly so – was inserting pieces of broken glass. Next, the passage itself had to be tightened. An astringent decoction of sloes or acorns, cypress nuts, Provençal roses, myrrh and other styptics were used as a method by which 'the normal female parts, now too wide, may be drawn together'. Otherwise, the steam produced when heated brick or a red-hot iron was dropped into vinegar was applied.

Walter, we have seen, was interested in virgins, but he was determined to have the real thing. One night, he raised the matter with a retired major at his club, whom he often lent money to.

> *I one night talked about virgins and of getting them. He said such things were done; that harridans got a young lass, if well paid for it, but that they generally sold the girls half a dozen times over, 'and', said he, 'they train the young bitches so there is no finding them out; you may pay for one who was first fucked by a butcher boy, and then her virginity sold to a dandy; you may pay for it my boy, and not find out you have been done.' I pondered much over this, and the next night returned to the subject. His opinion was that an old stager like*

him was not to be done; but that any randy young
beggar would go up to the girl, and flatter himself he
had had a virgin, if the girl was cunning. 'When you
see the tight covered hole with your eye, find it tight to
your little finger, and then tight to your cock, my boy;
when you have satisfied your eye, your finger, and your
cucumber, and seen blood on it, you may be sure you
have had one, and not otherwise.'

Could this major whom Walter often discussed sexual matters with and lent money to be Colonel Hughes-Hallett? They
almost certainly belonged to the same club. One of Walter's
regular mistresses, a Frenchwoman named Camille, also
encouraged him to take an interest in virgins.

Then although she knew every incident of my life, she
took to asking if I had ever had a virgin, saying, 'Are
you sure, did you see her cunt before you had her?
Would you not like one again, if I can get you one, a
young virgin French girl, one sure to be a virgin?', and
so on until she made me doubt if I had ever had one. At
last I thought that I should like to have another. Well,
she could get me a young French girl, but would have
to go to France, it would cost a large sum of money.
This talk went on for some time, and little by little
I agreed to give her fifty pounds to pay her journey, and
also to keep on her lodgings. She postponed the journey
for a long time, but at length she went. She made me
promise to do something for the girl besides paying
her – which meant something or nothing – but I prom-
ised to pay the journey of the virgin back to France,
should she want to go; and also whenever I had the girl,
to pay Camille a 'Victoria', 'because', said she, 'you will
have my rooms and prevent my bringing friends home.'

A Victoria, of course, was a sovereign. With Walter's £50,
Camille headed off to the Continent and disappeared. 'Thought

I, "I am going to be humbugged,"' wrote Walter. He told the major, who said: 'You are done brown my boy, done brown; that woman will never turn up again.' ('Done brown' is Victorian slang for being swindled.) 'He joked me so, that I avoided him, and kept the subject to myself afterwards,' said Walter.

Nevertheless, Walter continued to pay the rent on Camille's lodgings, although 'the landlady said she did not expect to see her again. I had now set my heart on having this virgin; ten weeks nearly had gone.' However, Camille did eventually return with a young French girl called Louise. She said she needed more money to cover her expenses. By that time, Louise had cost him £90. Although still young, Walter had no qualms about deflowering Louise.

> *I went to work to get into Louise, having no compunctions, it seemed to me the most natural thing in the world. I had read about the naughtiness of seduction, but my associates had taught me that every girl wanted fucking, and was longing secretly for it, high, or low, rich or poor, it was the same. As to servants, and women of the humbler class, that they all took cock on the quiet, and were proud of having a gentleman to cover them. Such was the opinion of men in my class of life and of my age. My experience with my mother's servants corroborated it; and so to get into Louise seemed both natural and proper.*

Walter paid Camille another £10 to get Louise insensible so that he could check that she was a virgin. He waited across the road until he saw a signal in the window. Louise lay on the bed in a nightgown, which Camille threw up. Then she opened the girls legs while Walter examined her. Satisfied by what he had seen, Walter wanted to touch Louise's genitals, but Camille prevented him. Nor would she give him sex that night, so Walter went out to pick up a woman in Regent Street, whom he took to a bawdy house. The next day, Walter grabbed hold of Louise.

I caressed her, and in spite of her struggles, got my hands on her breasts and half-way down her belly, spoke baudy, pulled out my prick, was repulsed, and gave her a sovereign. Camille came back and I fucked her.

Walter then paid Camille £15 to go away for ten days. He then went to see Louise, who told him that Camille had gone away. 'I expect Madame has gone off with some man,' said Walter, 'she will get a good lot of fucking.' Walter then plied Louise with champagne and got her to look at an album full of 'voluptuous pictures'.

I opened the book again; under her eyes was a picture of a woman undressed, laying at the edge of the bed, her legs open, her middle finger on her cunt; by her side a man with trowsers down, his prick out stiff and crimson-tipped, one hand on the woman's thigh, and intensely looking at her cunt.

'I want to do that with you,' I said. 'Fi done! C'est villain,' said she, and pushed the book violently away. It fell on the floor, and at the same instant she attempted to rise. I held her tightly, and pulling her back on to the big sofa, her legs flying up, I threw up her clothes in front, showing her fine pair of thighs, and the next minute I had my mouth and nose buried in the hair, kissing and sniffing it, my hands roving about wherever I could feel warm flesh.

With a shriek – then another – she twisted ... her petticoats fell down, she got across the room to her bedroom, and bolted the door.

I stood shouting, 'What a beautiful form, what thighs ... let me fuck you, have pity on me.' All that suggested itself to a man whose prick was ready to discharge in his breeches did I say, but fruitlessly, she made no reply. I went back to the sofa and considered what to do. Soon I heard her moving, crept to the door, and heard the rattle of piddle. 'You're piddling out of that dear cunt,' said I, 'how I wish I could feel it.' The rattle stopped, and again I went back to the sofa.

He invited her out, but she did not answer. Then he went to the outhouse, leaving the book out so that Louise would see it. When he returned it was plain that Louise had taken a look at its pages. After some badgering, she agreed to go out with him. First he took her to the boot maker to buy her some new boots, provided she let him feel her legs.

She was delighted, and in the cab did nothing but put up her feet to look at them. She let me feel her legs, after she had pulled her petticoats tight round the knee; I wanted to go higher, 'No, no', she said; but I pushed up, on to her thighs.

Then he bought her a more significant present.

I bought her a bonnet, but it had to be altered and was to be sent home in the evening; I got out of the cab and, going into a shop without her, bought (guessing the size) white silk stockings and showy garters, without telling her. Then I bought her gloves, a collar and one or two other things, and then we went to dine.

The shopping trip aroused him.

As I bought each successive article I told my wants coarsely enough. I felt her in the cab, and got so excited that I pulled my cock out, keeping it covered with my handkerchief, removing it from time to time as I thought the sight of the cock would excite her. 'The omnibus, the omnibus,' she cried out suddenly. Forgetting myself and all but my wants, I had exposed my randy doodle just as an omnibus passed, and as I looked up, there was the conductor laughing at me.

I went to the N ... n hotel, then just opened, and ordered a dinner; there the collars, cuffs, gloves and other things, she fitted on and looked at, and laid them down, so that she could see them when dining. Gloves she had never put on in her life before. The anticipation of the bonnet filled her with delight; it was handsomer she was sure, than any one she ever saw Madame wear; did I not think she would be handsomer than Madame, if as well dressed? She was wild with conceit, and told me again how Madame had refused to buy her things she wished; saying that a servant could not be allowed to wear them. This grievance had sunk deeply into her mind. Meanwhile talking, laughing, joking, sometimes saying, 'fi! fi ! donc', sometimes, 'oh! villain!' sometimes giving me a kiss, sometimes saying, 'be quiet', she ate a good dinner, drank more champagne than she was aware of, got more and more talkative, whilst I got more and more lewed.

The bonnet still had a crucial role to play.

'The bonnet will be home', said I, 'let us go.' 'Allons, allons', so off we went. It was dusk when we got in the cab. 'I am to put on the stockings if I give you a pair, and to feel,' I said. 'No man has, c'est trop fort, you ask too much; you may put on garters below the knee.' 'Why not above?' 'Oh! quite different,' said she, 'in the fields no girl minds putting her garter on before all the world below knee; but above, sh! that is disgrace.' Such is fashion, I have seen an Italian market-woman stoop forward and piss whilst talking to a man (a neighbouring stall-keeper): she saw no harm. An Englishwoman would burst first; yet if the Italian had put his hand rudely up her legs, that man might have been stabbed by the woman. Louise saw no indecency up to the knees, but above was a disgrace. 'Put your boots up,' I said, up they went. 'I

*may put garter to there?' said I feeling outside. 'Yes.'
I shoved my hand up her petticoats on to her thighs,
they closed, and down went the legs: a squeal, a
struggle, but on her thighs I kept it until I got to the
house.*

Walter is not put off by screams or struggles. The bonnet
and the mirror are still to play a pivotal role in his mission to
turn the virgin into a prostitute.

*We let ourselves in; the bonnet had not come. Louise
opened the window to look out for it, although it was
dark. A ring came, it was the bonnet; down she rushed
for it. 'Bring lights, bring lights,' said she taking one in
her hand herself, the bonnet in the other; and rushing
into Camille's room where there were large glasses,
she put on the bonnet, clapped her hands for joy, and
kissed me saying, I was so good. She put on her gloves
and collar, turning round to me each time, and asking
how she looked. 'Let me sleep with you, and I will buy
you a dress tomorrow morning,' said I. 'Impossible,
impossible, was I not going now?' said she thoughtfully
on a sudden. 'No.' I meant to sleep there; and as I had
fetched a valise, I pulled out my things, took off my
boots, put on a dressing-gown. 'There,' said I, 'I shall
sleep here till Camille comes home.' 'There will be a
row then, and what will I do? Madame Boileau (the old
woman upstairs) must know, and will tell Madame,'
and she looked hard at me.*

*Then she was attracted by my dressing-gown which
was showy, but soon began looking at herself again,
and took off all her finery with a sigh. 'I am so hot and
thirsty,' said she. It was not wonderful, for she had fed
twice heavily, and been champagning off and on for
hours, her hands were burning, heat was throughout
her frame. 'Let's have some more champagne,' said
I, and opened a bottle; I pulled my trousers off – it*

was so hot – being then in dressing-gown, drawers and
slippers, I made up my mind to force her, if I could do
it no other way. Then my eye caught sight of a white
muslin wrapper which Camille wore, it was tied down
the front with blue bows.

Walter's fetish requires him to steer the child into the very
clothes of the prostitute.

'Put on Madame's wrapper, if you are hot, you will
look handsomer than she does.' She went into Camille's
room, bolted herself in, and came out looking splendid,
and had only on beneath the wrapper her coarse
chemise, which I could see (as indeed I knew before)
just reached below her knees. My heart palpitated,
I was in my dressing-gown, she with but the thinnest
garments on. The champagne was before us, we were
on the sofa, my arm was round her waist; through
the thin folds of her light dress I could feel her firm
haunches and well-moulded body; I talked baudy,
squeezed her to me, pressed her thighs with one hand,
and put the other down her bosom.

The child is isolated, manoeuvred into the outfit of the prostitute who had supplied her. Psychologically positioned, Walter
renews his physical attacks.

Every now and then there was a scuffle, a cry, and
forgiveness; then resistance grew fainter, another glass
of champagne, and her head dropped on my shoulder,
subdued by amorousness, and when I asked her to
let me sleep with her, she only said, 'Oh! I dare not.
I must not.' I slipped my hand up to her thighs, she
put her hand down stopping its progress. 'If I could
only get her into the bedroom, and on to the bed,'
I thought and went to Camille's room; the candles were
still burning. 'Would you like silk stockings? Here they

are.' 'Is it so?' said she, bounding up. I held them up before her. 'Let me put them on.' 'The garters above knee, mind.' 'Yes, yes', said she impatiently, 'give them me.'

She sat down on the side of the bed, and let me put them on, putting one leg up after the other, pulled off her new boots and old stockings, I saw her thighs, but she never heeded, so anxious was she to get the silk stockings on. I had thrown off my dressing gown, and knelt in front of her as a boot maker does in fitting on boots. I was so slow, that impatiently she said, 'Give it me, give it me,' pulled it on herself, and then put on the boot. I sat down on the floor, lowering my head and looking. Her silks and boots engrossed her. My prick came out from under my shirt, stiff, standing and pointing up to her; she never saw it, but got up directly one garter was on, contemplated one leg in the cheval-glass, laughed with delight, turned round, kissed me; then on went the other. As I put that garter on, I kissed the thigh just above it, up she got, lifted her robe to see her legs, strutted up and down in front of the glass until tired of looking. Her fine limbs looked exquisite in the silks and boots.

I cuddled and kissed her, put my arm round her. 'Do let me, dear,' I said. I got my hand up her clothes and between her thighs, she crossed her legs without replying.

The long build-up ends with Walter tipping into violence, first in language and then in acts. Brutal words are followed by brutal actions, Walter recording exactly how the child will yield through fear and anticipation of the pain he is happy to inflict.

'I will fuck you, I swear I will,' said I as I forced my hand still closer in. 'Oh! oh!' she said, and nothing more. I pulled her backwards on the bed . . . my finger

slipped farther. 'Oh I, don't hurt me,' she said sharply.
Pressing her backwards on the bed, I lifted her limbs,
she was yielding, meant fucking. I ripped open at once
the slight blue bows which fastened the muslin gown,
threw up the chemise . . .

Walter's turn-on in the virgin rape was the screams: 'Is she virgin? A sharp cry, "Oh! don't hurt me". I felt an obstacle, pushed violently again and again; "oh! oh! don't".' But in the first attempt he had not succeeded in creating his ultimate visual fetish, so he continued. He did not describe gagging the child, nor subduing her screams by hand, or telling her not to cry out. He liked to hear proof of the pain he was inflicting.

Next was fear lest she should get up . . . With pride
and power I clasped her, feeling sure she was virgin.
There she lay in all her beauty, submitting to my will,
I enjoying my sense of power, wriggling gently for a
minute, till my prick demanded its right of entry.
I pushed, a sharp 'oh!' a harder push, a louder cry,
the obstacle was tight and hard indeed, I had never
had such difficulty before; my lust grew fierce, her
cry of pain gave me inexpressible pleasure, and saying
I would not hurt, yet wishing to hurt her and glorying
in it, I thrust with all the violence my buttocks could
give, till my prick seemed to bleed, and pained me. 'Oh!
mon Dieu! ne faites pas ça, get away, you shan't,' she
cried, 'Oh! o-o-oh !' . . . and I had finished the toughest
virginity I ever had yet.

The job was done, months of anticipation, hopes,
fears, and desire, were over; my prick was in the cunt
of a French virgin, at a cost of two hundred pounds.

Walter plainly did not mind using violence to get his way, whatever the cost. He even took pleasure in hurting her. There were other delights he savoured from deflowering a virgin; 'on the chemise beneath large spots of sperm, patches of blood, and spunk streaked with blood in quantity'.

It transpired that Louise was Camille's sister.

'You have promised me never to go into the bedroom with my sister again!' said Louise.

Walter promised. It was a promise he would not keep.

'This was a funny episode,' mused Walter, 'a funny conversation between a woman carrying her first male spunk in a bloody cunt, and a man with a cock still dripping with cunt-juices on to his shirt, sitting by her side. We talked by the side of the bed; then for a minute she put her head on my shoulder and cried; it was over-excitement, nothing else, no regret.'

Unaffected by Louise's tears, Walter wanted to make her feel more pain.

> *She prayed me not, she was sore, ill, it hurt her. Hurt her? I longed to hurt her, knew I was going to give her pain whilst I lied, saying that no pain more would she feel . . . up her orifice went my cock again, amidst murmurs and prayers to leave her alone, a glorious fuck.*

Even after that, the sight of 'spunk mixed with blood' and 'the bloody seminal marks of her virginity' aroused him once more.

> *I felt a pain in my prick, and found the foreskin a little raw. I had paid for hurting her by hurting myself; but what did that matter; I was the first that had been up that cunt, had torn it open, my spunk was in her then, the bloody indications were all around me. I awakened her.*

Walter revelled in taking Louise's physical virginity. Even more, he also liked to destroy the girl psychologically as well by taking away her pride. The dominating mind tricks are as essential to Walter as hearing the screams, a practical step to make his victim compliant for later sexual abuse.

All that she has been taught to hold most sacred from man he has seen, felt, kissed, pierced, violated and wetted in. The virginity she prided herself on he has destroyed, she no longer shuns him, but is ready to comply with all his wishes, hopes he will compel her soon to yield again. This is the work of a few hours, and as she sits drinking her coffee opposite to him she thinks with him, what a change has taken place.

Walter records the rape of Louise in such excruciating detail as it is a milestone in his secret life. Camille's sister is the first time he has actively sought a young girl to rape. He has invented a formula for domination, and tested it.

That was my state of mind with Louise. I had had virgins before without pride in having them, they came in my way, but never had I sought them. Two certainly had never been breached before, but it gave me no pride nor special gratification. This woman I had thought and thought about for months, coveted and paid for the sole pleasure of piercing her hymen. I had now the delight of experience, of leaving my sperm where man had never left it before. This girl of sufficient age, growth and form, I had bored with difficulty and pain, to her and myself, she had bled, I had bled ... I sat at breakfast with as much complacency and jollity as a man could; yet, beyond fucking, I felt that I did not care one damn about her, and even felt sorry. I cannot explain why I felt that, but recollect it.

Walter's plea at the beginning of his book is that it will be of value to 'psychology' as he cannot explain his own sexual aberrations. The detail of his attack on Louise is all the more remarkable as, he tells us elsewhere in the book, it was made nearly two years before he kept his sexual diary regularly. He had written down what he had done to Louise nearly forty years later, as it is a marker of his own addiction. Walter reports on the first wave of a cycle of violence that would follow him into old age. First months of pre-planning and mental savouring of a sexual assault, intense arousal at the sight of blood during the attack, to be followed only by complacent indifference, a state that could only be cured by a new scheme. Walter's rollercoaster of sexual violence was soon to be repeated.

When Camille returned, he paid her £50 for Louise's virginity and told Camille that he had promised Louise not to have sex with her sister again. But, at the first opportunity, he did just that. He kept both of them until Camille announced that she was getting married and Walter contracted gonorrhoea. 'By her advice I wrote to Louise, said I had the clap, and feared I had given it to her, that she would not forgive me I was sure, and so never meant to see her again.' He was tired of Louise and determined to get rid of her, anyway. He sent her a cheque then headed off to Paris with his cousin Fred.

My illness kept to me, so returned to London, got a little better, longed for Louise, stood opposite the house one night, nearly crossed over to have her, but resisted, and seeing a nice woman in Regent street went home with her. I was so impatient that I pushed her to the side of the bed directly I was in the room, felt for her cunt, and spent in her in a minute; she had not taken her bonnet off. My spending hurt me, my doctor had told me I could go with a woman without fear of injuring her, but that for my own sake I had better abstain. She got up and took off her bonnet, to see if lying down had hurt it. 'I'll have you again,' said I. 'Let me wash, you've spent such a lot, it's all running down my thighs.' Again I fucked her; and next morning my ailment came back. My doctor said it served me right.

Soon after, the sign 'lodgings to let' appeared in the window of Camille's apartment. He knocked on the door. Madame Boileau answered and said the two women had left.

I never heard of the women afterwards. I am aston-
ished now that I was wheedled out of so much money
for a French virgin. How I could have done much that
I did makes me now laugh, I must have been very
green, and Camille very cunning; but I was also rich,
and generous, which accounts for much.

It did not occur to Walter that the sisters had gone on the run
from the violence of their client. With Camille gone, Walter
showed what was to become a most important link in his
secret sexual life: his relationship to older prostitutes who
could procure children for him. This was no great legal danger.
British law then said girls could consent at twelve.

Walter now had a taste for virgins, so he asked his mistress
Betsy Johnson to get him another one. She complained, saying
that where she lived there was not 'a girl over fourteen who
had not had it done to her'. 'I'll get you half a dozen little ones
without hair, but they all know as much as I do about fucking,'
she said.

That offer I declined, for I knew there were plenty
like that about the streets, whom I could get without
her assistance. 'A virgin, a virgin, and with no hair on
her cunt, or nothing.' Well she would if she could, but
she shook her head. Her last words were, 'Just a little
hair on it you wouldn't mind, would you?' 'Perhaps if
only just shewing, but mind, I'll have a good look at
her cunt, with thighs open, before I have her. No virgin,
no pay. I won't be gammoned.' 'All right, me dear, but
you'll have to wait pretty long.'

However, Betsy found a virgin for Walter named Molly, whom
she had taken in. And so began a new type of relationship
between Walter and a procuress. The first had been Camille,
a skilled French courtesan, who was callous enough to sell
her sister. But when she saw her condition after Walter's
rape, Camille ran away from him. Betsy, however, was no

Parisian class act: the girl she brought Walter was plainly a child. Not even Walter's signature gift – a bonnet – would disguise it.

They took her to a bawdy house, but she was so young the woman on the door would not let her in. While they were arguing in the hallway, another couple came in through the street door and the doorkeeper rushed Walter, Betsy and the girl upstairs so that no one would see them. Walter gave her a sovereign.

> *Betsy had made up the girl in the oddest way with a big bonnet, and she looked almost a bundle of clothes too big for her. It was an error in the disguise I saw at a glance. But there we were, all three snugly in the best room in the house. Betsy pulled off her bonnet and shawl as quickly as possible. Then she pulled a great shawl off the little one, and a bonnet big enough for a grenadier, and I saw a lovely girl of about fifteen, looking up earnestly from rather deep-set eyes. 'This is the friend who sent you the boots and stockings, and he'll give you a lovely crinoline,' said Betsy, 'Won't you, sir?' 'Yes,' said I.*

Betsy stripped the girl down to her chemise, so that Walter could examine her. To encourage her, the older prostitute stripped off her own gown and:

> *. . . throwing up her own chemise rolled back on the sofa, threw up her legs, opened her thighs well, and pulled her cunt lips wide open. 'There look at that, me dear – there's a sight for a stiff prick.' 'Oh! Oh! Betsy, don't,' said the girl. 'Didn't we do so last night my dear.' 'Oh, not before a man,' said the girl, colouring up and trying to pull Betsy's chemise down.*
>
> *'Don't – for shame.' 'Shan't. Pough, all my eye, Molly, show him yours.' 'Shan't – you're dirty.' 'Didn't we look at each other's last night, Molly?' 'Not before*

*a man – don't now, Betsy. Oh, don't before him.' It was
said quite naturally.*

Betsy took off her chemise and the girl did the same, although
she still tried to hide herself. To the girl's horror, Betsy sat back
on the sofa, opened the lips of her vulva and urged Molly to do
the same. She then urged Molly to perform oral sex on Walter.

'Oh, ain't you dirty,' said Molly.

'Dirty, you little fool,' said Betsy. 'A prick's nice wherever
you put it, nice anyhow, and anywhere. You'll think so before
a week – you'll be ready to eat one a week after it's been up
your cunt, Molly.'

Molly was still reluctant, so they decided to get her drunk.

'I got out wine and liqueur which I had brought with me,'
said Walter. 'There was only a water tumbler in the room and
we all three drank out of it. I would not ring for glasses lest the
servant should come in, and see the youth of the lass.'

Even though the girl got drunk, she would not cooperate.
Walter opened her legs by force, but Molly fought him off.
Then he suggested they play a game. He would toss shillings at
her vulva and she could keep any coins that hit it. He demon-
strated on Betsy, but Molly would not join in. Betsy then got
cross, saying that if the girl would not cooperate, she would
not be allowed to go home with her and would have to sleep
on the steps. Eventually, Betsy pushed her down on the bed
and Walter began his 'investigation into her virginity'. She was
so young that she had no hair on her pudendum. Once Walter
was satisfied that Molly was a virgin, he agreed a price with
Betsy then licked the girl's vulva, despite her struggles.

*But she would not let me mount her. In vain Betsy
coaxed and bullied by turn. 'No, no,' she had altered
her mind. She was frightened it would hurt, it would
make her bleed. Then she burst into tears and cried.
I desisted, Betsy quieted her, for fear of the people of
the house, and when she had done she spoke to her in a
subdued voice as nearly as possible thus.*

But Betsy was angry and berated Molly. 'You bloody little fool. I had pricks up me twice as big as that, and longer than his, before I was your age – don't I get a living by fucking? Don't I get silk stockings and dresses by fucking? How are you going to live? Who's going to keep you, I want to know? What did you come here for? Didn't you promise me? Didn't you say you'd let him? Didn't you say you'd like to be fucked if it was nicer than frigging yourself.'

The girl made no reply, and was confused and shaking.

> 'All right, you may go, and you may get home as you can,' said Betsy. She jumped off the bed and rolled up in a bundle the girl's chemise and petticoat, which were quite new. 'You shan't have the things I've given you, damned if you shall.' Then she came to the bed, violently pulled off from the girl both boots and stockings, and rolled up the stockings with the petticoat. 'Now you may go – put on your dress and your boots, and go, you're not wanted here, my friend and I will stop all night.'
>
> The girl was scared out of her senses. 'Don't Betsy, where am I to go to?' 'Go the Hell and buggery, go and shit yourself, I don't care a bloody fart where you go to.' The girl blubbered and sobbed out, 'I will then, I will let him.' 'Hold your snivelling, and don't make that noise. Someone's at the door perhaps. Let him do it to you. If you don't, go – and you know. You know what.' Betsy, tho slanging in the foulest way (and I have not told a quarter what she said), did it all in a suppressed voice.
>
> But when it came to it, Molly refused again, saying it would hurt.
>
> 'You do it, Betsy, with him,' she said, 'you let him do it.'

Betsy and Walter began to have sex, while Betsy encouraged

Molly to join in. Walter whispered 'sham' in Betsy's ear and they both pretended to come.

'Let him now do it to you,' said Betsy, again coaxing and threatening Molly. Walter then leapt on Molly and raped her.

> *'Oho – hah – ar,' she screamed, 'You hurt – get off – I won't let you – har.' She screeched loudly, and struggled violently. 'Hish, you damned howling little bitch,' said Betsy, pushing a pillow right over the girl's head. I pressed my head on the pillow, the girl's head was hidden from me, but I could hear her cry.*

Despite Molly's tears and her cries of 'oh don't', Walter continued, relishing the 'tightening of the hymen round my prick, as it went through it with a cunt-splitting thrust'. Molly begged him to 'take it out, you do hurt'. But these very words aroused Walter again. When he had finished a second time, Molly lay there with her hands covering her face in shame. Walter delighted in the sight of blood on the girl, blood running down the counterpane and blood on his penis.

> *I was delighted beyond measure. She bled more than any virginity of her age which I ever yet have had, I think.*

Betsy tried to make light of what had happened. Molly cried. Betsy and Walter began drinking again.

> *Our talk was all about fucking, and we chaffed the former virgin, who sat without answering in a meditative way, seemingly wondering and upset by what had taken place. At length, looking at Betsy, 'What will mother do if she finds it out?' she said.*

Betsy told Molly to tell her mother that one of the local boys had done it and she should come back to her and she would show her how to make a living. Molly complained that her

vagina hurt. Betsy suggested that she wash it. But Walter
wanted her again as she was.

> *She would not consent, she would not be hurt again,*
> *but we persuaded her, got her on to the bed . . . 'No –*
> *no – no,' was all I got out of her.*

But Walter would not be dissuaded. In fact, he convinced
himself that Molly was actually enjoying it.

> *She laid so quiet and closed her eyes in such a manner,*
> *that I am sure it did give her pleasure, tho she might*
> *not have spent.*

Walter continued meeting Betsy and Molly to have sex until
Molly returned to her mother who had been in prison after
assaulting a 'Peeler' – a policeman. Then Walter saw no more
of her. He had fifteen-year-old Jemima Smith, but after a few
nights, 'I began to have had enough of her, and to be satisfied
with youthful cunts'.

> *Yet I met her again. She had told her sister, who only*
> *hoped she would not get in the family way, and advised*
> *her to wash it out directly I had finished up her. Then,*
> *saying I was going out of town, I did not see her for a*
> *fortnight, during which time I had a letch for another*
> *little virgin. Then I met and asked if she could not*
> *bring me one, offering her gold if she would. Her own*
> *compliment was now half a crown. She would try, she*
> *said, but there was only one gal she knew of, and she*
> *didn't work with her, but they often talked together*
> *about men and women doing it, and she'd like it done*
> *to her, she knew. Giving her a few days, again I met her.*
> *The girl would come, and Jemima said she was sure she*
> *hadn't had it done to her, for she had seen her cunt. But*
> *before Jemima, tempted by the gold, consented to bring*
> *her, she remarked, 'What do yer want another gal for?'*

One night soon after, she came with a girl of about her own size and age – her name was Eva Kelly, and she was, I think, Irish. I didn't like her, for she looked half starved, bony and dirty, besides she seemed cunning and much too knowing. Her first want was to know what I had done with her friend Jemmy, who at my request, shewed her cunt to me and to Eva, who also saw my prick go up it for a second or so, and seemed gratified by the sight. Then, yielding to my solicitations, and the sight of the gold, I got Eva on the bedside with petticoats up, and I examined her orifice.

It was a funny looking little cunt, wonderfully small it seemed for her age, and with four or five straggling short dark hairs about it. She let me pull open the lips, which were scarcely lips, and certainly she was virgin. But when I tried to put my finger up the interior, she closed her thighs sharply and got up, and tho at last I promised her two sovereigns, she would not let me have her. She felt my prick, and looked at it with seeming pleasure, let me pull up her clothes and feel about her, but lay down on the bed with me she wouldn't. In vain Jemmy said 'I'll let him do it if you will, you said you wanted it, didn't yer now?' 'Perhaps I did and perhaps I didn't,' she replied to every remark, adding at times, 'but I shan't tho, I'm afraid.'

Once again, Walter had to rely on the participation of his procuress to get what he wanted. Older prostitutes became complicit in his sex crime. If they did not help him, Walter would not pay them.

Jemmy laid down and I fucked her, Eva witnessing the operations, feeling my prick before it went in, whilst in, and also when it came out reeking from the cunt. All was of no use. I put my sovereigns into my pocket angrily, saying I'd give her nothing for coming. She looked,

I thought, disappointed but said nothing. 'Come Jemmy, let's fuck again,' said I after a time, and laid her at the side of the bed. 'I'll give you half a crown to let me see your little cunt whilst I fuck Jemmy.' 'Do,' said Jemmy. Eva consented, and I shagged Jemmy, looking at the other one's beggarly cunt. She held it open without any hesitation like any harlot. Again I begged and took out the gold, and fingered her little quim as well, but 'No, shan't — I'm afeared,' quite settled the matter, and I neither had her nor saw her after that night.

Jemmy said she could get me no other girl, for she wasn't friendly with many girls, but didn't she get quickly on to the bed when I said, 'Let's do it.' After one or two more meetings I got tired of her, and just at that time she said they were short of work, and she had nothing to do, her mother would keep her tight till she had work again, and she couldn't be out after dark.

Walter had begun by paying a wealthy French courtesan for her sister, but soon he was trawling for strangers on the poorest streets. Later in the same chapter, Walter reflects on having 'three girls all under sixteen and a little virgin'. Elsewhere he says:

All circumstances attending the deflorating this lass are evidence that most poor girls are fucked before they are sixteen. It is immaterial who does it, but they will be fucked. She is quite as willing to have it done, as he to do it, and probably it is the female who incites the male (unwittingly perhaps) following simply the law of nature quite as much as the male incites the female to the pleasure. What rot then this talk about male seduction, when it is nature which seduces both. Equally absurd also the sentimental bosh about young virgins being bought and sold. The results to the girl are the same whether she is fucked for money or love – or if the term be liked better – for lust. A prick up her she

will have before she's sixteen. She will have her sexual
pleasure, paid or unpaid for it. The poor alone are
philosophical in amatory matters.

Walter had set a template. He had an older woman, usually
a prostitute herself, procuring a prepubescent girl for him. In
this case, it was a woman called H or sometimes H*l*n.

H was impecunious, and having made money by the
lass whose virginity I took last spring, I shall always
think put this temptation in my way for further profit.

I found there one day a little servant about fourteen
years old, fairly pretty, sprightly and pleasing, and
thought I should like to investigate her privates as soon
as I set eyes on her. H said the lass was the daughter
of a sea-coast man, and had two sisters gay, had been
stopping with one in London who had let her see men
fuck her. 'She won't be long before she has it.' She had
found out that this girl frigged herself – I suppose all
girls of fourteen do – and wanted to be fucked, knew
all about it, had said so. H and she had already looked
at each other's cunts – women like doing that – and she
had frigged the girl who was virgo intacta warranted.
'If you don't have her someone will soon, her sister
won't let her stop here, she'll make money out of her,
and if not the girl will let some man fuck her.' 'I'll have
her,' said I and began courting the lass.

Soon after, H said she'd have nothing to do with it,
but still she would not hinder me. I reminded her of
what she'd told me. She replied, that certainly the girl
would have a man soon somehow, or somewhere, for
she was so lewed and curious, that a little persuasion
would get her. H's change of front, her object in holding
back now, was not very clear to me, but I felt sure she'd
like to see me fuck the lass for baudy pleasure if for
nothing else. Telling her so, she laughed and said she
should.

That day I kissed the slut, gave her a trifling present, and felt up to her navel. She let me readily, even seemed complimented by my attention. H was present. 'There's no hair on your dear little cunt.' 'Not yet,' she replied. I had then one of those long, exciting, preliminary, baudy, inductive conversations, so very delicious with an unpoked girl, and equally delicious to her. 'You know what fucking is, don't you my darling?' 'No,' said she, hanging her head and looking confused. 'What a lie,' said H. 'You've seen gentlemen doing it to your sister.' 'Oh.' said the lass. At length she confessed it. Then I felt freely all about her hidden charms, my hands roved up and down, I insinuated a finger between her thighs closed tightly, but it rubbed between the lips of the grove, and brought away the female aroma. Ah, how nice is the smell of cunt, which some fools say isn't nice. She was sitting on my knee, I wanted to see her naked but that she refused, I pulled up her clothes, she pushed them down, whining. H winked at me. 'Your cunt smells so nice,' said I. 'You're a nasty man,' she replied, colouring up and looking at H.

'Let me another day, dear.' Then, as customary, I gave money to buy shoes and stockings.

On the next visit, Walter got the girl to raise her chemise so that he could run his hand over her 'nascent bubbies' and check that she had no pubic hair. He also examined her hymen and performed cunnilingus on her. However, he could not get an erection with her, but persuaded her to participate, then he had sex with H.

The job of a procuress to Walter had already proceeded from a supplier to a joint participant. Now Walter came to rely much more heavily on his pander. When he could not get an erection, the procuress had to help him. Only then, Walter attained his delight – the sight of blood. He was even proud of himself, while the girl sobbed.

Never was a virginity at last taken with greater ease or
luxury than hers, never was a girl more anxious to lose
it. She washed her cunt under H*l*n's directions, and
the basin full of water got red. Again I looked at her
quim which would not stop bleeding. 'Yes I liked it,'
said she, and that was much nicer than frigging herself,
that she was glad she had been fucked. She kissed me
as if she wished her lips to eat into mine, did the young,
hot-cunted loving slut, whose willingness for fucking
was remarkable.

Walter was fully aware that his sex assaults on young girls
involved tears, bloodshed and screams. But by this point he
began to enter the delusional thought process of the criminal
paedophile. He began to convince himself that those he
attacked got what they were asking for – that their pain was,
in fact, pleasure.

I'll swear I have known full grown virgins fetched by
my gristly rammer, the first time it was put up them,
and that their pleasure followed the slight pain which
the splitting gives. I incline to the belief that breaking
thro the hymen really gives very little pain. I know as
much about it as most men, and am sure that many a
virgin spends with her first fuck.

Walter then remarked that the girl 'soon left H*l*n and took
to whoring with her sister, who had also her cunt plugged
before she was fourteen'. Out in the countryside with cousin
Fred, he had sex with a country lass who was a virgin, but he
found her a disappointment.

I had had none of that sensuous delight which both
mentally and physically is found in getting into a virgin,
had never thought of having her as one, nor did I rec-
ollect much cunt resistance to my penetration; but she
certainly was a virgin. In my furious lust, and with my

> *unbendable stiff prick I must have hit the mark, and*
> *burst through it at one or two cunt-rending shoves. She*
> *had given a loud cry in the midst of it, 'Oh! pray now,*
> *oh! Pray,' but I had heeded it not. What excited me was*
> *her youth, her size, and the idea of having a little cunt*
> *with but little hair on it, something smaller than Molly's.*

Walter described a signature to his cycle of crime. In the country he acted alone, or with his cousin Fred, a male accomplice. In London, he habituated himself to women procuresses. He would need them to fulfil a new and more awful fantasy.

> *In bed, thinking of, and funking consequences, I longed*
> *for a girl still smaller, for one with no hair on her cunt*
> *at all.*

The other constant in his fantasy was resistance. In *My Secret Life* he usually recorded these underage women saying 'oh, don't' before he forced himself on them. It seems to have turned him on.

In London, girls were usually supplied by older prostitutes such as Betsy, Sarah, H*l*n and Nell. The women would get the girl drunk then Walter would deflower them, usually employing a certain amount of force. In one case, Sarah says: 'Get into bed and do her – if she won't let you, I'll hold her – don't give her a minute to think about it.' Although it was plain that the girls did not want to have sex with him, he convinced himself that they did, saying in one case 'unconsciously she wanted fucking'. In another case, a girl fell silent after he forced her to hold his penis, 'now unconscious to all but sexual wants I expect,' he said. She was 'now under the spell of the prick – lewdness and curiosity well filled her, she wanted the prick but feared it . . . ' He liked the fact that he hurt the girls as he entered them ' and enjoyed the sight of them bleeding afterwards.

'How I gloried at the sight of the red on her chemise,' he said after deflowering a girl named Lizzie. 'The very idea of hurting her delighted me – the blood on her chemise made my cock stiffen.'

The sight of blood aroused him and he forced himself on her despite her protests and obvious pain. Again, he believed she enjoyed the 'mutual spasms of ecstatic pleasure, and murmurs of delight in the throes of fucking – in joys which those of Paradise cannot excel'. For Walter, it was a 'divine function of nature . . . to inject the precious life giving sperm into the cunt'. Even when a woman who was not a virgin bled after sex, it aroused him.

When he was having sex with a girl named Agnes, he remarked that he had frequently been struck with impotence. However, once he had confirmed that she was a virgin he instantly had an erection. Again, she refused to have sex with him, but he went ahead anyway, remarking: 'Girls, I find, whatever their struggles before, all lay quiet directly the prick has shed its balmy fluid up them; sperm is a delicious cunt-soother.'

Agnes was Nell's maid. She soon supplied another named Frances, whom Walter called a 'willing virgin' even though she refused him and complained that it hurt. But when H*l*n supplied an 'unfledged' fourteen-year-old who seemed genuinely to have wanted to lose her virginity, Walter was struck with impotence repeatedly.

Walter also noted that the women who supplied the girls often masturbated while watching him deflower their victims.

> *Women I think like getting girls fucked, take pleasure in initiating them into love's mysteries, tho there is nothing mysterious about it excepting in the psychology. Madame de Maintenon probably did the same as Sarah F., Nell L. and H*l*n did.*

Although Walter, for the most part, had professional prostitutes recruit children for him, when he found young girls on the street he got them to bring him their friends. After having fifteen-year-old Kitty, he gave her a few shillings extra to bring him a fourteen-year-old named Pol, who was coaxed and bullied into surrendering her virginity. When she howled in pain and tried to get him to stop, Walter said: 'Again I coaxed, promised, lied, and Kitty bullied.' After raping her, Walter upbraided Pol for whining and snivelling, and called her an 'ugly little devil'. Then he inspected her bleeding vagina and, leaving both the girls naked, made his escape.

'I had fear that I might be in trouble through my voluptuousness,' he said.

When he raped a servant girl called Jenny, who begged him to 'think of a poor girl's ruin', he threatened her, too, saying: 'Now don't be a fool, damned if I don't murder you if you are not quiet! By God, I'll shove my prick up your cunt if I'm hanged for it.'

He was disappointed afterwards that there was no blood. However, he said, with some satisfaction, that she was 'like a well-broken horse' even though she 'cried every ten minutes', and she slammed the door behind him when he left.

As Walter grew older, he became more obsessed with having sex with virgins. When Walter was nearly fifty, he had sixteen-year-old Carry, then asked her to procure fourteen-year-old Sally for him.

A mistress he called the Great Eastern – presumably after the steamship launched by Isambard Kingdom Brunel in 1858 – even got the mother who lived downstairs to get her young daughter to show him her maidenhead, on the pretext that he was a doctor. Afterwards, he had fevered sex with the Great Eastern, pretending she was the girl. Later, he paid the girl half a crown to show him again, this time without her mother being present and without her knowledge or consent. He paid her another half-crown to feel his penis and then persuaded her to watch while he had sex with the Great Eastern. Later, the Great Eastern arranged for him to see the girl naked. That time, he masturbated over her, but the Great Eastern would not allow him to have penetrative sex with her.

After getting married, Walter found himself short of money and began going with a lower class of prostitute in poorer districts, which would appear to be the streets of Whitechapel. By then, his obsession with finding virgins had become a dangerous compulsion. Walter described walking the dark streets of the East End groping thirteen- and fourteen-year-old girls. He would insert his finger, looking for virgins among the street children. He tried to take advantage of a girl whose mother had just died, but she cried out and was rescued by an older woman. However, the girl's rescuer was not shocked and let Walter try again to seduce the girl. He raped another virgin in the back of a cab. Even though she cried out for him to stop, the cabman took no notice. He rued that, normally, 'it is not the gentlemen who get the virginities of these poor little bitches, but the street boys of their own class'. This, he thought, was a waste.

But it was not just virgins he liked, it was little girls.

> *Now suddenly I desired a little one. At L**c**t*r S****e one night, a group of girls so little that I thought them at first only rude children, spoke to me; and it ended in my going to a house with one about half my height, but who stripped and talked as baudily as if she had been fucked twenty years. I fucked her, wondering at the little hairless quim my prick was closed up in.*

The most extreme case he recorded was when he had sex with a ten-year-old girl, during a period when he was going out a lot with his lecherous cousin, Fred. Again, he relished every detail of the vile story.

> *Theatre every night, heavy lunches, heavy dinners, much wine, and cigars never out of my mouth, that was the first few days' proceedings. Fred was keeping a woman named Laura, of whom I shall say more; she was always with us. I don't recollect having a woman for a few days, but it may have been otherwise. On the fifth or sixth night we went to Vauxhall Gardens to a*

masquerade. It was a rare lark in those days. A great fun of mine was getting into a shady walk, tipping the watchman to let me hide in the shrubs, and crouching down to hear the women piss. I have heard a couple of hundred do so on one evening, and much of what they said. Such a mixture of dull and crisp baudiness I never heard in short sentences elsewhere. Although I had heard a few similar remarks when I waited in the cellars of the gun-factory, it was nothing like those at Vauxhall, and it amused me very much. There were one or two darkish walks where numbers of women on masquerade nights went to piss, and many on other nights.

At supper, Laura said, 'Where have you been the last hour?' I laughed. 'Tell us.' 'Hiding in the shrubs where ladies go by ones, twos, and threes without men.' Laura understood. 'Serves them right, they should go to the women's closets; but you are dirty.' 'Well it was such a lark hearing them piddle and talk.' Fred, always coarse, said he never knew a woman piss so quickly as Laura. Laura slapped his head. She had not been gay, and was very modest in manner and expression; but loved a baudy joke not told in coarse language.

The signal sounded for fireworks. Off we ran to get good places. I cared more about women than fireworks, and lagged behind, seeing the masquers and half-dressed women running and yelling (fun was fast and loose then). I passed a woman leading a little girl dressed like a ballet-girl, and looked at the girl who seemed about ten years old, then at the woman, who winked. I stopped, she came up and said, 'Is she not a nice little girl?' I don't recollect having had any distinct intention at the time I stopped; but at her words ideas came into my head. She – what a small cunt – no hair on that. 'Yes, a nice little girl,' I replied. 'Would you like to see her undressed?' 'Can I fuck her?' I whispered. The little girl kept tugging the woman's hand and saying, 'Oh!

*do come to the fireworks.' 'Yes . . . what will you give?'
I agreed to give, I think, three sovereigns, a good round
sum for a common-place poke then.*

*She told me to go out of the gardens first, get a cab
and stop a little way from the entrance. In three minutes
the woman and child joined me. At about five minutes
drive from Vauxhall we stopped, walked a little way,
turned down a street and, after telling me to wait one
or two minutes, she opened the door of a respectable
little house with a latchkey, went in and closed it. A
minute afterwards she opened the door and, treading
lightly as she told me, I found myself in a parlour out
of which led a bedroom, both well furnished. Enjoining
me to speak in a low tone I sat down, and contemplated
the couple.*

*The woman was stout, full-sized, good-looking,
dark, certainly forty, and dressed like a well-to-do
tradeswoman. The girl's head was but a few inches
above my waist, and she certainly was not more than
ten years, but for such age as nice and fleshy as could
be expected. She had an anxious look as she stared
at me, and I stared at her. The last month's constant
desire to have a cunt absolutely without any hair on
it was to be realized, I was impatient but noticed and
remarked, 'Why you have gas!' – a rare thing then
in houses. 'Beautiful, is it not?' said the woman, and in
a voluptuous and enticing manner began undressing,
until she stood in a fine chemise, a pair of beautiful
boots, and silk stockings. Engrossed with the girl whom
I was caressing, I scarcely had noticed the woman; but
as she pulled up her chemise to tighten her garter, and
showed much of a very white thigh, I said, 'I've made
a mistake, I did not mean you.' 'No,' said she, 'but it's
all the same.' She came to me, pinched my cock outside
saying 'oho' as she found it stiff, and then undressed
the child to her chemise. I had white trowsers and
waistcoat on, and was anxious about rumpling them.*

At my request, she drew my white trousers off over my boots with great care; then divesting myself of coat and waistcoat I stood up with prick spouting. 'Look there – feel it Mary.' The girl not obeying, she took her little hand, and made her feel it. Sitting down I lifted the girl on to my knees, and put my hand between her little thigh.

'Give me the three pounds,' said the woman. All my life I have willingly paid women before my pleasure; but thought I was going to be done so demurred, and asked if she supposed I was not a gentleman, took out my purse, showed I had plenty of money, gave her one sovereign, and promised the others directly I had the child, and then pulled off my boots.

We went into the bedroom, she lighted candles, the gas streamed in through the open door. 'Lay down Mary', said she. 'Oh! he ain't going to do it like the other man, you said no one should again', said the girl whimpering. 'Be quiet you little fool, he won't hurt you, open your legs.' Pushing her back, or rather lifting her up, there I saw a little light-pink slit between a pair of thighs somewhat bigger than a full-sized man's calves; the little cunt had not a sign of hair on it. To pull open the lips, to push up my finger, to frig it, smell it, then lick it was the work of a minute. I was wild, it was realization of the baudy dreamy longings of the last few weeks. I was scarcely conscious that the old one had laid hold of my prick, and was fast bringing me to a crisis.

Pushing her hand away I placed my prick against the little cunt which seemed scarcely big enough for my thumb, and with one hand was placing it under the little bum, when the girl slipped off the bed crying. 'Oh don't let him, the other did hurt so – he shan't put it in.'

'Don't do it to her, she is so young,' said the woman in a coaxing tone. 'Why that is what I came for.' 'Never mind, it hurts her, have me, I am a fine woman, look,'

*and she flung herself on the bed, and pulled up her
chemise, disclosing a fine form, and to a randy man
much that was enticing. 'Look at my hair, how black it
is. Do you like tassels?' said she, and throwing up her
arms out of her chemise, she showed such a mass of
black hair on her armpits, as I have rarely seen in other
women, and rarely in an English woman at all.*

*'What the devil did you bring me here for? It was
for her, not you, I hate hair, I like a cunt without hair.'*

*'Have me, and look at her cunt whilst you do it, here
Mary,' and she pulled the young one to the bed cunt
upwards. But disappointed, lewed, and savage, I swore
till she begged me not to make a noise, and saying,
'Well, well, well, so you shall, hold your tongue (to
the girl), he won't hurt you, look his cock is not big.'
She pulled the girl on to the edge of the bed again, and
brought her cunt up to the proper level with the bolster
and pillows. Then said the woman, 'Let me hold your
cock, you must not put it far in, she is so young.' I
promised I would only sheath the tip; but she declared
I should not unless she held it. 'Wrap your handkerchief round it,' said she. I did so, and that left only
half its length uncovered. Impetuously I tore the white
handkerchief into pieces, wrapped round about an inch
of the stem of my prick with it, which then looked as
if it was wounded, and bound up; then hitting the little
pink opening I drove up it. I doubted whether I should
enter, so small it was. It held my prick like a vice, but up
her cunt I was, the woman promising the child money,
to take her to Vauxhall again, and so on, and then put
her hand over her mouth to prevent her hollowing, she
did not hollow at all really.*

*I spent almost instantly, and coming to my senses
held her close up to my prick by her thighs, there was
no difficulty so light a weight was she. There I stood
for a minute or two. 'My prick is small now,' said I,
'unroll the handkerchief.' 'No,' said the woman. 'I will*

give you ten shillings extra if you do, my prick can't hurt now.' The oddity of a woman attempting to unroll from a prick a slip of white rag, whilst the prick was up a cunt; but out came my prick from the little hole before she could accomplish it.

The mark of Walter's crime was the linen handkerchief – to him a fetish item as filled with erotic meaning as the bonnets he bought as a prelude to sex. Walter now had to relish what he had done.

Desire had not left me, holding the thighs open I dropped on my knees, my prick flopping, and saw the little cunt covered with thick sperm. There lay the girl, there stood the woman, neither speaking nor moving, till my eyes had had their voluptuous enjoyment. 'I will give you another sovereign now, and then fuck her again.' 'All right,' said the woman. 'But she must not wash.' 'All right.' I gave it, then took the girl up like a baby, one hand just under the bum, so that the spunk might fall on my hand if it dropped out, and laid her on the sofa in the parlour, where the gas flared brightly, opened her thighs wide, gloated, and talked baudily till my prick stood again.

Then I lifted her back on to the bed, and rolled the strip of handkerchief round the stem again; but I longed to hurt her, to make her cry with the pain my tool caused her, I would have made her bleed if I could; so wrapped it round in such a manner, that with a tug I could unroll it. The woman did not seem so anxious now about my hurting her.

Here, Walter is at his vilest. He wanted to hurt a ten-year-old child and make her bleed.

Sperm is a splendid cunt-lubricator, my prick went in easier, but still she cried out. Now I measured my pleasure. With gentle lingering pushes I moved up and down in her. Under pretence of feeling my prick, I had loosened the handkerchief, then tore the rag quite away, and afterwards lifted her up, and then with her cunt stuck tight and full with my pego, and both hands round her bum tightly, I walked holding her so into the sitting-room to a large glass. There seeing my balls hanging down under her little arse, I shoved and wriggled, holding her like a baby on me, her hands round my neck, she whining that I was hurting her, the woman hushing, and praying me to be gentle, till I spent again. I held her tight to me in front of the glass, her thighs wide apart, my balls showing under her little buttocks, till my prick again shrunk, and my sperm ran from her cunt down my balls. Then I uncunted, and sat down on a chair. We were both stark naked.

Walter felt no remorse. For him, it was merely a pecuniary transaction.

The girl sat down on a footstool, the woman sat in her chemise. I gave her the remaining money, and to the little one some silver. Although I had had her twice, I scarcely had looked at her; both fucks must have been done in ten minutes. Now I longed to see the little cunt tranquilly. 'Let me wash her cunt,' said I. 'You can,' said the old one. I took the girl into the bedroom, she left a large gobbet of sperm on the stool, which the old one wiped off. I washed her cunt, threw her on the bed, and looked at the little quim. It seemed impossible I could have been up it; but from that day I knew a cunt to be the most elastic article in the world, and believed the old woman's saying, that a prick can always go up where a finger can.

Even then, Walter could not stop. After having the child, he had the older woman. It is a union of sexual sadists.

He noticed that she had masturbated while watching the rape.

> *She was frigging her clitoris with her middle finger, and she smiled invitingly. 'Come and do it to me, I do want it so, I have not had a poke for a fortnight.'*
>
> *My love of a fat arse, and a big hairy cunt returned suddenly. I stood turning my eyes, first to the little hairless orifice, then to the full-lipped split, then to the little pink cunt, and then back again to the matured cunt. 'Come, do me.' 'I must go.' 'Why?' 'I came to have her.' 'So you have, now have me, you can have her again if you like after.' 'Can I?' 'Yes, oh! come, I am so randy.' 'It's late.' 'Stop all night.' I said I would. Off the bed she got, put a nightgown on the child, laid her on the sofa, told her to go to sleep, and throwing off her boots and stockings, got on to the bed again.*
>
> *I threw off my socks. 'Shall I be naked?' said she. 'Yes, it is very hot.' Off went her chemise, and the next instant, cuddling up to me, she was tugging at my prick, kissing me, and using every salacious stimulant. Though a hot night, naked as we both were we felt a chill, so covered ourselves with a sheet.*
>
> *'How old are you?' said I. 'Guess.' 'More than forty.' 'I am not thirty-eight, although I am so stout, feel how firm my flesh is, how my breasts keep up.' I threw down the sheet to see her fully. She was delighted, turned round and round, opened her thighs, pulled open her cunt, exposed herself with the freedom of a French whore, and by the time I had seen all my prick was at fever heat, and I fucked her. Our nakedness was delightful.*

Walter talked to the older woman, exploring the social circumstances that had brought him the child. Facing poverty, she was selling an orphan for sex. It was better than the workhouse.

*She was not the mother, nor the aunt, though the child
called her so; the child was parentless, she had taken
charge of her and prevented her going to the workhouse. She was in difficulties, she must live, the child
would be sure to have it done to her some day, why
not make a little money by her? Someone else would,
if she did not.*

Walter clearly knew what he had done was not only shameful,
but illegal under the consent laws of the time. But his mindset
was that of a sexual sadist. He was so far removed from
empathy for his victim, he was annoyed when the older woman
stopped him hurting the child some more and even found the
situation 'funny'.

*How funny to have that little creature on the top of
me; how funny to be able to feel at the same time a
big hairy cunt at my side. Such thoughts and emotions
finished me, and after spending in the little one, she
again went to the sofa, then with my arse to the aunt's
arse we went to sleep.*

*She was the youngest I ever yet have had, or have
wished to have. We laid abed till about mid-day. I fucked
as much as I ever did in my life, and found that a tiny
cunt although it might satisfy a letch, could not give
the pleasure that a full developed woman could. Tight
as it was, it had not that peculiar suction, embrace, and
grind, that a full-grown woman's or girl's has. When
I was getting drier and drier, the old one stiffened my
prick, and I put it into the child; but oscillate my arse
as I might, I could not get a spend out of me; then in
the aunt's clipping though well stretched cunt, I got my
pleasure in no time. A fuck is barely a fuck if a man's
prick is but half up a girl, it wants engulfing. A very
young girl never has the true jerk of her arse, nor the
muscular clip in her cunt; so if a languid prick be put
up it, it will slip out, unless the letch be strong; whereas*

a flabby, done-for prick, once in the cunt of a grown woman may be resuscitated, and made to give pleasure to both, if she uses the muscular power which nature has given her between bum-hole, buttocks, and navel.

We ate and drank, I paid liberally, and with empty ballocks and a flabby tool went away. White trowsers and a black tailcoat were then full evening dress at Vauxhall; but ludicrous in the day. I recollect feeling ashamed as I walked out in that dress in the sunshine.

Despite what he had done, Walter only felt ashamed because he had to walk down the street during the day in his evening clothes.

She would not fetch a cab as she was most anxious about noise. She gave me full instructions where to write and have the girl again. About a fortnight afterwards I made an appointment, but she did not keep it. I went to the house and asked for her; a woman opened the door. 'Do you know her?' said she. 'Yes.' 'She is not here, and I don't know where she has gone, perhaps you're as bad as she is,' and she slammed the door in my face. A few years passed away before I took a letch for a hairless cunt again, and then I was a poor man.

It was this encounter with the ballet girl that, in 1969, was declared by a British court to be 'the most evil thing you have ever read.' But as bad as it was, it may not be the worst of it. In numerous places in *My Secret Life*, Walter mentioned that he had destroyed part of the manuscript, so sex with virgins and underage girls may be the lesser of his evils. In one place, he said:

The narrative of some adventures, tho carefully written, will be destroyed. Unfortunately, soon after they occurred, I made them the subject of conversation at my clubs, and told some of the incidents to friends and relatives. To repeat them here would be to declare myself, and others still alive. So to the flames they go – how many, many pages of manuscript have been so destroyed.

Was this how news of his nocturnal adventures reached the ears of Hughes-Hallett? In another place he noted:

More manuscript must be destroyed for mere abbreviation will be useless. Eighty pages must go to the flames. The narrative thus curtailed cannot show clearly the gradual development of abnormal eccentric tastes, and necessitates an epitome of some years to supply the hiatus. Some of the most conspicuous incidents I shall keep as originally written or nearly so, and they will take their place chronologically.

One can only wonder at what these 'abnormal eccentric tastes' were, especially when compared to the ones he talked about. That these tastes were even more bloodthirsty is a reasonable assumption.

It would take the muckraking news editor Stead to provoke Walter's epitome. After years of stalking virgins in London's sexual underground, the hunter was about to become the hunted.

6

THE LONDON MINOTAUR

In 1885, W.T. Stead set up a secret commission to look into prostitution in the capital. During its investigations, he came across a wealthy 'English gentleman' with an insatiable desire for young women, whom he called the London Minotaur.

As in the labyrinth of Crete there was a monster known as the Minotaur who devoured the maidens who were cast into the mazes of that evil place, so in London there is at least one monster who may be said to be an absolute incarnation of brutal lust. The poor maligned brute in the Cretan labyrinth but devoured his tale of seven maids and as many boys every ninth year. Here in London, moving about clad as respectably in broad cloth and fine linen as any bishop, with no foul shape or semblance of brute beast to mark him off from the rest of his fellows, is Dr ———, now retired from his profession and free to devote his fortune and his leisure to the ruin of maids. This is the 'gentleman' whose quantum of virgins from his procuresses is three per fortnight – all girls who have not previously been seduced. But his devastating passion sinks into insignificance compared with that of Mr ———, another wealthy man, whose whole life is dedicated to the gratification of lust. During my investigations in the subterranean realm I was constantly coming across

> *his name. This procuress was getting girls for* ———*,*
> *that woman was beating up maids for* ———*, this girl*
> *was waiting for* ———*, that house was a noted place*
> *of* ———*'s. I ran across his traces so constantly that*
> *I began to make inquiries in the upper world of this*
> *redoubtable personage. I soon obtained confirmation*
> *of the evidence I had gathered at firsthand below as to*
> *the reality of the existence of this modern Minotaur,*
> *this English Tiberius, whose Caprece is in London.*

The Roman Emperor Tiberius was renowned for his sexual
excesses with young boys and girls on the island of Capri, or
Caprece. But despite the excesses of the London Minotaur,
Stead did not name him.

> *It is no part of my commission to hold up individuals*
> *to popular execration, and the name and address of this*
> *creature will not appear in these columns. But the fact*
> *that he exists ought to be put on record, if only as a*
> *striking illustration of the extent to which it is possible*
> *for a wealthy man to ruin not merely hundreds but*
> *thousands of poor women, It is actually Mr* ———*'s*
> *boast that he has ruined 3,000 women in his time. He*
> *never has anything to do with girls regularly on the*
> *streets, but pays liberally for actresses, shop-girls, and*
> *the like. Exercise, recreation; everything is subordi-*
> *nated to the supreme end of his life. He has paid his*
> *victims, no doubt – never gives a girl less than £5 – but*
> *it is a question whether the lavish outlay of £3,000 to*
> *£5,000 on purchasing the assent of girls to their own*
> *dishonour is not a frightful aggravation of the wrong*
> *which he has been for some mysterious purpose per-*
> *mitted to inflict on his kind.*

Stead told the Liberal MP, Reginald Brett: 'The Minotaur is
a man, as you are perfectly well aware, of no education or
position, whose power of mischief depends upon the accident

of wealth having been accumulated in hands unfit to use it.' In reply, Brett said: 'I was sorry to hear in the H[ouse] of C[ommons] Labouchere tells people that you came across the tracks of Mr Gladstone in the course of your exposures. He also had told people the name of the 'Minotaur'. Labouchere was Radical MP, Henry Du Pré Labouchere, who added an amendment to the 1885 Criminal Law Amendment Act outlawing 'gross indecency'. It was this amendment that led to the arrest and trial of Oscar Wilde. Labouchere regretted that Wilde was sentenced to only two years' hard labour. His original proposal would have permitted seven.

Wilde himself was part of a ring called the Order of Chaeronea that procured underage boys for sexual purposes. He also boasted among his circle men like Leonard Smithers, whom Oscar called the 'most learned erotomaniac in Europe' and whose tastes included 'first editions, especially of women'. 'Little girls are his passion,' Oscar said.

Stead's description of the Minotaur closely matches Walter, who did not go to university and owed his considerable wealth to two large legacies. Even if Stead's Minotaur was not Walter, the fact that the name of such a man was being bandied about in the House of Commons was certainly a threat to Walter's reputation, if not his liberty. All those involved in the virgin trade and having sex with underage girls might be named and shamed and, possibly, prosecuted.

As well as the prostitutes Walter got to procure for him, he was in contact with a madam he called the abbess. According to Walter, the abbess was 'an expert in flagellation' who 'either tickled or bled the masculine bums, and women's as well, or superintended men flogging female bums'. She set up all manner of orgies, where Walter indulged in both heterosexual and bisexual activities, although flogging held no appeal for him.

It seems likely that the abbess was the notorious madam and procuress, Mary Jeffries, who was involved in white slavery and child prostitution. She had brothels in Kensington and Chelsea, as well as a flagellation house in Hampstead and a torture chamber in Gray's Inn Road. During his investigations, Stead visited one of her houses:

> *Flogging or birching goes on in brothels to a much greater degree than is generally believed. One of Mrs Jeffries' rooms was fitted up like a torture chamber . . . There were rings in the ceiling for hanging women and children up by the wrists, ladders for strapping them down at any angle, as well as the ordinary stretcher to which the victim is fastened so as to be unable to move. The instruments of flagellation included the ordinary birch, whips, holly branches and wire-thonged cat-o'-nine-tails.*

Jeffries would drive out into Hyde Park in her carriage to pick up girls, and had among her clientele a number of aristocrats including, reputedly, Leopold II, King of Belgium. Walter was well aware that the use of prostitutes was common even in the highest reaches of society. He once attended a huge prostitutes, ball at a fashionable address in Great Portland Street.

The police knew of Mary Jeffries' activities – one of her brothels was across the road from the police station – but she was not prosecuted. However, one policeman, Inspector Minahan of T Division, did amass evidence against Jeffries and others, which he reported to his superintendent. He was mocked for not taking the hush money like the rest of the force, and warned to hold his tongue. When Minahan persisted in his allegations, he was demoted to the rank of sergeant and resigned from the force in disgust when his superiors refused to prosecute her.

In 1880, the Quaker Alfred Dyer set up the London Committee for the Exposure and Suppression of the Traffic in English Girls for the Purposes of Continental Prostitution, after rescuing an eighteen-year-old English girl from a brothel in Brussels, who talked of police complicity in the trade. Four years later, the committee learned that Jeffries was running a high-class brothel in Chelsea. They had employed ex-Inspector

Minahan as a private detective. He had spent a year gathering evidence against her. By March 1885, the committee were ready to bring a private prosecution. The only crime with which they could charge Jeffries was the common-law offence of keeping a disorderly house. However, they hoped to gain valuable publicity when their evidence was heard, especially as one of their witnesses was a former housemaid at the brothel who was ready to testify that a thirteen-year-old girl had been raped and flogged by a customer. The trial was held on 5 May. Jeffries arrived at the court escorted by a group of rich young army officers and pleaded guilty by prior arrangement with the judge so that none of the evidence against her would be heard. The judge let her off with a fine of £200, which was immediately paid by some of her rich customers, and she left the court in triumph with the army officers forming a guard of honour. Stead alleged that Jefferies pleaded guilty in order to 'save her noble and Royal patrons from exposure'.

Another famous procuress was on the streets of London at that time. Her name was Rebecca Jarrett. She was the youngest of thirteen children. Her father was a rope-maker with a shop off the Old Kent Road. He left when Rebecca was young. Her mother turned to drink and, by the time Rebecca was twelve, her mother was selling her to men in Cremorne Gardens, Chelsea. This was one of the areas Walter visited to pick up prostitutes.

When one of Rebecca's brothers returned from sea and discovered his sister was a prostitute, he threw her out of the family home. By the time she was sixteen, Rebecca was running a brothel. For twenty years, she roamed the country drinking heavily, living off men and running brothels in Manchester, Bristol and Marylebone in London, where she procured young girls who were drugged before being deflowered. In 1884, she was living with a man in Northampton, where she fell dangerously ill from excessive drinking. She collapsed outside a Salvation Army meeting. An officer rescued her and sent her to London for ten weeks' drying out in Whitechapel Hospital. She was then transferred to the Rescue Home in Hanbury Street. It was run by Catherine Booth, wife of William Bramwell Booth, the general of the Salvation Army.

Whitechapel was the home of the Salvation Army. Its founder, William Booth, set up his first Christian mission there. Under the influence of his wife, Catherine, the Salvation Army quickly became a leading force in the women's movement by offering women positions of leadership within the organization, which they were denied elsewhere. However, the Salvation Army, with its agenda of temperance and moral purity, was not unopposed. Pub owners and brothel keepers set up a 'Skeleton Army' to disrupt their meetings. Angry mobs would pelt them with dead rats and cats, tar, rocks, rotten vegetables and even burning coals and sulphur to show their hatred of the new movement. The Skeleton Army had its own banners and publications. In 1882, 669 Salvationists were brutally attacked. One of them, Mrs Susannah Beatty, was viciously kicked in the stomach and left for dead in a dark alleyway. Others were killed. There was a war going on, and on to the battlefield would step Walter and Jack the Ripper.

Threats against Jarrett's life forced her to find sanctuary with proto-feminist Josephine Butler, whose husband was a canon of Winchester Cathedral. Josephine Butler was fighting for the repeal of the Contagious Diseases Act, which sanctioned the enforced medical examination and imprisonment of women thought to have a venereal disease. She likened her campaign to the fight against slavery. Not only did the Act permit the violation and humiliation of women, it tacitly gave official sanction to prostitution and the keeping of brothels where, she maintained, women were kept as slaves. Her supporters, she said, were 'for downtrodden women what the American Abolitionists were to the despised Negro'.

Butler had also risked male violence by her stance. At the 1870 Colchester by-election, she had campaigned against the Liberal candidate Sir Henry Storks, who supported the Act. As governor of Malta, he claimed to have stamped out 'the disease incident to vice'. A special office had been created for him in the War Department and the government was eager to find him a seat in the House of Commons. At Colchester, the hotel where Butler was staying was attacked by a mob led by the city's brothel keepers.

'It must be observed that these were not of the class of honest working people, but chiefly a number of hired roughs, and persons directly interested in the maintenance of the vilest of human institutions,' Butler said.

The windows were smashed and she was forced to dim the lights and hide in the attic. Supporters who had risked going outside were manhandled. Their clothes were torn and they were pelted with 'mud, flour and more unpleasant things'. Some were wounded. Eventually, for her own safety, she had to flee the hotel and, later, sought refuge from the mob in a disused warehouse. Two years later, when Butler was holding a rally in Pontefract, a violent mob 'led by two persons whose *dress* was that of gentlemen' set bundles of straw on fire while the police, 'Metropolitans who had come from London for the occasion of the election . . . simply looked at the scene with a cynical smile and left the place without an attempt to defend us'. Two or three working women managed to hold off their attackers while Butler made her escape. Mrs Butler was sympathetic to the plight of prostitutes, particularly those, like Rebecca Jarrett, who had reformed. And when Jarrett proved successful performing rescue work among prostitutes in Portsmouth, the Butlers helped her set up her own rescue home at Hope Cottage in Winchester.

Meanwhile, Mrs Booth had been touched by the stories she heard from Rebecca Jarrett and others. Many of the girls in the home were in their teens, some only eleven or twelve. They had been seduced by men like Walter, then abandoned to be arrested and harried by the police as common prostitutes. At the time, the age of consent for women was thirteen, after the 1875 amendment to the 1861 Offences Against the Person Act had raised it from twelve. The indecent assault or rape of a girl under the age of consent was a misdemeanour with a penalty of up to two years' imprisonment. Unlawful carnal knowledge of a girl under the age of ten was a felony, which invited severe penalties. Change was afoot. In 1881, legislation to raise the age of consent to sixteen and allow children under eight to testify against their abusers was introduced. Called the Criminal Law Amendment Bill, it was passed by the House of Lords in 1883, but was blocked by the House of Commons. Reintroduced the following year, it again failed. The Earl of Dalhousie tabled the bill a third time in April 1885. Again, it was passed by the House of Lords, but the Commons had not voted on a second reading when it adjourned for the Whitsun break in May and supporters feared that it would be put aside again unless some drastic action was taken. However, General Booth thought that if the public could be made aware of the plight of girls deflowered then abandoned, Parliament would be forced to act. He invited Stead, who had also fought for the repeal of the Contagious Diseases Act, to come to Hanbury Street for a meeting with Josephine Butler and the anti-vice campaigner and Chamberlain of the City of London, Benjamin Scott. Booth was promoting the bill and explained to Stead that it might fail again unless some drastic action was taken. Booth then told Stead that he had four fallen women in the next room whom he could interview himself. Three of them were girls under sixteen. Rebecca Jarrett was later sent to meet Stead. As a result, Stead learned firsthand about the plight of prostitutes in London and agreed to agitate to get the bill passed.

'I do not know if you can do it,' said Scott, 'but if you cannot, then we are beaten. No one else will help us. You might be able to force the bill through. Will you try?'

Stead said he would. They prayed together. But Stead was a man of action. It was then that he set up his Special and Secret Commission of Inquiry to gather more evidence on child prostitution and the white slave trade. Among its members were Josephine Butler and representatives of the Salvation Army and the London Committee, which was then chaired by Benjamin Scott. As part of the investigation, two women, an employee of the *Pall Mall Gazette* and a girl from the Salvation Army, posed as prostitutes and infiltrated brothels at great risk, getting as much information as they could and escaping before they were forced to render sexual services. It has even been said that Butler spent ten days walking the streets of London with her son, Georgie, posing as a brothel keeper and a procurer, and that together they spent a total of £100 buying children from high-class brothels. Stead consulted ex-inspector Minahan and interviewed brothel keepers, procurers and traffickers, including Mary Jeffries. During his investigations, the name of the London Minotaur kept surfacing.

The Reverend Benjamin Waugh, who, in 1889, founded the London Society for the Prevention of Cruelty to Children (later the NSPCC) recorded Stead's travails:

> *He got valuable introductions from good names to the fashionable brothels; he personated a wealthy voluptuary; he won his way into the lady keepers' private rooms; and through the good names he had and the free spending of money, he heard confidential secrets. He made acquaintance of procuresses; priced and bought their virgins; he entered the shuttered and cloth-curtained rooms, where shrieks were drowned of maddened girls; saw the chambers of children, the chloroform which the tender mercies of the wicked administered to 'very little things', and the women that healed them; he heard their inhuman laugh at his suggestions of pity, their confidence as to being 'within the law'.*
>
> *'But do gentlemen like girls unwilling?'*
> *'Some like them a little unwilling, it is pleasant, you see, to persuade; and some like quite a stir. There's no fun in a fox that wants to be caught.'*
> *'Can you get me an unwilling girl?'*
> *'Give me time, and I can get you anything.'*
> *'But how about the law?'*
> *'Oh, we know the law. Then who'll believe them? Men have a kind of liking for seeing a fine girl go down.'*
> *The keepers of brothels knew flesh and blood very*

well; but they did not know him: he was the son of a Puritan, a child of the Father in Heaven: the room was moving round, the furniture swam. Again and again did he break down and stumble out into the dark street, giddy, with a bursting brain. It seemed as though it would kill him; and yet he returned again. He had but one thought – it must be done.

Under the quiet stars, in the awful stillness of the London night, he walked streets and parks, and got close to the hearts of the pitiable women and girls who there made their bread. To his gentle, childlike ways, their brazen bearing vanished; their eyes grew soft with genuine tears, their daring spirit grew humble: they were girls and women again; and they told him their tale of home and ruin: and he cried. They had been slain by a coward; a coward had killed the feeble; it was done when they were girls. It was all a dream, a nightmare; he became a madman.

'But you hate me!' said one. 'You mock me!' she shrieked and, flinging him from her with her arm, she rushed away into the darkness.

They were all weak enough and sinful enough, as the world counts sin; but overwhelmed by the pity of it all, he can never bear to hear unfeeling denunciations of these famished, silent strollers of the night, who light their candles in their attic-room as the stars fade.

'Oh, if ever a child of mine should be like that,' he murmured, as he bent his head upon his arm on the table of the office to which he had returned as the summer's sun was gently rising over the still sleeping city. His investigations closed.

But compiling the facts was not enough for Stead. He knew his craft as a journalist and had an eye for a sensational story. He persuaded Rebecca Jarrett to return to her old haunts to procure a girl for him. She paid brothel keeper Nancy Broughton £5 for thirteen-year-old Eliza Armstrong – £3 down and £2 after her virginity had been professionally certified. Eliza's mother, a drunk who lived in Lisson Grove, west London, got £1. Eliza was then taken to an abortionist named Louise Mourez, who was paid to certify her virginity. Mourez did so, but then took pity on Eliza and her forthcoming defloration, telling Jarrett: 'The poor little thing – she is so small, her pain will be extreme. I hope you will not be too cruel with her.' To dull the pain, she sold Jarrett a bottle of chloroform and promised to patch up the girl afterwards. Eliza was then taken to Nancy Broughton's brothel where she was undressed, put to bed and knocked out with chloroform. When she came round, she found Stead in her room and screamed. The teetotal Stead was said to have swigged a bottle of champagne to play the part. He fled. Eliza was then handed over to General Booth's son Bramwell, who sent her off to France under the care of a Salvationist family.

Stead had his story. He proved that you could buy a virgin girl from her mother for a trifle, drug her and deflower her – if that was your inclination.

7

THE MAIDEN TRIBUTE OF
MODERN BABYLON

On Saturday, 4 July 1885, the *Pall Mall Gazette* published a
short piece headed: 'Notice to our Readers: A Frank Warning'.
It warned that the Criminal Law Amendment Bill was about
to founder. Consequently, the *PMG* had set up the Special and
Secret Commission to examine the subject of sexual criminality
the bill was supposed to address. From the following Monday,
6 July, Stead intended to publish the Commission's report, in
full. However, the following warning was first given:

> *we have no desire to inflict upon unwilling eyes the
> ghastly story of the criminal developments of modern
> vice. Therefore we say quite frankly today that all those
> who are squeamish, and all those who are prudish,
> and all those who prefer to live in a fool's paradise of
> imaginary innocence and purity, selfishly oblivious to
> the horrible realities which torment those whose lives
> are passed in the London Inferno, will do well not to
> read the Pall Mall Gazette of Monday and the three
> following days. The story of an actual pilgrimage into a
> real hell is not pleasant reading, and is not meant to be.
> It is, however, an authentic record of unimpeachable
> facts, 'abominable, unutterable, and worse than fables
> yet have feigned or fear conceived'. But it is true, and
> its publication is necessary.*

As promised, publication began on the Monday. The series was called 'The Maiden Tribute of the Modern Babylon'. In it, Stead deliberately evoked the Greek myth of the Minotaur, the half-man half-bull confined to the labyrinth on Crete and which, being a creature of unnatural passions, had to be supplied every nine years with seven youths and seven maidens. The first instalment covered the sale, purchase and violation of children, the procuring of virgins, the entrapment and ruin of women, the international slave trade in girls and other 'atrocities, brutalities and unnatural crimes'. It included tales of the violation of willing and unwilling virgins, the confessions of a brothel keeper, a depiction of the London slave market, a description of how the law abets the criminals involved and ended with the tale of the purchase of Eliza Armstrong, whose identity Stead protected by renaming her Lily.

Stead claimed that during his research he wallowed in degradation and filth.

'For days and nights it is as if I had suffered the penalties inflicted upon the lost souls in the Moslem hell,' he wrote, 'for I seemed to have to drink of the purulent matter that flows from the bodies of the damned.'

But he had emerged triumphant.

'The sojourn in this hell has not been fruitless,' he said.

The next day, Stead followed up with more tales of young girls forced into prostitution, a long interview with Mesdames X and Z and the story of how he had ordered five virgins from them, at £5 a head, although two of them had failed certification as neither was technically *virgo intacta*. The next day they had brought four more still, three of whom had failed certification. Girls were duly handed over outside Madame Tussaud's. They were to get £2 or £2 10s (£2.50). One girl had been blackmailed into selling her virginity by Madame Z, who had advanced her mother money. Another said she was prepared for the pain, but would drown herself if she got pregnant. A third dreaded being undressed and had been told that 'babies never came from the first seduction'. They cried.

On Wednesday, Stead said: 'We feel as if our Commissioners had stirred up hell to heave its lowest dreg-fiends uppermost, in fiery whirls of slime.'

Stead castigated those who opposed the bill. Some contended that prostitution below the age of fifteen had practically ceased, by quoting the declining numbers of girls who had turned up at the Rescue Society on Finsbury Pavement saying they had lost their virginity between twelve and thirteen. In response, Stead related the tale of a girl who had been raped at the age of five. He said he had even been told of a house supplying little children that was visited by a cabinet minister and he quoted the Reverent J. Horsley, a chaplain in Clerkenwell, who said:

> *There is a monster now walking about who acts as clerk in a highly respectable establishment. He is fifty years of age. For years it has been his villainous amusement to decoy and ruin children. A very short time ago, six-teen cases were proved against him before a magistrate on the Surrey side of the river. The children were all fearfully injured, possibly for life. Fourteen of the girls were thirteen years old, and were therefore beyond the protected age, and it could not be proved that they were not consenting parties. The wife of the scoundrel told the officer who had the case in charge that it was her opinion that her husband ought to be burned. Yet by English law we cannot touch this monster of depravity, or so much as inflict a small fine on him.*

Again, the law seemed to abet those who abducted and impris-oned young girls in brothels. It was then that Stead revealed the existence of the 'London Minotaur'.

In the final instalment published by Stead, he accused the police of turning a blind eye to the trade, having been bought off by the likes of Mary Jeffries. Even the lowest street girl had to tip the local constable if she wanted to stay out of jail. He wrote of the collusion between the police and brothel owners when a man had tried to save a child from them. The police, too, used prostitutes, as Walter also attested. In *My Secret Life*, he mentions a policeman who kept a 'well trained' seventeen-year-old prostitute called Betsy as a mistress, as well as others who used prostitutes casually.

Stead pointed out that even while he was publishing these damning articles, Mesdames X and Z continued delivering virgins and signed a contract to supply a foreign brothel – although the police could now hardly pretend that they did not know the nature of their business. During the six weeks of investigation undertaken by the secret commission, no one they had spoken to had even been 'inconvenienced' by the police. The only involvement of the police in the investigation came when Stead and another member of the secret commission attempted to rescue a German girl of about sixteen and suffering from tuberculosis, who had been fraudulently trafficked from Cologne to be put to work as a prostitute in the Strand. Her pimp reported them to the police, who sent a detective sergeant to interview them.

Following the publication of 'The Maiden Tribute of Modern Babylon', Stead was accused of flooding London with filth and obscenity. W.H. Smith & Son, the newsagent and distributor, banned its sale but this only increased the clamour for copies. The *Pall Mall Gazette*'s office in Northumberland Street was besieged by news vendors trying to get more copies and the presses ran ceaselessly. Eleven newsboys arrested in the City and 'had up before the London mayor' were released on the understanding that they would sell no more in the City. They returned directly to Northumberland Street to pick up more copies. The *Pall Mall Gazette* begged the authorities to prosecute the paper, not those who sold it, and thanked W.H. Smith for 'reducing a demand which we were still utterly unable to meet'. In Parliament, Cavendish Bentinck asked the Home Secretary to prosecute the *Pall Mall Gazette*. Instead, fearing riots, the Home Secretary asked Stead to cease publication of the articles. Stead said he would do so only if the bill was carried without delay. But the Home Secretary could not give that guarantee, so Stead ordered the *Pall Mall Gazette*'s presses to continue. Stead said he welcomed prosecution as the case against Mary Jeffries had been curtailed without the evidence being heard.

'There would be no such abrupt termination to any proceedings which might be commenced against us, [the newspaper]' he said.

On Wednesday, 8 July 1885, when the third part of 'The Maiden Tribute' came out, there was a riot. The police moved in to guard PMG offices in Northumberland Street. Windows were smashed. Eventually, officers organized a system to allow vendors to enter through one door, purchase their copies and exit through another. The paper was sold out by 8 p.m. News vendors were still turning up asking for copies at midnight, but the *Gazette* had run out of paper.

In an effort to calm the situation, the publication of the fourth part of 'The Maiden Tribute' was delayed until Friday. French and Belgian papers had already picked up the story. American journals reprinted the articles in full, but the other British papers remained extraordinarily quiet, although *The Times* mentioned the complaints in Parliament. That Sunday, 'The Maiden Tribute' was the subject of sermons, but in the *PMG*'s Monday edition, Stead reported: 'Of course all reference to this great outpouring of righteous indignation is ignored by the morning papers.'

On 13 July, a mass meeting of women was held at Prince's Hall, in Piccadilly, demanding action. By then, feelings were running so high that the new Conservative government under Lord Salisbury could not ignore the matter. On 30 July, the Home Secretary, Sir Richard Cross, opened the debate in the House of Commons on the third reading of the bill.

'This question has stirred England from one end to the other,' he said.

There followed a heated debate. Old rakes such as Cavendish Bentinck argued that prostitution was a necessary and inevitable evil, while others argued that the young women used in the trade were already defiled by the sordid and vicious circumstances of their birth. Prostitution gave them a way to improve themselves. Nevertheless, the Criminal Law Amendment Bill was passed on 10 August 1885, including the Labouchere amendment that would lead to the downfall of Oscar Wilde ten years later.

Meanwhile, Cavendish Bentinck was accused of being the London Minotaur by the Gospel Purity Association, although they did not substantiate their accusations. He wrote to the papers complaining that the agents of the Purity Association refused either to back up their allegations with solid evidence or withdraw them. Everyone was also curious to know who was the author of a series of letters defending libertine behaviour, published under the byline 'A Saunterer in the Labyrinth'. To encourage debate, the *Pall Mall Gazette* allowed the publication of anonymous letters. At the time, it was reported: 'It is generally believed that Labouchere, who certainly has had a very extensive experience in this particular labyrinth, wrote them.'

The passing of the Criminal Law Amendment Bill was not the end of the matter. On 21 August, Stead addressed a meeting at St James's Hall to spur the faithful. The following day, a demonstration was held in Hyde Park. Billed as a 'meeting of the inhabitants of London', people came from all over the city to show their support for the newly passed Act. They carried placards proclaiming 'War on Vice', 'Protection of Young Girls' and 'Shame, Shame, Horror'. The contingents from the East End and Pimlico marched through the West End, which they considered enemy territory. Normally, the streets there bustled with prostitutes. Even the upmarket Burlington Arcade off Piccadilly had to be avoided by respectable women from lunchtime onwards. The area of clubs and bachelor chambers to the north of Green Park was a forbidden zone for unchaperoned women as the male pests who inhabited the West End were not tradesmen or errand boys but 'gentlemen'. Walter, by his own admission, was one of them and it was often difficult to tell the difference between West End prostitutes in their finery and the 'fast' daughters of the upper middle class who had abandoned the mute colours favoured by their mothers for a more 'racy' style.

On the day of the Hyde Park rally, though, it was noted that club land was deserted and the 'great ladies on the balconies of Belgravian mansions' were notably absent. Numerous bands played and it was estimated that 250,000 people turned out. Newspapers were struck by the large numbers of women and working men in the crowd. Members of the Ladies National Association for the Repeal of the Contagious Diseases Act, dressed in black and carrying white flowers, arrived by carriage. Women trade unionists were followed by wagonloads of young virgins, dressed in white, under the banner 'Innocents will they be slaughtered'. Male trade unionists and socialists also rallied to the cause on the grounds that the 'Maiden Tribute' revealed the corruption of the upper classes. Religious and moral tracts were circulated. However, members of the Skeleton Army also turned out with the pornographic journal, *The Devil*, the front page of which showed three ladies 'displaying their voluptuous charms'.

Speeches called for the 'lynching' of men who offended against the Act, while a police officer was asked why he did not arrest all men who interfered with women in the streets.

'I should have to run my own magistrate,' he replied.

At the end of the rally, the following resolutions were declared to have been carried:

> 1. *That the people of London hereby express their shame and indignation at the prevalence of criminal vice in their midst.*
> 2. *That this meeting pledges itself to assist and stimulate the public authorities in the vigorous enforcement of the Criminal Law Amendment Act, and to support any strengthening of the law which may be found necessary for the protection of young girls.*
> 3. *That it is the duty of all good citizens to face resolutely the evils, social and moral, in which these*

*crimes against girls have their root, in order that their
extirpation may be secured.*

Stead did his part in helping enforce the Criminal Law
Amendment Act by calling for the establishment of vigilance
committees under the National Vigilance Association. In the
wake of the 'Maiden Tribute' articles, the *Pall Mall Gazette*
published a pamphlet called *Vigilance Committees and their
Work: Containing the New Law for the Protection of Girls.
With suggestions as to its Enforcement by The Chief Director
of the Secret Commission.* The pamphlet was designed to put
the new law into action. On the first page, guidelines for the
committees were spelt out. These were:

> *That publicity in most cases is better than prosecution.*
> *That everything depends on individual effort.*
> *That all attempts to deal with this subject by men
> alone must fail.*
> *That the fallen woman is a sister to be saved, rather
> than a sinner to be punished; and that, while attaching
> the greatest importance to all efforts to discourage vice
> and to promote the purity of life, vigilance committees
> will be most useful if they primarily direct their atten-
> tion to the repression of criminal vice.*

This sent the sisters to the barricades. Until then, there had
been a schism in the social purity movement. There were those
who saw prostitutes as the wellspring of vice and those who
saw them as sinners to be saved. Now they were urged to
concentrate on the 'repression of criminal vice' – that is, the
trade in underage girls – and the vigilance committees were
to be a spy network to gather news on the virgin trade. Stead
pointed out:

> *Another reason for refusing resolutely to run amok
> at vice as vice is the necessity of obtaining informa-
> tion from the older women on the streets as to the*

whereabouts of these juvenile prostitutes. An adult harlot resents the competition of the child and if she is not treated as an enemy she will often be the most effective ally of the Vigilance Committee. Nor is that by any means the only service which she can render if she is given to understand that she will not be interfered with so long as she is on her good behaviour. These girls are usually very kind-hearted and sympathetic and would gladly cooperate privately in bringing to light and helping to secure the punishment of brothel slavery as well as those crimes of trapping, ruining and violating innocent girls which are constantly being committed in the trade. The fact is that without assistance from the women of the town and those who consort with them it will be almost impossible for vigilance committees to secure the information which they need to repress the crimes, the prevention of which is the primary object of their being.

And he again boasted that 'our Commissioners had stirred up hell to heave its lowest dreg-fiends uppermost, in fiery whirls of slime'.

The pamphlet also pointed out, unashamedly, that the Criminal Law Amendment Act was a blackmailer's charter. It said:

The fear that girls under sixteen will attempt blackmail upon men who have had intercourse with them, enforcing payment by threats of informing that man had rendered himself liable to a penalty of two years imprisonment with or without hard labour ... would be more efficacious in reducing the demand for juvenile prostitutes than the directly deterrent effect of the threatened penalty. Any man who has intercourse with a girl over thirteen and under sixteen places himself under the power of that girl ...

This was directed at Walter and his ilk. Walter already disguised his identity because he was terrified of being blackmailed.

Advertisers in the pamphlet included the Minors' Protection Committee at Stonebuilding, Lincoln's Inn WC (i.e. the West End), the Female Mission to the Fallen and the Children's Aid and Refuge Fund at 32 Charing Cross Road, and Hatchards at 187 Piccadilly, which had just published *Works for the Promotion of Purity of Life*. The enemy were closing in on Walter. However, he did not yet take them seriously. He even mocked 'The Maiden Tribute'. In *My Secret Life* he wrote:

> *She came to the sitting room, had a glass more wine, for an hour we talked and kissed. The most luscious conversations I've ever had have been with virgins just after defloration. Open a woman's cunt and you open her mouth. Our talk was all about fucking, or what leads to it – about her being virgin – how she'd kept one so long, what her longings had been, what her sensations as my prick broke through the membrane, what as it stretched and spent in her. Then cuddling, kissing, showing my prick, feeling her cunt, looking at its ragged bleeding edges; within the hour I done all this. She'd felt my stiff prick, I'd fucked her again, she had given down her maiden tribute to mix with her ravisher's, and our spendings had mingled in our pleasures.*

But Walter did not need to take the new law seriously. The first person the police would hunt down after its passing was not the Minotaur, but Stead himself.

After reading 'The Maiden Tribute', neighbours had turned on the mother of 13-year-old Eliza Armstrong, the girl Stead had bought as part of his investigation, accusing her of selling her daughter. Mrs Armstrong recognized aspects of the story in the *Pall Mall Gazette* that matched her daughter and went to Marylebone Police Court to demand that her daughter was returned to her. A reporter from *Lloyd's Weekly News* picked up on the case and, on

12 July, published a story under the heading 'A Mother Seeking Her Lost Child'. Soon after, the *Daily Telegraph* published the story of Eliza's father Charles Armstrong. He claimed that his wife had not told him about the sale of his daughter and that he had beat his wife when he heard that she had allowed Eliza to go off with a stranger. As Eliza's legal guardian, he had not been consulted when his daughter was taken and had not given his consent.

Eliza was returned to her parents on 23 August. By then, plans to prosecute Stead and his accomplices, including General Booth, for abduction were already well advanced. Stead, Rebecca Jarrett, the abortionist Louise Mourez and Samuel Jacques, an ex-war correspondent and agent of Stead, were also charged with indecent assault over the examination to determine Eliza's virginity. When the defendants appeared at Bow Street Police Court to answer the charges, the police were powerless to control the mob, who threatened to lynch Booth and Jarrett. Members of the Salvation Army who arrived that morning were hooted and jostled by the crowd on their way to the courtroom. Stead was singled out for censure for bringing the British Empire into disrepute. Released on bail, Stead and Jarrett were hissed at as they left court. The crowd tried to overturn General Booth's carriage and molested other members of the Salvation Army. It took a dozen policemen to put Rebecca Jarrett in a cab as a crowd of around 100 people clamoured to get at her. But the cabman stopped not far from Bow Street, saying he would take them no further. Jarrett was convinced that he wanted to abandon them to the rabble where there would be no police to protect her.

The defendants were sent for trial at the Old Bailey where the Attorney General, Richard Webster, himself acted as prosecutor. The backlash was so strong that the Hanbury Street Rescue Home was closed down. Word reached Josephine Butler that an assassin squad was hunting the Hanbury Street whistle blower. Four brothel keepers went down to Winchester intending to kill Jarrett, who had dared to tell the secrets of the virgin trade. One of them was a man named Sullivan from the brothel in Marylebone. He had been Jarrett's lover and she had procured girls of thirteen and fourteen for his establishment at 24 Marylebone High Street, where she drugged them so they could be deflowered.

'The girls were brought to these houses, not knowing what they were, and drugged and violated,' she admitted.

Fearing for her life, Jarrett agreed not to name them in court. For her own safety, she was sent abroad to track down Mary Jeffries, who was in Brussels, and to offer her a large sum of money to return to England to testify about the virgin trade and leading members of the government's knowledge of it. Jeffries said she would not return unless she was given immunity from prosecution. She later cut her own deal and stood trial on lesser charges.

Involving Jeffries in the Armstrong case would have brought the investigation perilously close to Walter. He was saved from exposure on 10 November, when, after twelve days of testimony, the jury handed down its verdict. General Booth was acquitted, but guilty verdicts were returned on the other four defendants. Stead was sentenced to three months' imprisonment; Jacques to one month. Jarrett was sentenced to six months' imprisonment; Mourez six months with hard labour. She died in jail.

In his speeches defending his actions, Stead referred to Eliza Armstrong throughout as 'Lizzie', a name that Walter uses repeatedly. It is also the name he gives to a virgin procured for him by his mistress, Sarah.

Despite Stead's imprisonment, the campaign against the virgin trade did have its effect. A special cable from London dated 19 October says: 'Under the orders of the Home Secretary, the police have prohibited the sale of gutter-sheets and raid Haymarket and other haunts of abandoned women, and clear the streets nightly.'

Walter also noted the change:

> *The London public had a fit of virtue to which it is subject periodically. It commenced a crusade against*

*gay women, and principally those frequenting Regent
and Coventry Streets, and others in that neighbourhood. Many nice, quiet accommodation houses were
closed, and several nice gay women whom I frequented
disappeared. Indeed, for a time, the police were set
on with all their brutality. Women by dozens were
taken before magistrates ruthlessly, and altho mostly
cautioned and set at liberty, some were imprisoned;
and the effect was that for a short time the streets
named, and a few others, were all but cleared of gay
women.*

*Among the women who disappeared was one named
Betsy Johnson, a lovely little creature under twenty,
and in the perfection of her youth. Just before she
disappeared, she said one night to me in her jocular
way, 'Fucking is done for here except for love, so I shall
take to washing for my living.' She disappeared, and
I was now to meet her again some nine or ten years
after.*

And it was not just England that was affected by the sudden
change in the moral climate. Brothels in France, Germany,
Italy and the Netherlands were raided by police looking for
underage girls and women who had been trafficked.

With Stead in jail, the National Vigilance Association
was taken over by William Alexander Coote. He was a
hardliner who encouraged the police to close brothels and
hound prostitutes. At this point, Josephine Butler split with
the movement. In 1886, she finally succeeded in getting the
Contagious Diseases Act repealed, but her objective remained
to save fallen women, not to persecute them. Coote would not
be deflected. Even though Sir Charles Warren, who became
chief commissioner of the Metropolitan Police in 1886, tried
to initiate a policy of laissez-faire towards prostitution, in
the summer of 1887 alone 200 brothels in east London were
closed, rendering thousands of women homeless, on the street
and vulnerable to attack. Coote went on to try and have the

works of Emile Zola and a production of *Lady Godiva* at the Palace Theatre banned. Bernard Shaw said that Coote was in 'artistic matters a most intensely stupid man, and on sexual questions something of a monomaniac'.

8

BLOOD SPORTS

Walter experienced sexual problems from an early age. He remembered that his nursemaid used to hold his penis for him when he was a child. 'Was it needful to do so?', he wondered, in *My Secret Life*.

> *She attempted to pull my prepuce back, when, and how often, I know not. But I am clear about seeing the prick tip show, of feeling pain, of yelling out, of her soothing me, and of this occurring more than once.*

He also remembered playing with her.

> *As she played with me and the toys, we rolled over each other on the floor in fun, I have a recollection of having done that with others, and of my father and mother being in that room at times with me playing. She kissed me, got out my cock, and played with it, took one of my hands and put it underneath her clothes. It felt rough there, that's all, she moved my little hand violently there, then she felt my cock and again hurt me, I recollect seeing the red tip appear as she pulled down the prepuce, and my crying out, and her quieting me.*

She played ride-a-cock horse with him between her legs until he cried. He remembered seeing her legs naked, her thighs, one cheek of her backside and possibly her vulva. She kissed him to calm him. Walter was convinced that she was masturbating. He also remembered as a child sleeping with a woman – probably the nursemaid – and enjoying the smell of her body. He recalled the sound of her peeing in a chamber pot and seeing her naked. Later, his mother dismissed the woman, whom she called 'a filthy creature, whom she had detected in abominable practices with one of her children; what they were my mother never disclosed'.

Until he was sixteen he could not retract his foreskin without pain, 'nor well then when quite stiff unless it went up a cunt'. It was a problem he suffered throughout his life. His penis would become sore or even lacerated unless his lover's vagina was well lubricated – often with urine or semen, his own or someone else's. However, the problem did ease slightly after his penis was lacerated and bled when he roughly deflowered Louise. Walter grew obsessed with blood – blood on the penis, blood on the vagina, blood stains on a woman's chemise and, particularly, blood mixed with semen. Blood eased the pain caused by his deformed manhood.

When other boys compared penises, Walter was embarrassed to show his because of the problem with his foreskin. The first occasion seems to have been with cousin Fred.

The next thing I clearly recollect, was one of my male cousins stopping with us. We walked out, and when piddling together against a hedge, his saying, 'Shew me your cock, Walter, and I will shew you mine.' We stood and examined each other's cocks, and for the first time I became conscious that I could not get my foreskin easily back like other boys. I pulled his backwards and forwards. He hurt me, laughed and sneered at me; another boy came and I think another, we all compared cocks, and mine was the only one which would not unskin. They jeered me, I burst into tears, and went away thinking there was something wrong with me, and was ashamed to shew my cock again, tho I set to work earnestly to try to pull the foreskin back, but always desisted, fearing the pain, for I was very sensitive.

It was Fred who told him that women did not have penises, although he had already been in a position to observe that for himself. They were particularly interested in how girls peed and if it wetted their legs when it came out. Then, for fun,

> *one day Fred and I pissed against each other's cocks, and thought it excellent fun. I recollect being very curious indeed about the way girls piddled after this, and seeing them piddle became a taste I have kept all my life. I would listen at the bedroom doors, if I could get near them unobserved, when my mother, sister, the governess, or a servant went in, hoping to hear the rattle and often succeeded.*

Fred and Walter managed to catch a peddler woman squatting down in a side road to relieve herself. They took delight in taunting her. She threw a stone at them and, when they threw one back, it smashed the large basket of crockery she had for sale.

Walter also took any opportunity to stick his hand up the dress of his governess or other servant girls to explore. Encouraged by Fred, Walter pulled up the clothes of his nine-month-old sister to examine her. 'I pulled one leg away to see better,' he said, 'the child awakened and began crying, I heard footsteps and had barely time to pull down her clothes, when the under-nursemaid came in.' He had had only a momentary glimpse and, although he denied any wrongdoing, received a severe telling off. Years later, when Walter's sister died, he was still fantasizing about what he had seen.

Walter's bedroom overlooked the yard outside the kitchen, where there was a wash-house, a knife-house, the servants' privy and, beyond, a garden shed. One morning, the adolescent Walter spotted a servant emerging from the garden shed and decided that he could play a 'baudy trick' on her. The following morning, he got up early and laid in wait for the maid. When she came in from the kitchen yard, he shoved his hand up her dress.

> *She pushed me away, then caught hold of the hand with which I had touched her cunt, and squeezed it hard with a rubbing motion, looking at me as I recollected (but long afterwards), in a funny way. 'Hish! Hish! here is the old woman,' said she. 'Oh it is not, I'm sure I heard the wires of her bell,' and sure enough there came a ring. Up I went without shoes, like a shot to my bedroom, began to smell my fingers, found they were sticky, and the smell not the same. I recollect thinking it strange that her cunt should be so sticky.*

Soon after, the maid and the gardener were sacked. Walter concluded that they had been dismissed for having sex in the garden shed. Later, he used the small room off the kitchen yard to have sex with cooks and housemaids.

In the countryside, Walter and his cousin Fred made free with the farm girls. Walter raped fifteen-year-old farm hand Nelly 'in the root-shed in the Twelve-Acre field'. She threatened to tell the magistrate. The foreman threatened her with the sack if she did, saying that he would ensure that she would not get work anywhere else in the parish if she told. Now off the hook, Walter eyed Nelly's sister, fourteen-year-old Sophy, who was pregnant.

Walter suspected she had got pregnant after being raped. He seduced her so he could get the story of her attack. During sex, he pressed Sophy for details that would plant a dark fantasy.

> *Persuasion, kisses, promises, and she answered my questions again. 'He cuddled me, he was big and strong, and I could not help it; and then he pulled up my shimmy, and his shirt was up, and he put his belly close to mine.' 'Then his prick was up against your belly?' 'I shan't say', said she with a modest fit, no sham.*

By this time, Walter was playing the role of the rapist.

> 'Was it? Was it just as my prick now is?' Her story was
> exciting me. I pulled her belly up to mine, and my prick,
> a right good stiff one was between us. 'I suppose it
> were,' said she, 'I don't recollect, all seems in a muddle,
> he hurt me dreadful, I screamed, he put something over
> my mouth, and I don't know no more; but he was doing
> it right up, and I were hollowing, and then I cried.'
>
> 'Are you sure you cried out?' 'I hollowed, I know,
> but I knowed there was no one to hear.' 'Then you were
> in the house alone?' 'Yes.'
>
> 'I don't recollect more,' she went on, 'but he lay
> on me, oh! a long, long time.' 'Not up you?' 'Yes oh!
> a long time.' 'Did he keep on fucking?' 'He kept on a
> doing it and stopping; no he never pulled it out. At last
> I fainted or slept I suppose, for when I recollect more
> he was out of bed. Then he got into bed, and he did the
> same I can't say how many times. When it were day
> I said, "Ain't you going to work?" and he said, "No. If
> anyone comes they will think I am gone, and if you say
> a word if anyone knocks I will murder you." Then he
> got up, and showed me his razor, and said, "Do you see
> that? I bloody well mean it, mind." Then he got into
> bed again, and he did it again.'

This was an horrific story, particularly as the rapist was
Sophy's brother-in-law. But all Walter could think of saying
was: 'Did you like it?'

> 'I don't know, I was all pain, but I think I must at last;
> I was so muddled like and ill I could not move. Then
> he dressed and says he, "If ever you tell I'll cut your
> bloody throat; now you say you were ill, and stopped
> at home from work" and he went away to his work.'
> I guessed she had been raped . . . Sophy had said there
> would be murder if she told who the father was.

Walter loved every detail of this story, which he got Sophy to tell him over and over again, with him playing the part of the rapist, she the victim. He filed the scene in his mind and used it to arouse himself later.

In volume six of *My Secret Life*, Walter gave a whole chapter over to a story he was told by a woman named Gertrude, who he had had an affair with in Paris. She had been in Lombardy during the War of Italian Independence and she said her sister had been gang raped at sword-point by Austrian soldiers before the Battle of Solferino in 1859, 'the incident of which I talked over and over with her for a few months, in fact until our liaison came to an end'. Again, sex and blades aroused him.

Throughout his life, Walter was a keen hunter and was familiar with killing and skinning game. He associated this activity with sex. As a young man, he would get his penis out in the woods and examine it before the kill.

'Once I recollect shooting at a rabbit with my prick out of my trowsers,' he wrote.

He would go hunting in Darlington – famous deer-hunting country. Weardale in County Durham was England's second-largest hunting ground after the New Forest. Later he went to Scotland. In nineteenth-century hunting manuals, hunters were told to move in on a felled deer as quickly as possible, then cut its throat to put it out of its misery before draining the carcass of blood, which spouted from the wound. It was a bloody business. With the deer laying on its back with its legs open, it should then be disembowelled. This process, called gralloching, continued with the hunter emptying out the entire contents of the carcass. To do this, he used a good, sharp knife to make a cut the length of the torso. The cut should extend downwards from the sternum right round to the base of the tail, then upwards to the neck and chin so that the windpipe could be removed. This was done so that the internal organs did not taint the meat. The carcass was then skinned and cut into joints of meat. The sweet meats were kept and the head was cut off and thrown to dogs as a reward.

When Walter and Fred used a knife to cut through the wallpaper to spy on his young cousins bathing, they were on a hunting trip. Was it his hunting knife? On another occasion, when visiting his aunt in Darlington on a hunting trip, he took the opportunity to seduce his cousin, who was married, and force himself on the maid. When shooting in Scotland, 'my lust for the common, coarse, vulgar females revived . . .'. In Dundee, he went what he called 'cunt-hunting', dressed in a 'well-worn shooting suit'. In France, he was out early one morning going shooting when he picked up a woman and went with her instead. Sex and hunting were, in Walter's mind, inextricably mixed.

Walter was a fan of the ballet, too, up to a point. He had sex with a ballet girl 'for the pleasure of fucking thro a cut I made in her tights'.

It is not hard to draw a comparison between the gralloching of a deer and the mutilation of Mary Ann Nichols and Annie Chapman. But W.T. Stead saw a political motivation in the butchery. In the *Pall Mall Gazette* of 19 September 1888, Stead wrote a piece called 'Murder as Advertisement'. He posited that the murders were the work of a 'scientific humanitarian'.

'We may be in the presence of a Sociologist Pasteur,' he wrote, 'capable of taking a scientific survey of the condition of society, and absolutely indifferent to the sufferings of the individual so long as he benefited the community at large.'

The murderer at large in Whitechapel may be a 'scientific sociological Jesuit', wrote Stead. In the East End, he said, 'tens of thousands of our fellow creatures are begotten and reared in an atmosphere of godless brutality, a species of human sewage, the very drainage of the vilest productions of ordinary vice'. Philanthropists had repeatedly called attention to their existence. 'The Bitter Cry of Outcast London' – an 1883 inquiry into social conditions by the Reverend Andrew Mearns – had fallen on deaf ears. Prayer, entreaty and warning all were in vain. When social reformers had tried to call attention to the 'malebolgic pool of the Metropolitan inferno' at the Trafalgar Square rally the previous year, Metropolitan Police Commissioner Sir Charles Warren 'rode them down with his cavalry, smashed their heads with his bludgeons' in what had become known as Bloody Sunday.

A scientific sociologist, Stead reasoned, would look for other ways to bring the devastating social problems of poverty in the East End to public attention and 'ask himself by what means a maximum effect could be produced with a minimum of expenditure in money and in life'.

'There must be blood,' Stead wrote. 'That was indispensable. The warning must be printed in letters of gore. But mere bloodshed would not suffice. There must be more than murder. The public cannot be impressed by a mere commonplace killing. There must be mutilation. That is where the sensation comes in.'

The scientific sociologist would have such a supreme devotion to the welfare of the community, Stead reasoned, he would not for a moment hesitate in sacrificing a few worthless lives in order to attain his end. He would argue it is sometimes expedient that one should die for the sake of the multitude. Having arrived at that decision, he would naturally select as his victims those whose lives were the most worthless to themselves and the state, and most vividly illustrated 'the vicious horrors of the criminals' lairs'.

'The victims belong to the class which of all others suffers the most hideous and tragic fate in the human lot,' he wrote. 'None of them found life worth living. All were drunken, vicious, miserable wretches, whom it was almost a charity to relieve of the penalty of existence.'

In Whitechapel, the murderer had picked the very centre of the problem that he sought to publicize. Believing that the victims had been strangled before they were stabbed, Stead said he had 'killed them with the merciful painlessness of science, so that suffering was reduced to a minimum, and death came as a welcome release from the insupportable miseries of existence'.

'After killing his victim he mutilated her,' said Stead, 'well knowing that a knife's slit in a corpse makes more impression on the vulgar mind than the greatest cruelties, moral or even physical, on the living.'

The killer then waited to see what effect the murder had. Finding that the first murder had not achieved its objective, he killed again, and again. 'Not, however, until his fourth experiment did he succeed.' Then the public was at least aroused. Thousands of sightseers poured into Whitechapel after the murder of Annie Chapman and '*The Times* and *The Morning Post* vie with each other in writing articles of almost unmitigated socialism'. The 'indefatigable Christian worker for the regeneration of Whitechapel', the Reverend S.A. Barnett, Vicar of St. Jude's, said: 'Whitechapel horrors will not be in vain if at last the public conscience awakes to consider the life which these horrors reveal.'

'What then is more reasonable than to suppose that these horrors may have been produced in this scientific sensational way to awake the public conscience?' concluded Stead. 'If this should after all turn out to be the case, the defence of the scientific sociologist at the Old Bailey will be a curiosity in the history of criminal trials and may mark the beginning of the scientific era in social development.'

The killer did have a political agenda. However, his motives were much more sinister.

9

The Murder of 'Long Liz' Stride

On the night of 30 September 1888, the Ripper struck again. Elizabeth 'Long Liz' Stride was murdered in Berner Street, off Commercial Road, the closest yet to Walter's underground lair. Born Elisabeth Gustafsdotter in Torslanda, near Gothenburg in Sweden on 27 November 1843, she was forty-five when she died. In 1860, she moved to Gothenburg where she worked initially as a domestic servant. In March 1865, she registered with the police as a prostitute. The following month she gave birth to a stillborn child. By October she was being treated for a venereal chancre, but was given the all-clear in November.

Walter records visiting Sweden as a young man, but was enraged by the refusal of the prostitutes there to show him their genitals on the street. It was one of his favourite fetishes.

In 1866, Liz Stride moved to London and possibly worked in service. When she married in 1869, she gave her address as 67 Gower Street in the West End. She moved out to Poplar, where she and her husband managed a coffee shop until it was taken over in 1875. She claimed that her husband and their two children died aboard the *Princess Alice*, a steam ship that sank after a collision in the Thames in 1868 with the loss of some 700 lives. This story has been discounted, as no one meeting their descriptions was among the dead, and the death certificate of one John Stride showed that he died of a heart condition in the Sick Asylum in Bromley in 1884.

From 1882, she lived on and off in the common lodging house at 32 Flower and Dean Street, though she intermittently lived with waterside labourer Michael Kidney in Devonshire Street. He told the inquest: 'During the three years I have known her she has been away from me about five months altogether . . . It was drink that made her go on previous occasions. She always came back again. I think she liked me better than any other man.'

Dr Thomas Barnardo, street preacher and founder of the homes for destitute children, moved into Hanbury Street. He visited 32 Flower and Dean Street, where he found the women 'thoroughly frightened'. They were discussing the Whitechapel murders. One woman, possibly drunk, cried bitterly: 'We're all up to no good, no one cares what becomes of us! Perhaps some of us will be killed next!'

This is a stark contrast to the long conversations Walter records having with prostitutes, none of whom ever seem to mention the Ripper or even acknowledge his existence – a strange omission on his part.

Barnardo recognized Liz Stride as one of the women present at that meeting. She was attempting to reform, with mixed results.

> *'Accustomed to live entirely without control, she found the discipline of this place more than she could endure, and she left,' a missionary said. 'We saw nothing of her for a time, but she came to us again, and still seemed sick and weary of the wretched life she led. If she could only find something to do she really would try, but of the "Home" she seemed to have a positive horror. We could find her no work, and she tried charring and washing, and I believe did her earnest best to maintain herself that way. But it was gradual starvation; often we found she was whole days without a bit of food; and those she lived with say that only at the last extremity did she allow herself to be driven again to her old courses. I am afraid, however, she drifted back, but still she would come to our meetings and listen very*

*earnestly to all that went on, and would borrow from
our library books that you would never imagine she
would care to read.'*

Liz Stride had been to a meeting at the mission in the week
that she was murdered. Dr Barnardo later identified her body
in the mortuary.

Also using the mission's readings rooms was 'another of the
same class, and who used to be an associate of the poor creature
murdered in Berner-street'. These women were trying to give
up prostitution and 'regain respectability'. Tracts produced
by Josephine Butler emphasized that the reclamation of fallen
women was not just a religious duty, it was a political struggle.

Liz Stride's body was found in Dutfield's Yard beside the
International Working Men's Club, where plays by Russian
revolutionaries were put on. Russian, Polish, Czech, Italian,
French, British and Jewish radicals met there. The night she
was killed a debate was held there. The subject: 'Why Jews
should be Socialists'.

Several people saw Liz Stride with a man that night, though
their descriptions of her companion do not tally. At around
11 p.m., two workmen named J. Best and John Gardner saw
Stride leaving the Bricklayer's Arms in Settles Street, just north
of Commercial Road and almost opposite Berner Street. She
was with a man wearing a mourning suit and a coat.

'He was hugging and kissing her,' said Best, 'and as he
seemed a respectably dressed man, we were rather astonished
at the way he was going on at the woman.'

The couple stood in the doorway for some time hugging
and kissing. The workmen tried to get the man to come in for
a drink but he refused. They taunted Stride, shouting: 'That's
Leather Apron getting round you.' Stride and her companion
then moved off towards Commercial Road and Berner Street.

Police Constable William Smith saw her outside the
International Working Men's Club in Berner Street at around
12.30 a.m. This time she was with a man wearing a deerstalker
hat. He also said that the man was carrying a parcel wrapped

up in newspaper, about eighteen inches long and six to eight inches wide.

Mrs Fanny Mortimer, a housewife and mother of five who lived at 36 Berner Street, saw a man carrying a shiny black bag. William Marshall, of 64 Berner Street, gave a description of a man that in many ways matched the description given by PC Smith, but he added that the man was middle-aged and looked like a clerk. He wore a 'black cutaway coat and dark trousers'. Again, he saw them kissing and cuddling, and Marshall overheard a snippet of their conversation.

'You would say anything but your prayers,' the man said. The woman laughed. Then they continued walking unhurriedly down the street.

Marshall said the man he saw wore a round, peaked cap, 'something like what a sailor would wear'.

Another witness, James Brown, saw Stride later with a man in a long coat and had overheard her say: 'No, not tonight. Maybe some other night.'

The *Star* printed an article the day after the murder, saying: 'From two different sources we have the story that a man, when passing through Church Lane' – opposite the Gunmakers' Proofing House – 'at about 1.30 a.m., saw a man sitting on a doorstep and wiping his hands. As everyone is on the lookout for the murderer, the man looked at the stranger with a certain amount of suspicion, whereupon he tried to conceal his face. He is described as a man who wore a short jacket and a sailor's hat.' Others described a man wearing a black peaked cap.

When Walter made excursions into the East End he was similarly attired to the man described in the *Star*. Describing one evening's outing, he said:

> *My friend knew sailors' necessities, and their habits, and those of their female acquaintances ashore, for he was a large ship owner. He had been to the dancing places and taprooms, which sailors frequented, and knew the quarters where the women were to be found.*

To amuse me and satisfy my curiosity, we dined together a few days afterwards, and after our dinner, visited several of the public houses. To avoid remark and possibly offensive behaviour towards us, we dressed in the shabbiest possible manner, and with caps bought just opposite the docks, and such as were worn largely by the working people in the neighbourhood, we flattered ourselves that we looked as common a couple of men, as ever rolled barrows along the street.

Thus costumed, we spent the evening at public houses, among sailors, whores, and working men – in an atmosphere thick and foul with tobacco smoke, sweat and gas.

Matthew Packer, who ran a grocer's store at 44 Berner Street, two doors from Dutfield's Yard, said that a woman with a white flower pinned to her jacket came into his shop around 11.45 p.m. with a man who bought half a pound of black grapes. Packer's description matched Liz Stride, and he identified her at the mortuary. In fact, Liz seems to have been wearing a red rose with white maidenhair fern behind it. She was not wearing it when she left the lodging house and no one knows who gave it to her.

The man with her looked like a clerk, Packer said, and was young – but then Packer was very old.

'He spoke like an educated man, but he had a loud, sharp sort of voice, and a quick commanding way with him,' Packer told the *Daily News*.

He thought they were on their way to Commercial Road, but they crossed the street and talked for about half an hour. When they had finished talking, they crossed back and walked off past the International Working Men's Club.

Walter frequently had long conversations with prostitutes in the street when he was trying to track down girls he had lost touch with and Walter mentions grapes in *My Secret Life*, which may have been some sort of erotic fetish. On one occasion, Walter was at an orgy with his cousin Fred who, wearing only a shirt, stood on his head. 'Lady A took up a bunch of grapes, and dashed it on his ballocks.'

At Liz Stride's inquest, the police surgeon said: 'Neither on the hands nor about the body of the deceased did I find grapes, or connection with them. I am convinced that the deceased had not swallowed either the skin or seed of a grape within many hours of her death.'

But he also said: 'The Coroner also desired me to examine the two handkerchiefs which were found on the deceased. I did not discover any blood on them, and I believe that the stains on the larger handkerchief are those of fruit.'

Two journalists from the *Daily News* claimed to have found a grape stalk, stained with blood, which had been washed down the drain when the police cleaned up the yard.

A knife was found on a doorstep in Whitechapel Road on Monday morning. It had blood on the blade. Dr Phillips identified it as an instrument called a slicing knife commonly used in a chandler's shop. It had a blade nine or ten inches long with a rounded tip. Dr Phillips and Dr Frederick Blackwell, who had been called in to assist in the post-mortem, agreed that this could not be the murder weapon. Phillips concluded that Stride had been killed using a 'short knife, such as a shoemaker's well-ground knife'. The knife employed by deer-hunters typically has a sharp pointed blade four or four-and-a-half inches long.

Phillips also remarked at the inquest on 1 October: 'In this case, as in some others, there seems to have been some knowledge of where to cut the throat to cause a fatal result.'

A deer-hunter would certainly possess this knowledge. *The Times* had only recently pointed out that despite the improvement in guns, the knife was essential for the kill: 'The excitement is rather increased than diminished. The operation of the gralloching – that is, of disembowelling the slaughtered stag on the spot to save the venison from taint – is not the less necessary.'

The grocer Matthew Packer had more intriguing evidence to impart. On 27 October, four weeks after the death of

Liz Stride, he was standing by his barrow at the corner of Greenfield Street and Commercial Road, when he saw the man who had accompanied Liz on the fateful night. The man gave Packer 'a most vicious look'. The grocer sent someone to fetch a policeman, but the man jumped on a tram heading for Blackwall. Walter did not confine his activities in the East End to the hours of darkness. He went out during the day to the sailors' quarters 'along the line of docks from Tower Hill eastwards', as the women there were cheap – typically five shillings.

'I put on the same shabby things I had used when out with my friend,' he said, 'and took a cab to the locality, feeling much ashamed at my costume, and sorry that my servant should see me, but there was no help for that.'

On 13 November, a man came into Packer's shop to buy rabbits and told him that he believed his own cousin was the murderer. Curiously, on the hunting trip when Walter had shot a rabbit with his penis out, he had been with his cousin Fred.

Like Mary Ann Nichols, Liz Stride was carrying a piece of a comb, along with a complete comb. She was also carrying two handkerchiefs. As we have seen, Walter sometimes paid for sex with handkerchiefs. And Liz Stride was wearing white stockings. Walter had a fetish for white stockings and shied from other colours, especially black. In *My Secret* Life, he recalled trying to seduce a young girl called Mabel.

> *I recollect the conviction coming over me that she was no virgin, and if I had doubts before, the way my finger slipped from her clitoris up the love-pit and plugged it, confirmed them. She lay with her eyes fixed on me, palpitating gently with voluptuousness. Her petticoats up to her knees, I saw legs in black stockings, one in wrinkles, the other halfway bagging down the calf, and her feet in shabby slippers.*
>
> *I had at that time a horror of black stockings, which affected me at times so much as to deprive me of all*

> *desire. Once with a gay woman who had black stock-*
> *ings I was unable to poke her, in spite of her blandish-*
> *ment, till she put white ones on. As I now saw Mabel's*
> *legs a disgust came over me, desire left me, and my*
> *prick began to shrink . . .*

Liz Stride was wearing a checked silk scarf. The knot had
been turned to left and pulled very tight. The long gash of
the wound 'exactly corresponded to the lower border of the
scarf,' said Dr Blackwell. It was as if he did not want to cut
the scarf, although 'the border was slightly frayed, as if by a
sharp knife'. Walter, of course, had a thing about silk scarves.
They came up in conversation with his friend, the Major, who
was 'older, poorer, and more dissolute than ever'.

> *'He is the baudiest old rascal that ever I heard tell a*
> *story,' was the remark of a man at our club one night.*
> *Ask him to dinner in a quiet way by himself, give him*
> *unlimited wine, and he would in an hour or two begin*
> *his confidential advice in the amatory line, and in a*
> *wonderful manner tell of his own adventures, and give*
> *reasons why he did this or that, why he succeeded with*
> *this woman, or missed that girl, in a way as amusing,*
> *and instructive to a young listener, as could be imagined.*

The Major was ever eager to impart advice.

> *'If you want to get over a girl,' he would say, 'never*
> *flurry her till her belly's full of meat and wine; let the*
> *grub work. As long as she is worth fucking, it's sure*
> *to make a woman randy at some time. If she is not*
> *twenty-five she'll be randy directly her belly is filled,*
> *then go at her. If she's thirty, give her half an hour. If*
> *she's thirty-five let her digest an hour, she won't feel*
> *the warmth of the dinner in her cunt till then. Then*
> *she'll want to piss, and directly after that she'll be ready*
> *for you without her knowing it. But don't flurry your*

*young 'un, talk a little quiet smut whilst feeding, just
to make her laugh and think of baudy things; then
when she has left table, get at her. But it's well,' the old
Major would say, 'to leave a woman alone in a room
for a few minutes after she has dined, perhaps then
she will let slip a fart or two, perhaps she'll piss, she'll
be all the better for the wind and water being out. A
woman's cunt doesn't get piss-proud like a man's prick
you know, they're differently made from us my boy, but
show any one of them your prick as soon as you can,
it's a great persuader. Once they have seen it they can't
forget it, it will keep in their minds. And a baudy book,
they won't ever look at till you've fucked them! – oh!
won't they! – they would at church if you left them
alone with it.' And so the Major instructed us.*

Bearing this in mind, Walter began stalking his prey.

*About three days afterwards, taking a pair of garters,
two small showy neckerchiefs, and [a copy of] Fanny
Hill with me, I knocked at the door. 'Oh! you!' said she
colouring up. 'Yes, is everything right?' 'Yes! all right,
what should be the matter sir?' She stood at the street-
door holding it open, though I had entered the hall. I
turned, closed the door, and caught hold of her.*

The girl, whom he called Jenny, refused him, but he gave her
a sovereign to buy some stockings in exchange for a kiss. To
arouse the girl, Walter told her a story of how he had sexually
molested a housemaid while his wife was upstairs. The girl
had been fired, along with a fellow servant who had reported
what was going on to Walter's wife.

*Thus I talked to Jenny till I expect her quim was hot
enough; then said I, 'Here is a pretty neckerchief, put it
on.' 'Oh! how pretty.' 'I won't give it you unless you put
it on.' She went to the glass and unbuttoned the top of*

> *her dress, which was made to button on the front. I saw*
> *her white fat bosom, she threw the kerchief round the*
> *neck, and tried to push it down the back. 'Let me put*
> *it down, it's difficult.' She let me. 'You are not unbut-*
> *toned enough, it's too tight.' She undid another button,*
> *I pushed down the kerchief, and releasing my hand as I*
> *stood at the back of her, put it over her shoulder, and*
> *down in front, pushing it well under her left breast.*
> *'Oh! what a lovely breast you have, let me kiss it.'*
>
> *A shriek, a scuffle. In the scuffle I burst off a button*
> *or two, which exposed her breast, and getting my*
> *hand on to one of the globes began feeling and kissing*
> *it. Then I slid my hand further down, and under her*
> *armpit. 'Oh! what a shame, don't, I don't like it.' 'How*
> *lovely, – kiss, kiss – oh! Jenny what a lot of hair I can*
> *feel under here.' 'Oh! – screech, screech – oh! don't*
> *tickle me, oh! oh!', and she crouched as women do*
> *who can't bear tickling. I saw my advantage. 'Are you*
> *ticklish?' 'Yes, oh! – screech, screech – oh! leave off.'*

Walter did not leave off. He continued tickling her and buried his face in her breasts. He showed her the pictures in the illustrated edition of *Fanny Hill* he had taken with him. He then persuaded her to let him put on the garters. Naturally, he took advantage of the situation and ran his hand up her thigh, only to discover that she had her period. Walter was not fond of 'poorliness' in women, but the sight of blood on his fingers turned him on.

Liz Stride had not had her abdomen ripped open like a butchered animal, like Mary Ann Nichols and Annie Chapman. But, once again, the killer had attacked the throat. It is generally assumed that the killer did not start gralloching her, as he had his earlier victims, because he was disturbed. It was surprisingly busy in Berner Street that night. Morris Eagle, a Russian Jew who had been chairing the debate on socialism at the International Working Men's Club that night, left at 11.45 p.m. to take his young lady home, but he returned through Dutfield's Yard at 12.35 a.m., shortly after Liz Stride had been seen in the street by PC Smith. There was no body in the yard then.

Israel Schwartz, another Jewish immigrant, said he was in Berner Street at around 12.45 a.m. 'and having gotten as far as the gateway where the murder was committed, he saw a man stop and speak to a woman, who was standing in the gateway. He tried to pull the woman into the street, but he turned her round and threw her down on the footway and the woman screamed three times, but not very loudly,' the Home Office file says. Schwartz later identified the woman as Liz Stride.

Schwartz crossed over to the other side of the street, where he saw a second man lighting his pipe. He could not tell if they were together, nor did his descriptions of them match with those others had given. These men, he said, both had moustaches. Walter says he had a moustache at a time when few men did, although it seems cousin Fred also wore 'whiskers'. Later, Schwartz told the *Star* that the second man came at him with a knife and he quickly made off.

The man who was attacking the woman shouted out 'Lipski'. It was assumed, at first, that he was addressing the other man. However, Inspector Frederick Abberline, who was head of detectives in Whitechapel, noted: 'I questioned Israel Schwartz very closely at the time he made the statement as to whom the man addressed when he called Lipski, but he was unable to say.'

At the time, the name Lipski was on everyone's lips. On 28 June 1887, Israel Lipski, a Polish Jew, had been executed for the murder of Miriam Angel, who had been forced to drink nitric acid. She was six months' pregnant at the time. The case had stirred up anti-Semitism and the term 'Lipski' was used as an insult to anyone who looked Jewish.

'As Schwartz has a strong Jewish appearance, I am of the opinion it was addressed to him as he stopped to look at the man he saw apparently ill-using the deceased woman,' concluded Inspector Abberline. 'Schwartz being a foreigner and unable to speak English became alarmed and ran away.

The man whom he saw lighting his pipe also ran in the same direction as himself, but whether this man was running after him or not he could not tell. He might have been alarmed the same as himself and ran away . . . Inquiries have also been made in the neighbourhood but no person with the name Lipski could be found.'

10

THE YOUNG WALTER

From *My Secret Life*, we can piece together a detailed picture of Walter. His public face was that of an upper middle class gentleman. His early memories are of a large house with horses and grooms, aunts with manor houses, and a family tree of landed gentry. A lord or two came to visit. However, Walter's branch of the family fell on hard times. His father lost money, fell ill and died before Walter was sixteen. The family moved to a smaller house. He was sent to a local school. Walter's collapse into relative poverty coincided with his growing fixation on sex. Like any boy, he had frequent erections, masturbated regularly and had wet dreams – but unlike most he took to voyeurism. He stared up petticoats, put his hand up the shirts of servants and went to any length to see or hear women urinating. At home, his peeping bred further fetishes – for women's underarm hair and white stockings. Outdoors, Walter took to stalking and flashing his genitals at passing washerwomen. Sex and death became mingled in Walter's mind when he encountered his first prostitute at the time both his father and godfather died.

> *One afternoon after my father's death, and that of my godfather, Fred was with me, we went to the house of a friend and were to return home about nine o'clock. It was dark, we saw a woman standing by a wall. 'She is a whore,' said Fred, 'and will let us feel her if we*

pay her.' We both gave her money. 'You'll let us both feel?' said Fred. 'Why of course, have you felt a woman before?' Both of us said we had, feeling bolder. 'Give me another shilling then, you shall both feel my cunt well, I've such a lot of hair on it.' We gave what we had, and then she walked off without letting us. 'I'll tell your mothers, if you come after me,' she cried out. We were sold; I was once sold again in a similar manner afterwards, when by myself.

This was Walter's first encounter with a prostitute and he had been cheated.

While the family had already moved from their country estates nearer to London, they still had servants. They had a cook named Mary, who was twenty-five or twenty-six and 'fresh as a daisy'. Then a new housemaid arrived on her father's cart.

'Down she stepped, her clothes caught on the edge of the cart, or step, or somehow; and I saw rapidly appear white stockings, garters, thighs, and a patch of dark hair between them by her belly; it was instantaneous, and down the clothes came, hiding all. I stood fascinated, knowing I had seen her cunt hair,' he wrote.

The girl was unconscious of the fact – few English women wore knickers or panties in those days. They did not become fashionable until the early twentieth century.

She was a little over seventeen years, had ruddy lips, beautiful teeth, darkish hair, hazel eyes, and a slightly turn-up nose, large shoulders and breast, was plump, generally of fair height, and looked eighteen or nineteen; her name was Charlotte.

Walter was smitten.

I went to bed, thinking of what I had seen, and stared whenever I saw her the next day, until, by a sort of fascination, she used to stare at me; in a day or two I fancied myself desperately in love with her, and indeed was. I recollect now her features, as if I had only seen her yesterday, and, after the scores and scores of women I have fucked since, recollect every circumstance attending my having her, as distinctly as if it only occurred last week; yet very many years have passed away.

He spoke to her kindly, touched and, when his mother was not looking, pinched her backside. Gradually they began kissing and cuddling. 'I told her I loved her, which she said was nonsense.'

One day when his mother was out and the cook was upstairs, he grabbed her and said: 'I wish my prick was against your naked belly, instead of outside your clothes.'

She pushed him off.

'I will never speak to you again,' she said.

He then told her what he had seen when she stepped down from her father's cart, and pulled out his penis.

'How stiff it is,' he said, 'it's longing to go into you, "cock and cunt will come together"' – this was the refrain from a song the boys sang at his college.

Without a word, she fled. Walter followed her into the kitchen and repeated what he had said. She threatened to tell cook. He responded that 'she must have seen your cunt, as well as me.' The girl began to cry. Then he pushed both hands up her skirt and grabbed her. She screamed and ran upstairs. Walter was unrepentant. 'The ice was quite broken now, she could not avoid me.'

He promised not to repeat what he had said and done, but broke his promise repeatedly. On occasions he got a slap on the head for his efforts. One day, when his mother and the cook were out, Walter molested Charlotte in front of his little brother Tom. He got his hand up her skirt and refused to let go, while with the other hand he pulled out his penis. She was crying and begging him to stop. She called him a brute and pulled his hair until 'I thought my skull was coming off' to try and free herself from his grip.

> *I told her I would hurt her as much as I could, if she hurt me; so that game she gave up; the pain of pulling my hair made me savage, and more determined and brutal, than before.*

After half an hour's struggle, he had to let her go. While she went about the house attending to her chores and attending to Tom, he taunted her, saying that her vagina had got wet when he touched it, and exposed himself. Later, he was terrified that she would tell his mother.

The kissing and cuddling continued and he pulled up her skirts on every possible occasion, despite the obvious threat to her job. Eventually, Walter found himself alone in the house with Charlotte. He molested her again, while still protesting his love for her. Next time they were alone in the house again, he did the same thing, but she locked herself in her bedroom. Walter pretended he was going out. Then, when she opened her bedroom door, he raped her.

'Oh! you hurt, I shall be ill,' said she, 'pray don't.'

But Walter did not care.

'Had she said she was dying I should not have stopped,' he wrote.

She was his first virgin.

Afterwards Charlotte wept hysterically. Walter got some brandy and water to calm her. While she drank it, he pulled up her shirt again. Later, he noticed that there was blood on his shirt. His penis was sore and she had been bleeding. That night he examined himself.

'I . . . looked sadly at my sore prick, I could not pull the skin back so much as usual, it was torn, raw and slightly bleeding.'

He thought that Charlotte had given him some sexually transmitted disease. Every time he thought about sex the pain came back again. When he went to the chemist, the pharmacist pulled back the foreskin, causing Walter to howl. He advised that Walter be circumcised. Instead, Walter bought some lotion and left reassured that he had only torn his foreskin while taking Charlotte's virginity.

When he tried to molest Charlotte again, she continued to try and fight him off, but then gave way as there was nothing she could do to prevent him. When he asked when they could have sex again, she said: 'Never.' But there was little she could do to stop him.

He got a sovereign from his aunt and, on Charlotte's day off, he said he would take her to a pub. Instead he took her to a bawdy house. There, with some difficulty, he managed to get her naked, then had sex with her.

'All this I recollect as if it occurred but yesterday, I shall recollect it to the last day of my life, for it was a honeymoon of novelty; years afterwards I often thought of it when fucking other women.'

They had lunch in a pub, then returned to the bawdy house. From then on, according to Walter, they made love whenever they had the opportunity – even in front of his infant brother Tom. When he began to talk of it becoming a danger to them, they started having sex in the servants' privy. The cook, Molly, almost caught them there.

One day, the conversation came around to Molly who, as they shared the servants' quarters, Charlotte had seen naked.

'Had she much hair on her cunt?' said I. 'What's that to you?' said she, laughing, but went on: 'Oh! twice as much as I have, and of a light brown.' 'I suppose her cunt is bigger than yours?' said I reflectively. 'Well, perhaps it is,' said Charlotte, 'she is a much bigger woman than me, what do you think?'

Walter continued probing Charlotte about Molly. She confided in Walter that in the bed the two servants shared, Molly sometimes masturbated. And Charlotte said she had once seen Molly, drunk on sherry, undress and throw herself back on the bed with her legs akimbo – 'the description of the big bum, white thighs, and hairy belly bottom, the jog, jog of the elbow, and all the other particulars, sank deep into my mind,' he said. Meanwhile, Walter and Charlotte became reckless.

'We fucked more than ever, recklessly. It is a wonder we were not found out, for one evening, it being dark, I fucked her in the forecourt, outside our street-door; but troubles were coming.'

Charlotte's father began to notice that she was not coming home on her days off.

'No man and woman could have liked each other more, or more enjoyed each other's bodies, without thinking of the rest of the world.'

Her father turned up, insisting that she get married to the son of a well-to-do baker. An anonymous letter had arrived, saying she had been seen at the waxworks with a young man, 'evidently of position above', and her mother threatened to have her examined by a doctor to see if she had been 'doing anything wrong'. Charlotte was frightened of getting married as her husband would find out that she was not a virgin. She accused Walter of ruining her, and cried. They talked of drowning themselves.

But Charlotte had no choice but to return to her family. She wrote to Walter. His mother tried to open the letter, but Walter snatched it from her hand.

'I am not a boy, I am a man,' he said, 'if you ever open a letter of mine, I will go for a common soldier, instead of being an officer.'

Charlotte married the baker. The letters ceased. Walter followed her to the bakery where she was working. She fled into a back room.

> *I dared not go in for fear of injuring her . . . Thus I lost my virginity, and took one; thus ended my first love or lust, which will you call it? I call it love, for I was fond of the girl, and she of me. Some might call it a seduction, but thinking of it after this lapse of years, I do not.*

The new housemaid was as ugly as sin, so Walter turned his attention to Mary, the cook. But she was a full ten years older, and many pounds heavier than both Walter and his first conquest. Walter's sex attack on Mary would take advance planning. He caught her coming back from the privy, drying herself with her skirt. He leapt out, kissed her and pestered her for sex. She grew angry. When Walter put his hand up her skirt, she pushed him downstairs. Days later, after hearing her peeing in a chamber pot, he burst into her room to find her half-naked. He grabbed her and started kissing her breasts. When she pushed him off, he fell to his knees and stuck his head up her chemise. And when she pushed him off again, he tore the chemise. In the struggle, the cook fell on top of him, overturning the chamber pot and spilling her urine over his head and neck. She told him to go, cursing him as a 'black-guard'. Even though his nose was bleeding, he begged her to show him her cunt. When she refused, he tried to molest her again, only retreating when the housemaid came to see what was going on.

A few days later, he tried to molest her again. This time, he grabbed hold of her pubic hair so she could not push him off.

'I had found my courage, and used the words cunt and fuck,' he said.

But the older woman had the measure of him.

'So young and yet so cruel,' Mary said, 'five minutes ago you were saying you were so fond of me, and now you are trying to hurt me; you promised you would not touch me again, now you are doing it; you are all alike, young and old, cruel and liars.'

But Walter would not give up.

'Kiss me, feel me, and I will indeed leave off,' he said. 'I have seen your belly, let me feel it, and I will leave off.'

'You will break your word again,' said she.

'I swear not.'

She kissed him and touched his penis. The young Walter came in her hand and fled in shame. However, when he returned, Mary let him have sex with her, or so he said. Afterwards, she begged him not to come near her again for fear of losing her job, but Walter continued his advances. Again she agreed, saying: 'May God forgive me for my weakness.'

Then a letter came. After that, she refused him on the grounds that she was a married woman. She had been lying to him all along. Mary was not even her real name. Her husband, she said, had been chronically unfaithful to her, but she forgave him until he gave her a venereal disease. She went back to her mother's, but her husband broke in and raped her. He then went to America where he had earned a lot of money. Now he was returning and she went back to him. Walter felt aggrieved. He had been used by the older woman for sexual amusement, then abandoned. Charlotte, his first love, had deserted him. He had been twice betrayed. He felt suicidal and confused. But the one thing he had learnt was that, in the quest for sex, aggression – even violence – paid. For the rest of his life, Walter would bounce between virgins and older women, seeking satisfaction.

He went to stay with his aunt and his cousin Fred, who introduced him to the ways of country girls.

'Kiss and grope, and if they don't cry out, show them your prick and go at them,' Fred advised.

Behind Fred's back, Walter went to see one of Fred's girl-friends named Sarah, and offered her five shillings for sex. It was more than she got for a week's work in the field. She agreed to do it for seven shillings and sixpence, provided he was quick and did not tell Fred. It became a regular thing. One day, they were interrupted by Sarah's younger sister Martha, who was not yet sixteen. Walter sent Sarah away to buy shrub, gin and peppermint, and molested her sister. When the alcohol came, he got Martha drunk. Then he raped her. She was a virgin and Walter, again, saw blood. Walter so enjoyed the sight, he was prompted to rape Martha again, she all the while protesting that he was hurting her.

'Be quiet, I can't hurt you, my prick is right up you,' he said, although it was clear that she was in pain. He left her crying, but gave two sovereigns to her sister Sarah. Fred, for the second time, introduced Walter to prostitutes – 'gay women'. And, unlike the first, they were not to be cheated. Walter and Fred paid for a foursome. The encounters taught

Walter money could buy not only sex, but goodness itself; 'virtue'. Before Martha, he said, 'I don't think that I had ever heard of tempting women's virtue by money, but I never forgot the lesson and much improved on it as time went on'.

Back in London, a friend lent him a copy of *Fanny Hill*. During his lifetime, he bought numerous – usually illustrated – copies. He tried to molest the ugly housemaid, who threatened to tell, and took to masturbation. It was then that he joined his friend Henry in the 'gun factory'.

'Meanwhile there was either no servant at my home worthy of a stiff one, or those who would not take one; and I had no alternative but to frig,' he said. This did not stop him trying though. One maid he molested fled in tears, and quit the day after.

It was after that he met the poor woman who gave him sex for just two shillings. Another gave him a feel for a silk handkerchief. He had her several times again until he could persuade her to show herself in the light. He found that she was one of the ugliest women he had ever seen. From then on he avoided her, crossing the road if he saw her. A few days after their last encounter, he came down with a venereal disease. By then, he had given up his ambition of joining the army and, just as he was getting well, 'my long promised appointment came from the W. Office'. His uncle then pointed out that he was set to inherit in a year and a half's time, so his mother gave him a reasonable monthly allowance.

> *I now found out that women of a superior class were to be had much cheaper than my great friends used to talk of, but at the time I write of, a sovereign would get any woman, and ten shillings as nice a one as you needed. Two good furnished rooms near the Clubs could be had by women for from fifteen to twenty shillings per week, a handsome silk dress for five or ten pounds, and other things in proportion. So cunt was a more reasonable article than it now is, and I got quite nice girls at from five to ten shillings a poke, and had several in their own*

rooms, but sometimes paying half a crown extra for a room elsewhere.

And if he could not pay with money, he gave them silk handkerchiefs.

'Passing a brothel off the Waterloo Road where the girls used to appear in the windows half-naked, he was dragged inside by a woman who insisted on having sex with him even though he did not have any money,' he said. And when he could not perform, she 'fell on her knees, and began sucking my prick violently, made it stiff in spite of me'.

Then his mother took on Charlotte's sister Mary as a housemaid. One day when he was coming home from the 'W. Office', he was stopped by a woman dressed in black, wearing a veil. It was Charlotte, who had heard that he had been kissing and fondling her sister. Charlotte begged him not to ruin her. By subterfuge, he got Charlotte back to a room and raped her. Although Walter could not see it, Charlotte was sacrificing herself to save her younger sister. After that, Walter went to the baker's store twice to see her. Instead, he was met by her husband, who exchanged stares.

'I never saw Charlotte again, though I still may do so,' he wrote in *My Secret Life*, 'but to this day I have an affection for her, and although she must be forty, should like to poke her.'

New staff arrived. The young housemaid Harriet snubbed him, so he turned his attentions to the middle-aged cook whose name was Brown. At the first opportunity, he began to molest her. Brown called him 'a young devilskin' and agreed to sex a few times, before suggesting Walter try again with Harriet. The housemaid was, after all, having sex with the baker and had seen Walter naked. There was a cheval-glass in his room and if the servants looked through the keyhole they could see him having a bath. Next day, he had a bath, stood up, played with his penis until it was erect, then opened the door suddenly to catch Harriet stooping.

The cook teased Harriet about this, then one night told Walter to come to their room after they had gone to bed. Walter obliged. He threw off his nightshirt and, despite Harriet's protests, got into bed with the two of them. Harriet appealed to the cook to protect her, but she just laughed. Eventually, Walter managed to pull up Harriet's nightdress and the cook got up and went to sleep in his room, leaving them to it. Harriet was furious, but there was nothing the young housemaid could do – to cry out would be to lose her job and reputation. Walter got on top of her and pinned her down with all his weight. She kept her legs closed, but eventually, to get rid of him, relented. In the morning, they were woken by the cook. Back in his room, Walter found his foreskin was torn, but not bleeding. Later, when they had sex again, it did bleed. She said she had been a virgin until he had forced himself on her, but when she stayed out nights with the baker, Walter slept with the cook. Harriet said that she was going to marry the baker, protesting that Walter never gave her presents. He responded with 'some article of jewellery'. After she had been with the baker, he noted 'her quim did not seem to need so much wetting as usual'.

Soon after, Harriet and the cook were fired. Walter thought he had been found out, but he had not.

'I saw at once I was not implicated, so asked no more,' he wrote, 'nor did I ever see them again; though about ten years after, I met in the streets a tall gaunt haggard woman who stared at me, and I think it was Harriet.'

He explained his heartlessness by saying: 'Harriet was a lewed bitch. I never liked her, and her cunt always gave me pain as well as pleasure, but she was at hand, and so I got into her, of course.'

What fascinated him was the cook inciting him to have Harriet, 'but I have since found girls anxious to get others into the same way as themselves. Many I am sure like doing that, and all girls who have been fucked illicitly like other girls to do the same.'

A middle-aged charwoman then came to help in the house. Her eighteen-year-old daughter sometimes came to stay. Through a keyhole Walter could watch the older woman pee in a chamber pot and sometimes saw the daughter naked, once examining her vulva with a hand mirror. The next day, Walter told the young girl what he had seen and tried to molest her. When he got rough, she squealed. He offered her money. She refused.

Concerned at nearly being exposed by the servants, he returned to the prostitutes at Waterloo Road. Sometimes he 'offered a shilling for a feel and met with but few refusals in any part of London. Sometimes it ended in a fuck. Once or twice to my astonishment they took mere trifles, and, as I think of it, there is wonderfully little difference between the woman you have for five shillings, and the one you pay five pounds, excepting in the silk, linen, and manners.'

One woman introduced him to anal sex.

Two new servants came to the house – twenty-six-year-old Sarah and her sister Susan, who was eighteen. Walter spied on them, seeing them both naked, and kissed and molested both of them. But neither succumbed. Walter was slowed by another dose of the clap he caught off a woman in the street. Then one Sunday, when everyone was out, he raped Sarah in his mother's bedroom, almost getting the girl sacked. Instead, he got her pregnant. When she returned home to see her mother, Walter raped her sister, too, and she too fell pregnant. Susan had a miscarriage, but Sarah gave birth. Walter borrowed fifty pounds 'from a Jew' and sent them to Canada.

'This ended my intrigues with servants for some time, for my fucking took quite another direction. Harlots of small degrees amused me till I came into what was a pretty fortune in those days,' wrote Walter.

Walter was twenty-one, a practised rapist and a rich man.

Once Walter had money, he gave up his intended career and headed to the West End to spend his inheritance. In Waterloo Place, he met the Frenchwoman Camille, who took him to a house on the corner of 'G-I-n Square'. Camille introduced him to threesomes, then brought in more and more women.

'At last I had six altogether at once, and spent the evening with them naked, flicking, frigging, spending

up or over them, making them feel each other's cunts,
shove up dildos, and play the devil's delight with their
organs of generation, as they are modestly called. Then
came other suggestions. "I know such a little girl, not
above this high," she said. I ballocked that little girl.'

After he had raped the child, Walter was brought a man to
'frig'. Then he watched as the man had sex with Camille. This
was just one part of a smorgasbord of sexual practices the
Frenchwoman sold Walter. But his favourite was a throwback
to his childhood – he paid Camille to urinate into a basin
balanced on his chest. In all, Camille provided Walter with
sixty women, he estimated. Then Camille suggested one of the
priciest treats of all – a virgin – and she went off to France
to get Louise. But the inevitable happened: Walter caught
gonorrhoea. During the convalescence, he went out to stay
with his aunt in 'H..tf..dshire', where he began molesting a
seventeen-year-old farm girl named Pender. She had recently
been married, and tried to avoid the persistent house guest.
Walter stalked her and spotted her peeing. This pushed him
over the edge. He threw her down in a half-built haystack
and had sex with her, even though, in his condition, it hurt
him. She was terrified that her husband would find out, but
Walter continued pursuing her. Eventually, she contracted
gonorrhoea, too. That did not stop him taking advantage of
other women farm workers. When he caught the nursemaid
with the page, he threatened to tell his aunt unless she had
sex with him. He recorded in his memoir how he 'hurt' the
nursemaid and made her bleed.

'I did not like the girl nor her manner, didn't feel kind as I
always do towards a woman I have had,' he said. Nevertheless,
he had her again. Later, he got her to kiss the penis of the child
she was tending, while he had sex with her from behind.

Then he met sixteen-year-old Molly, a dairy maid 'who
used to curtsy to me'. Walter blackmailed her into having sex
with him, otherwise he would tell her mother that she had
had a farm hand – a 'bumpkin', Walter called her boyfriend

Giles. She cried, but then Walter had her a second time against her will with a mixture of threats and coaxing. That done, he turned his attention to girls in the fields beyond the manor.

'Some were apparently not more than twelve years of age. I longed to see their cunts, and joked with one or two of the larger girls; but a decided longing for young cunts had set in on me.'

By then, Walter had spent a large part of his fortune on Camille's city prostitutes, so he stayed in the countryside where he could often get sex for free. It was then that he raped the fifteen-year-old virgin, Nelly, ensuring her silence with the collusion of the foreman. Walter also gave her a sovereign. Directly afterwards, he began to fantasize about having sex with an even younger girl, one without any pubic hair. He then took a fancy to Nelly's fourteen-year-old sister, Sophy, who was pregnant after being raped by her brother-in-law. Walter examined her, as if he were a doctor, and got her to tell the story over and over. It turned him on.

'It delighted me to hear about her virgin offering,' he wrote, 'it made my cock stand.'

Walter returned to London's Vauxhall Pleasure Gardens, where he spied the ten-year-old dressed as a ballerina. She'd become his youngest victim, an urban rape that followed an extended schooling in rural sex attacks.

He now had so little money that he could not afford to go to Paris with Fred. Instead, he returned to his aunt's manor house with his mother. The nursemaid he had forced to have sex had been sacked for misconduct. And seventeen-year-old Mrs Pender, the farm manager's wife he had raped, was newly pregnant. She begged him to take her away. When he said he could not, she said she would drown herself. This did not put Walter off having sex with more farm hands. He was amazed at his success with country women.

'Here I no sooner attacked than the females fell to me,' he wrote. Again he used the word 'attacked'.

When rainy weather stopped him having sex in the open air, he headed back to London. Molly, the dairy maid, was on the train. She was going to stay with her aunt. When they went through tunnels and it was dark, he seized the opportunity to molest her. He managed to get out of her the address where she was staying in London, but decided to follow her anyway. However, Molly's aunt did not turn up to meet her at the station, so he took her to a bawdy house. He coerced her into having sex with him a second time, although he knew she did not like him. The affair continued as Walter deliberately corrupted her with money. Eventually her aunt, sensing she was in moral danger, sent her back to her mother. Later, when Walter saw Molly back in the country, he said dismissively that she was 'as modest as a whore at a christening'. By then, she had taken up with his cousin Fred. Nevertheless, Walter compelled her to go to his room and had sex with her forcibly, directly after Fred had had sex with her. Although she refused him, Walter had her a second time and promised her a new bonnet if she would do it again. She fell pregnant. Walter denied paternity, saying the 'bumpkin' Giles must have done it. Molly returned to London and, to support herself, became a prostitute. It was little more than a year than Walter had overseen her fall from curtsying dairy maid to whore. She soon had gonorrhoea. Walter had sex with her anyway, then wrote an anonymous letter to her mother for her to come and get her daughter. By then, she had a child, and everyone assumed Giles was the father.

Nelly was also pregnant. She and her sister Sophy left the village. After Walter's ravages, they became prostitutes. Walter said that a village abortionist took them to London and blamed the 'German Jewess' for their downfall. In another version of the story, Walter said he met Nelly again in the Argyle Rooms, a popular hangout for prostitutes in the Haymarket. He slept with her a few times, but by then he was on his uppers and could not afford her prices. However, when his fortunes revived he had sex with her again. And this time, he would get Nelly to procure virgins for him. But that would be years in the future.

11

THE HUNTSMAN

Walter grew tired of farm girls. He returned to London, where he now had a 'terrace house' away from his mother. Walter went out with cousin Fred and Laura, who were now married, and Laura's friend from Plymouth, Mabel. After Fred and Laura went to bed, Walter and Mabel began to kiss. However, Walter lost his erection at the sight of Mabel's black stockings. He could not get the image of them out of his head even when she dropped her skirts, covering them. He only managed to have sex after watching her urinate. Then he blew out the candle and they did it in the dark. Afterwards, he told her that he loathed black stockings.

Inside the bedroom, an increasing range of fetishes was gripping Walter. Outside the house, a new one provided opportunities to find yet more darker ones. Walter took up blood sports. His wealthy uncle was a hunting enthusiast who leased his farm field for game. Walter would holiday there and go hunting with his uncle and Fred. It was after a hunting trip that Walter watched Fred use first a gun-screw and then a knife to cut a slit in the wallpaper to spy on the women of the household bathing. It was here Walter experienced the contrary impulse that drove him to, but repulsed him from, middle-aged women. As he peeped through the slit, Walter recalled: '[One] was ugly and middle-aged. I would sooner have fucked any one of the young women than her, and yet I recollect feeling the most furious baudiness about her, and frigged looking at her.' He watched while two of the women had sex with each other. When he told Fred about it, Fred said that, in India, he had bought three virgins from their parents and kept them in a bungalow where they 'satisfied their letches' in that manner.

'His girls, he said, did it, and did it before him,' Walter said. 'I was amazed and wondered, and half-thought him lying.'

Walter had always imagined that women had done such things for his amusement, not out of desire for each other. As a youth, he had been repulsed by homosexuality and 'was approaching middle age before I realized the fact that frigging another fellow's doodle was agreeable, and that some women find similar pleasures with their own sex'.

Fred bought some erotic engravings that he intended to throw over the wall into the neighbouring girls' school, but he suffered a sprain. Walter went back to London alone and rushed to Fred's wife Laura's lodgings, where Laura and Mabel were sleeping together for company. Walter stripped off and got into bed with them. He had sex with Mabel, then when Mabel was asleep, had Laura too.

After amusing himself with a number of prostitutes, he went back to the country to see Mrs Pender. She was now hugely pregnant, but that did not stop Walter having sex with her. She told him that her husband suspected that Walter was the father of the child. This would be Walter's first brush with the law.

> About a month after this, I received a letter from a lawyer in London saying he wished to see me. I went, and found that he was instructed to bring an action against me for seducing Mrs Pender. I denied all, but it was of no use. I at once went to my solicitor, who after a time feared the case could be proved against me. The action would be brought for damages (there was no divorce possible then), and there would be the scandal, the annoyance to my aunt, and the horror of my mother.

Walter's reaction was typical.

> *The only chance of getting a word with Mrs P. was waylaying her in the laurel-walk. When I saw her she looked the picture of misery, her husband had refused to sleep in the same bed with her. At about five o'clock one evening, it being quite dark, she had given me a signal during the day. I went to the privy. There I fucked her, she said how utterly miserable she was, and asked me to take her away. Uprighters were never to my taste, and now her big belly made it far from pleasurable.*

Then, the prospect of public exposure hit home.

> *I got worried, and at length after much legal annoyance, agreed to give five hundred pounds, on condition that I had a letter from Pender saying that he was very sorry for what he had done, that he was convinced he had made a mistake, and was then sure of his wife's fidelity, or something to that effect.*

Five hundred pounds was a huge amount of money. A few hundred would buy a country cottage. Walter then suspected he had been the victim of a blackmail plot. He again went looking for Mrs Pender – and this time not for sex, but to force a confession from her when she was naked.

> *Before this was quite settled, Mr Pender got leave of absence, and went away somewhere. My solicitor asked me whether I had any reason to suspect that Mrs P. had told her husband. Immediately I became savagely suspicious, went to the cottage under pretence of asking for Pender himself, although I knew he was away, and insisted she should meet me at the town. I thought of nothing until we met, but how I should entrap her into a confession, and worked myself up into a belief that the couple were making a market of me.*

She undressed, I caressed her, with hand on her cunt, looked at her and said, 'Your husband means to make a fortune out of me.' 'What he, – ho, ho, ho', she cried, 'the wretch, – oh ! I shall be exposed, – ho, ho', and was as white as a sheet. When she got better, I told her all. She knew nothing about what her husband had done, and begged I would pay nothing – she would drown herself – and I left, convinced that the poor woman was true to me. Pender gave notice to leave, and forfeiting wages left his place, and went to the north of England.

This was the first of a series of sudden disappearances that were a feature of Walter's memoirs. Walter viewed Mr Pender's legal action as a challenge to his right to be a sexual predator in the countryside. Forfeiting the huge sum of damages he was about to hand over to them, the Penders simply 'went to the north of England'. The only evidence the Penders were even alive, he said, was a note that came into Walter's hands.

Months afterwards I received a scrawl saying that the child was exactly like me, that P. was not unkind, but she was unhappy, would like to see me; and if I wished it she would run away, and be as good as a wife to me. There was no name or address to it, and I never heard of her afterwards.

Their disappearance saved him a bundle, but the incident left Walter with a lifelong fear of blackmail and exposure – although he was happy to use these tactics himself to get women into bed.

Walter continued seeing Mabel, but she was educated and the marrying kind. So he soon went back to 'harlotting'.

I had fits of great incontinence, and as many as three different women on the same day, at times. Exceedingly nice women were then to be met in the Quadrant from 11 p.m. to 1 a.m. in the morning, and 3 p.m. till 5 p.m.

*in the afternoon. I would have one before luncheon, get
another after luncheon, dine, and have a third woman.*

He also picked up women in the Opera colonnade, opposite
the United Services Club. Between prostitutes, Walter enjoyed
himself at the very height of English society. Walter, Fred,
Laura and Mabel had an orgy with 'Lord and Lady A'. At
the time, Walter, Fred and Mabel were living at Laura's apart-
ments, but Walter found himself short of money after making
a tour of the best brothels of Paris. He dropped Mabel and
went back to live with his mother. He still had women by the
dozen, although he tried to reduce what he paid them. Walter
was then twenty-six. He married. His wife had money, but was
otherwise unappealing.

*I tried to like, to love her. It was impossible. Hateful in
day, she was loathsome to me in bed. Long I strove to
do my duty, and be faithful, yet to such a pitch did my
disgust at length go, that laying by her side, I had wet
dreams nightly, sooner than relieve myself in her. I have
frigged myself in the streets before entering my house,
sooner than fuck her.*

He avoided her 'as he would a corpse', but he had little money
of his own to spend on other women. So he vowed to be chaste,
although he was troubled with constant erections. His health
declined. He had sleepless nights and contemplated suicide. He
was thinking of throwing himself in the canal when he found
himself in an area of town inhabited by cheap prostitutes. So
instead of killing himself, he decided to give way to his lusts.

The woman was kind to him and, afterwards, bought some
gin for them to drink. Her name was Mary Davis. After they
had had sex, she invited him to stay the night, but he was still
trying to maintain the appearance of propriety at home and
left. She even lent him a shilling for his fare. He returned the
money the next evening. They talked. Mary was nineteen and
'altogether as nice a little woman as one could have wanted'.

However, he did not understand why she had settled down in a neighbourhood of costermongers and sold herself for just five shillings, when she could have been a two-sovereign woman in the West End. That night, he did not go home. He stayed every night for a week. It cost him £2, although even that modest sum was more than he could afford. He stopped seeing Mary Davis for a while, fearing that he might lose her the regular clients that kept her. But the affair continued. Walter donned shabby clothing to visit her. He got to know Mary's landlord, an elderly carpenter, and his wife. When Mary was away ill, the landlady saw a business opportunity. She got Walter a 'beautifully shaped girl'. Walter wanted more. He asked the landlady to find him a virgin 'of about fourteen'. This, he was told, was an almost impossible task. Girls in that area had lost their virginity by then. But Walter was determined and sated himself with street molestation in an effort to find a hymen. 'I afterwards groped several young girls in those dark streets, and there was certainly no obstacle to my fingers searching their cunts.'

When Mary was away, ill again, the landlady brought Walter another girl whom she claimed was a virgin. They plied her with gin. Walter managed to get her to feel his penis, but she would not let him touch her. The landlady thought that Mary Davis might be able to persuade the child, but when she returned Mary refused to have anything to do with such a thing.

Over the course of two or three years, Walter got to know Mary well, although he estimated he had had some fifty other women in the seven surrounding streets. One of them was fifteen. She sent her mother to buy Walter a condom when he requested one. When he entered her, she cried out – to Walter's delight.

'Her cry of pain gave me pleasure, and fetched me,' he said.

At the time of his affair with Mary Davis in her one-room bordello, Walter was living in a 'small eight-roomed house' with only one servant, a housemaid named Mary. Another bout of venereal disease and lack of money made him abstinent.

'I worked at my occupation to get money and forget my troubles,' he said.

He lost his appetite, grew thinner and more miserable. One summer's day he came home early. His wife was out. He tried to read to take his mind off his woes, but broke down and cried. The housemaid, Mary, came to comfort him. He threw his arms around her and kissed her. One thing quickly led to another, but Walter suffered one of his occasional bouts of impotence. The next day, he returned home early again. This time, master and maid made love. Walter's wife was out of the house to tend a sick relative. For a few days they had free reign. Then, when Mary had a day off, he took her to a bawdy house. Despite Walter's wife's growing suspicions, the affair continued until Mary got pregnant. His wife then dismissed her.

Walter kept in touch for some time, sending her what little money he could. Then she disappeared. She was kept by the son of her new employer until he married. Seven years later, Walter bumped into her opposite the National Gallery and took her to a bawdy house in 'J . . . s Street'. Five years later, she wrote saying she was badly off. He sent two pounds. That was the last he heard from her.

After Mary first disappeared, Walter said he 'missed greatly her kind, sympathetic association'. He could think of nothing but her. For a while he went through alternate periods of 'indiscriminate cheap whoring' and abstinence. The neighbours had two daughters, one nineteen, the other twenty. The houses shared the same cesspool. When the girls went out to the privy, Walter followed suit so he could hear them pee. It aroused him and he masturbated. Soon he got tired of this and returned to paying prostitutes, once picking up a sixteen-year-old in the Lowther Arcade, opposite Charing Cross Station and not far from the offices of the *Pall Mall Gazette*. He had to turn 'savage' with a servant girl he met in the Strand. She made him promise not to come inside her. He agreed, but 'forgot my promise, even if I ever meant to keep it . . . my spend made doubly pleasurable, because she did not wish it in her cunt'.

Sometimes a request to control his sex acts, however slight, brought an extreme reaction. Once when he was unable to afford full sex, a pick-up agreed to masturbate him if he promised not to ejaculate on her silk dress. Walter deliberately came all over her finery, and flung semen in her face.

> *'Serve you right, you cheating whore,' said I putting on my hat, and leaving her with a towel wiping off my sperm, and cursing me as she did it. I don't know when I felt so spiteful against a woman as I did against her.*

As Walter could only afford cheap whores, he scoured the area between Charing Cross and Temple Bar, feeling up women who came out of the houses in Exeter Street. At night, the theatre side of the street was one large flock of prostitutes and there were dozens of bawdy houses in the side streets. The women would piss in the side streets and, sometimes, he would go and piss beside them. He would give them a shilling for a feel, then beat them down to five shillings for sex. Sometimes, they would do it up against the wall in the street. He found it humiliating when the women jeered at him for offering such a paltry sum.

Once again, he caught gonorrhoea, which 'made it again needful to open my piss-pipe by surgical tubes'. Afterwards, he tried to use condoms again, unsuccessfully.

A relative died, leaving him a small amount of money. It was then that he had the dress-lodger whose mirror he smashed. Afterwards, he had an affair with Brighton Bessie, which dragged on for ten years. She fell in love with him, he said, but he was never faithful.

'I don't know why my erotic fancies took the desire for a young lass,' he wrote, 'but they did.'

During his periods of promiscuity, Walter would study intently women whom he wanted for sex before he acted. He called it 'seeing how the cat jumped'. Again, as well as having mature women like Bessie, he was constantly on the hunt for young victims – 'black kittens'.

One afternoon in June (Walter gives no year, just the month), he saw two young girls outside a sweet shop.

'I'll buy you whatever you want if you will come with me,' he said.

They backed away from him. He continued watching them for a bit, then walked past, saying: 'Come with me and I'll give you money.'

He walked back and said: 'I'll give you three and sixpence.' Then he waited for the children at the corner of the street that was full of bawdy houses.

The younger girl was reluctant to follow, but the older one, Kitty, went with him. The woman who ran the first bawdy house let them in. Walter got the girl to strip and was delighted to find that she had not yet grown pubic hair. She said she thought she was fifteen, although her aunt said she was younger. Walter had sex with her anyway.

'If Kitty was not a harlot before, she was from that minute she had her spend with me,' he said.

He quizzed Kitty about the younger girl, Pol. She was fourteen. When Walter had established that she was a virgin, he told Kitty to bring her next time. Kitty was keen for Walter to have Pol as she was very poor and Kitty kept calling her a 'foule' for not making money from men. Next time, Kitty brought Pol. When Walter got to the bawdy house with these two very young girls, the landlady said nothing, simply charged him double. Walter thought Pol ugly. The only thing that appealed to him was that she was a virgin. When she howled in pain and tried to get him to stop, Walter said: 'Again I coaxed, promised, lied and Kitty bullied . . . ' At the sight of her 'unfledged' vulva, Walter was mad. His lost his vision and heard a voice in his head: 'My eyesight failed me, the demon of desire said, "It's fresh, it's virgin, bore it, bung it, plug it; stretch it, split it, spunk in it", and I laid hold of her . . . '

Walter's mindset then crossed from rape to murder. Pol was held down and screaming. Walter was 'determined to have her if I killed her', repeating his curse into the child's face; 'I'll murder you'.

Acts of serial rape and murder require the fantasy of rape and killing. No premeditated murderer kills without imagining the act of murder first. That is the definition of premeditation. Similarly, it is remarkably rare for men – other than sex killers – to fantasise about murder and death. Walter, however, ascribed to himself the urge to have sex 'even if I killed her'. It is beyond a turn of phrase. The extremity of the language is evidence of the fantasy to kill. The threat of murder had the practical effect of allowing him to commit the rape. It is akin to characters such as Ian Brady and Fred West, who bring enabling women into the rape and murder fantasy. Walter could only write that he was determined to have Pol 'even if he killed her' because it had crossed his mind to kill someone for sex. Within the same description of the sex act with Pol, he abused her saying, 'damn you I'll murder you'. The scene with Pol and Kitty was a joint rape with a threat to murder.

> *I then fell with the full weight of my body on her, grasping her thin buttocks, and nearly stifling her on that hot afternoon, determined to have her if I killed her. The girl gave howl after howl . . .*

He was 'blindly battering' Pol while Kitty held her down. Walter cursed and threatened he would kill her.

> *'Damn you, if you are not quiet I'll rip your dress into ribbons, and you may go home, and tell your mother what you like, damn you I'll murder you, – I'll give you ten shillings.' 'You fool he'll give you ten shillings.' I heard no more.*

The encounter ended, as Walter hoped it would – with blood-shed. Once he had penetrated Pol, he got off. Kitty saw the blood first. 'She is bleeding,' she said. Walter cursed Pol for making a fuss, then checked that Pol was 'bleeding freely'.

> *I saw the ragged edge my intrusion had made, and*

not feeling inclined for more fucking gave the girl half-a-sovereign in gold, Kitty five shillings, and went off leaving them still naked, Kitty from time to time looking at her friend's wounded orifice . . . I had fear that I might be in trouble through my voluptuousness, although a girl of twelve years is competent to judge of her own fitness for fucking, and many not a month over that age are plugged daily in London.

Walter left the girls to attend 'a disagreeable interview' with his solicitors. When he came out, he saw a crowd. In the middle of it were Kitty and Pol.

'Oh! Lord,' thought I, 'here is a row about what I have been doing.'

Walter jumped in a cab and made off, deciding not to see them the next day as he had promised.

'There will be a row about that ugly little lump having been pierced,' he wrote. 'I will go no more.'

However, three days later, he could not resist and, again, took them to a bawdy house. Once more, Walter took delight in making little Pol howl. But he soon got tired of Pol, although he continued seeing Kitty who needed money to eat. Costing only three and six a time, this was economical for Walter. He fed her sausage rolls and bought her white stockings. One day, when she was with Walter, Kitty – who was Pol's senior by a year – had her first period.

That night I had Brighton Bessie, and told her about it. Bessie said the dirty little bitch ought to be flogged by the hangman; if she had her way all such young bitches should be sent to prison, and the men who had them ought to be punished as well.

Bessie later complained that she herself had been arrested because she refused sex to a policeman.

Walter then had to go abroad for seven months. When he returned, he bumped into Kitty in the Strand. She had become a prostitute.

His home life continued to be a misery, so Walter spent a lot of time back at his mother's house, now his brother was away and his two sisters were married. He also stayed with one of his sisters whose husband he liked. At his mother's he would climb the gardener's ladder to spy on a place where men and women urinated: 'the greatest fun I had was once seeing a female bogging, who turned round and gathered two or three of the largest leaves from the lime trees in our gardens that overhung the wall and wiped her arse with them'.

For years Walter had two artist friends – one a sculptor who drank himself to death, the other a painter. He would visit their studios to see the nude models and took to sketching them – 'therefore by training, instinct, and a most voluptuous temperament become a good judge of beauty of female form'.

Walter wrote this in the introduction to an interlude with Sarah Mavis. He spotted her in the Quadrant one summer morning about midday but could not tell if she was gay or not. When she stopped to look in a shop at the corner of Beak Street, he met her eye and began to follow her. At Tichborne Street, he asked: 'Will you come with me?' She made no reply. When she stopped to look in another shop, he asked: 'May I go with you?'

'Yes, – where to?'

'Where you like, I will follow you.'

She took him to 13 J . . . s Street: 'which I entered that day for the first time, but many hundreds of times since'. He offered her ten shillings. She said she would not go upstairs with him for less than a sovereign. He agreed. Even so, she resisted, then only gave him the briefest encounter. He implored her to see him again that night. He arrived back at 13 J . . . s Street half an hour before they were to meet, taking the same room. It cost seven and six an hour, or twenty shillings for the night. 'Scores of times I have paid both fees.' The room was full of mirrors. He pulled his penis out, then began worrying whether she would find it too small. This was a constant anxiety. After an hour, she arrived. Then, when she refused to strip off or be pulled about, Walter got angry.

'You're one of those beasts, are you?' said she.

Walter saw Sarah Mavis once or twice a day for the next week, although she still refused to strip or spend any length of time with him. She was often in and out of the house in ten minutes, leaving him angry. One day, he stormed out, picked up another woman in the street and took her back to J . . . s Street. Sarah had already gone. Then he began to economize again, taking ten-shilling rather than twenty-shilling women, although he still used J . . . s Street, even though it was expensive.

After a fortnight, he saw Sarah Mavis again. But, in the house in J . . . s Street, she was not more forthcoming. She asked him whether he had been with other women. He lied and said he hadn't. She said she had seen him going up the stairs in J . . . s Street with one. This sparked a row but they were then reconciled and Sarah became more compliant.

One night he persuaded her to go out to dinner with him and drink champagne. Afterwards, they had sex and, for the first time, Sarah appeared to enjoy it. But still she would not take off all her clothes. Eventually, Walter got her to strip down to her chemise. Then he offered her one, two, three sovereigns to take it off. He even tried to rip it off her.

'I've got an ugly scar, I don't like it seen.' 'Never mind, show it.' Slowly she dropped the chemise, and stood in all her naked beauty, and pointing to a scar just below her breasts, and about four inches above her navel. 'There,' said she, 'is it not ugly? Does it not spoil me! How I hate it!'

I told her no, that she was so beautiful, that it mattered not. Yet ugly it was. A seam looking like a piece of parchment which had been held close to a fire and crinkled, and then glazed, star-shaped, white, and as big as a large egg lay between her breasts

and her navel. It was the only defect on one of the
most perfect and beautiful forms that God ever had
created.

Afterwards, he often saw her naked. They had sex again and
Walter wanted her to stay.

'If I'm not home by half-past ten I shall be half-mur-
dered.' She had let expressions like that drop more than
once; but I got no explanation excepting that she lived
with her father and mother, and at that time I believed
it.

Walter was with Sarah Mavis 'almost exclusively' for three
years. Sarah fell pregnant and miscarried. He began to believe
that she had another lover. Then she announced that it was
true, and they were going abroad together.

I sank back on the sofa sobbing; it came home to me all
at once that I was madly in love with her. I was dazed
with my own discovery, I in love with a gay woman!
One whose cunt might have had a thousand pricks
up it! Who might have sprung from any dung-hill!
Impossible!

Walter cried and begged her to stay. He felt his heart breaking.
They had been so happy together that he had forgotten the
misery of his home life. She said that he might be happier at
home after she left. Then she dropped the bombshell.

'I am a married woman,' she said, 'and have two children,
and am going with them and my husband.'

Walter was crushed.

Until she left, they saw a lot of each other. She told him that
she had been an actress in the *poses plastiques*, where beautiful
girls and young men posed near-nude in figure-hugging silk
in artistic tableaux, and had modelled for the artists William
Frost and William Etty, both well-known painters of luxurious

nudes. He bought a painting of her, although he had spent so much during their time together, he was now deeply in debt. When she eventually left, he was distraught and went home very drunk.

'For some days I was prostrate in mind, and almost in body,' he wrote.

> *It was well nigh three weeks before I touched or saw a cunt after Sarah left. Then one Sunday I had erections all day long. After dinner, lust drove me nearly mad; so I went to my room, took a clean sheet of white paper, and frigged myself over it. My prick only slightly subsided, I frigged again, and then as the paper lay before me covered with sperm-pools I cried, because it was not up my dear Sarah's vagina, laid my head on the table where the paper lay and sobbed with despair, jealousy and regrets, for I thought someone would fuck her if I did not, that it would be her hateful husband whom she had helped to keep with my money.*

Walter took up with a mulatto woman. After a time, he plucked up the courage to go back to J . . . s Street again, where the landlady told him that Sarah was not married. She had gone away with another woman's husband whom she supported, along with the rest of the family. And the father of her children was the husband of the aunt, the woman who ran the *poses plastiques*. The money Sarah had earned from him was going to set up a new *poses plastiques* troupe on the Continent.

Walter sought comfort in other women, and returned to rape. Walter also took to visiting an old couple in a distant suburb, who sympathized with him over his unhappy marriage. They had a servant girl named Jenny. When Walter was left alone with her, he attacked her and she lost consciousness.

> *She sank back in the chair, seemingly unconscious and deadly white. I withdrew my hand, then came a mental*

*struggle; my first impulse was to get cold water, the
next to look at her cunt.*

When she recovered, Jenny said she would drown herself if her
boyfriend found out what Walter had done to her.

'You must be a bad man to take advantage of a poor girl in
the house alone,' she said.

Walter was unrepentant. When he caught her sister Jane
alone in the house, he forced himself on her, too. He continued pestering Jenny and had sex with her in the garden
when the family returned. Her employer complained that
some man had got over the wall and said he would call the
police.

Eventually, Walter's fortunes began to revive. He moved
into a new home, 'a larger house with only three servants'.
He was away touring the Continent when a special messenger
caught up with him.

'Death had done its work,' he recorded. 'Hurrah! I was free
at last.'

It seems his wife had died.

'I travelled home night and day, hurriedly arranged affairs,
gave carte blanche to solicitors and agents, and with lighter
heart than I had had for years, went abroad again,' he said.

He then enjoyed 'four years of freedom', before falling in
love again. Much of his time was spent abroad. He recorded
over thirty trips, including 'a long voyage across the sea',
which is thought to have taken him to America. He certainly
visited Russia, the Far East, Denmark, Sweden, Belgium, the
Netherlands, Germany, Spain, Switzerland, Italy and France –
particularly Paris – repeatedly.

'Winifred terminated my four years of freedom,' he noted
in the bracketed text he added at proofreading stage. 'I fell in
love and was changed, yet my amorous frailty clung to me. I
loved deeply, truly, shall love to my dying hour, and, in spite
of my infidelity, would at any time have slain any one of my
paramours rather than have give her pain.'

But he could not help himself.

Why with this feeling I sought the Cyprians, demireps,
sluts and strumpets, which I have done, I cannot
explain, nor the frame of mind which led me into
lascivious vagaries and aberrations, fancies and
caprices, yet to be told of.

As Walter aged, conflicting desires brought on murderous
impulses. Walter was repulsed by homosexual sex, but wanted
it badly. The tension between these two impulses made him
violent to men and, later, to women. The conflict began after
Walter masturbated a man during an orgy and found himself
'excited beyond measure'. He then wanted to go all the way.
The prostitute and procuress Sarah found him a man to bugger
in her sitting room for £10.

I closed on him half mad . . . my brain whirled, I wished
not to do what I was doing, but some ungovernable
impulse drove me on . . . I held him to me, grasping
both his prick and balls tightly. He gave a loud moan.
'Oho I shall faint,' he cried. 'Ho, pull it out.'
'It's in, don't move or I won't pay you, or something
of that sort,' I said, holding myself tight up to him.
'Ohooo, leave go, you're hurting my balls so' – I sup-
pose I was handling them roughly but his bum kept
close to my belly. I recollect nothing more distinctly.
A fierce, bloody-minded baudiness possessed me, a
determination to do it – to ascertain if it was a pleasure.

Walter ejaculated, but said he wanted to kick the man he had
sex with and kill anyone who knew about it.

Immediately I had an ineffable disgust at him and
myself – a terrible fear, a loathing – I could scarcely be
in the room with him, could have kicked him. He said,
'You've made me bleed.' At that, I nearly vomited. 'I
must make haste,' said I, looking at my watch, 'I forgot
it was so late – I must go.' All my desire was to get

> *away as quickly as possible. I left after paying him and*
> *making him swear, and swearing myself, that no living*
> *person should know of the act.*

This is proof that Walter considered murder to hide a shameful sex act. He wrote a memoir of sex that contained imaginings of murder. These were not the cheeky words of a lively author but homicidal urges described by a repeat rapist. Such wanderings in the mind of a self-confessed serial rapist, blood fetishist and prostitute-stalker must be considered as more than colourful phrasing. They are clues to murder itself. Sarah, who had set up the sodomy, was plainly at risk. Walter's wife had also been a victim of his violent – if not homicidal – urges after unusual sex. The episode in question, as usual, began with an erotic notion.

'The idea of catching a couple fucking made me more randy,' wrote Walter.

When he saw a prostitute and a penniless sailor arguing, he stepped in. He paid the woman five shillings and offered the sailor five shillings to watch then join in. After the sailor had had the woman up against a wall, Walter entered her. Then the two men took turns, with Walter holding the sailor's genitals as he penetrated. Eventually, the approach of a policeman's lantern stopped the action. As ever, Walter was terrified of exposure.

> *My lust went off. What if the policeman saw and*
> *knew me! I got to the road, turned to the left along the*
> *crunching gravelled path, walking very quickly, and so*
> *soon as I turned the corner took to my heels, and ran*
> *hard home, ran as if I had committed a burglary.*
>
> *Letting myself in with my latchkey I found I had left*
> *my umbrella behind me. Then a dread came over me. I*
> *had fucked a common street nymph, and in the sperm*
> *of a common sailor, both might have a pox, – what*
> *more probable? I could feel the sperm wet and sticky*
> *round my prick, and on my balls.*

Walter washed himself. Then he entered his wife's bedroom. He found himself so excited about what he had just done, he brutally raped his wife.

> *I jumped into bed and, forcing her on to her back, drove my prick up her. It must have been stiff, and I violent, for she cried out that I hurt her. 'Don't do it so hard, – what are you about!' But I felt that I could murder her with my prick, and drove and drove, and spent up her cursing. While I fucked her I hated her – she was but my spunk-emptier. 'Get off, you've done it, and your language is most revolting.'*

During his attack, Walter had suffered memory loss.

> *Off I went into my bedroom for the night. What I said whilst furiously fucking her, thinking of the sailor's prick and the spermy quim of the nymph, and almost mad with excitement, I never knew.*

Walter's manuscript continued with his experiments with sex. He watched flogging, took to masturbation with a glove, attempted intercourse, he said, with a woman with two vaginas, built a device with hooks and ropes to examine genitals. But his memoir always returned to what he had come to crave most – sex with 'unfledged' girls. Walter took to calling his penis 'the piercer'. He would pierce girls to make them bleed. *My Secret Life* overflows with blood.

> *My sperm rises, I love her, could drink her piss, her blood . . . I longed to hurt her, to make her cry with the pain . . . a bloody sacrifice, scarcely any hymen I've slaughtered caused so much blood-letting . . . patches of blood, and spunk streaked with blood . . . blood on my handkerchief which I had put under her bum . . . 'You've made me bleed,' she whimpered . . . my fingers were smeared with blood . . . blood on my*

> *finger and her pain gave me a voluptuous shiver . . . a*
> *red stream followed . . . a violent jerk, and there was*
> *blood . . . satisfaction of finding my fingers well blood-*
> *stained . . . A mass of blood-streaked sperm filled the*
> *mouth . . . pouring down blood copiously, and drop-*
> *ping on to my shirt. The sight of blood always made*
> *me furious . . . the jagging seemed fresh, raw, and signs*
> *of blood just showing on it. I touched it . . . I got home*
> *and found my shemmy bloody . . . you bloody bitch,*
> *look out for yourself . . . 'She'll bleed – oh joy, that*
> *blood.'*

In his book, Walter described making twenty different women bleed. Almost all descriptions were of blood from the broken hymen of a raped girl. So how could these be considered the mark of a murderer?

The link between blood fetish, sex and murder had been noted two years before the Ripper killings. The German researcher Richard von Krafft-Ebing published the fantasies that drove killers such as Case 25, Mr X: 'Bloody thoughts were constantly present, and induced lustful excitement'. Killings were driven by 'imagining representations of blood and scenes of blood . . . without (these) no erection was possible'. The Viennese psychiatrist discovered the mindset of sex killers: 'following lust-murder . . . sight of the victim's blood are a delight and pleasure'.

Modern researchers have seen it too. Candice Skrapec, professor of criminal psychology at California State University, has studied blood fetish in historical serial murderers. She investigated Peter Kurten, the so-called 'Monster of Dusseldorf', convicted of the murders of nine people and attempted murders of seven others between 1913 and 1930. She wrote:

> *The murders Kurten confessed to involved strangula-*
> *tion, stabbing, and/or blunt force trauma over a period*
> *of time . . . However, if one examines the modus*
> *operandi closely . . . the killings appear to be incidental*

*to a perverse drive for sexual gratification. Many
of Kurten's assaults appear to have been directed by
a need to cause and witness the flow of blood from
his victim. While Kurten's paraphilic "blood lust"
did result in the deaths of nine people it does not
appear that the death of a victim was a determining
factor in his emotional satisfaction and/or sexual
release.*

The fetish has figured in notorious modern crimes. Jeffrey
Dahmer murdered and cut up seventeen young men between
1978 and 1991 in Wisconsin. His elaborate masturbatory
fantasies involving blood, led him to kill repeatedly, to dissect
his victims' bodies, to drink their blood, and to devour their
flesh. In 1982, he even took a job at a blood bank but was
eventually fired.

To see slit throats as a sexual turn-on may seem too
extreme, even for a man such as Walter, who would delight
in bringing blood to the genital slits of children. But Walter
told us he had long ago taken that step. He described how
his first sight of a vulva had conjured up the 'slit throat of
a dog'. Small surprise that his mind wandered to murder
during the rape of Pol, the attack on his wife and his
embrace of sodomy. Walter's hand wandered to the blade
to make spy holes for sex. To think Walter did not use his
knife to bring on the blood he craved gifts this sex attacker
with self-control and human empathy not evident in his
memoir.

'Blood and power intoxicate', wrote Russian novelist
Fyodor Dostoyevsky in 1862. 'Callousness and vice develop;
the most abnormal things become first acceptable, then sweet
to the mind and heart.' The year Dostoyevsky noted that
sweetness, the author of *My Secret Life* was making diary
entries of his joy of spilt blood.

Throughout Walter's long sex life, his desires became
increasingly bizarre and violent. Although he did not say so
specifically, on checking the various dates in *My Secret Life*,

Walter would have been around sixty-seven in 1888, the year he printed the first volume – the year Jack the Ripper was at large. And, as we shall see, he was not necessarily too old to be the killer.

THE MURDER OF
CATHERINE EDDOWES

On the same night he killed 'Long Liz' Stride, the fiend at large on the streets of Whitechapel also murdered Catherine Eddowes. On 28 September 1888, two days before she was killed, she returned from hop-picking in Kent and told the superintendent of the workhouse in Shoe Lane where she was staying: 'I have come back to earn the reward offered for the apprehension of the Whitechapel murderer. I think I know him.'

The superintendent warned her not to get murdered herself.

'No fear of that,' she replied.

The *East London Observer* also reported this conversation, but said that this exchange happened at the Mile End casual ward.

Later that day, Catherine Eddowes, or Kate as she was known to friends, met up with John Kelly, her common-law husband, at Cooney's Lodging House at 55 Flower and Dean Street, where they had lived together, on and off, for seven years. They had no money and pawned Kelly's boots to pay for breakfast. At around 2 p.m., they parted company in Houndsditch. He was going to look for work in the markets; she said she was going to see her daughter Annie in King Street, Bermondsey, to see if she could borrow any money. Kelly said he warned her to be careful.

'Don't fear for me,' she said. 'I'll take care of myself and I shan't fall into his hands.'

But Kate did not find her daughter Annie, who had moved twice since her mother had last visited her. However, Kate found some money somewhere, and by 8.30 p.m. she was drunk; PC Louis Robertson found her lying in a heap on the pavement outside 29 Aldgate High Street, surrounded by a crowd. He asked whether any of them knew her. No one replied. With the help of PC George Simmonds, he took her to Bishopsgate police station, where Sergeant James Byfield noted that she smelt strongly of drink. When asked her name, Eddowes replied: 'Nothing.' She was put in the cells to sleep it off.

At 11.45 p.m., PC George Hutt visited her and found her awake and singing. At 12.30 a.m., she asked to be released.

'When you are capable of taking care of yourself,' Hutt replied.

'I can do that now,' said Kate.

Half an hour later, she was let out of the cells.

'What time is it?' she asked Hutt; it was 1 a.m.

'Too late for you to get anything to drink,' said Hutt.

'I shall get a damn fine hiding when I get home,' said Kate.

'And serve you right,' said Hutt, 'you had no right to get drunk.'

She gave her name as Mary Anne Kelly and her address as 6 Fashion Street, then she was discharged. However, when she left the police station, she did not turn right towards Fashion Street or Cooney's, where she would expect to find Kelly. Instead she turned left, towards Houndsditch and Mitre Square. The City police were left with the impression that she had an appointment. After all, she had a cell for the night – for free – if she had wanted it and was concerned about the time when she left. Because of the murders, the police had been told to look out for men with prostitutes. So it seems she did not pick up someone on the street. Instead she hurried alone towards a rendezvous with her killer in the deserted area around Mitre Square.

A woman answering her description was seen with a man on the corner of Duke Street and Church Passage, the short alleyway that runs through into Mitre Square.

At about 1.35 a.m., Harry Harris, a furniture dealer, and Joseph Hyam Levy, a butcher, were leaving the Imperial Club at 16–17 Duke Street with commercial traveller, Joseph Lawende. Harris and Levy avoided the unsavoury couple on the corner. Levy could not give a description of them, apart from that the man was about three inches taller than the woman. However, Lawende, who walked a little closer, said the man had a moustache and the 'appearance of a sailor'. Major Henry Smith, acting commissioner of the City police, also recorded that Lawende told him that the man was wearing a deerstalker cap, although otherwise he would not recognize him.

At 1.44 a.m., just three-quarters of an hour after the body of Liz Stride had been found in Dutfield's Yard, PC Edward Watkins found the body of Catherine Eddowes in Mitre Square. None of the residents, which included a City police officer and a night watchman who was an ex-policeman, had heard anything. PC James Harvey walked past the square not five minutes before. 'I saw no one, I heard no cry or noise,' he said.

As before, the victim's throat had been slashed. She had been split up the middle and her entrails pulled out. Her uterus had been removed, along with a kidney. But this time, the killer had slashed her face, severing her nose completely. When she was stripped in the morgue, part of her ear fell out of her clothing. The killer had done his work quickly and, once again, disappeared apparently into thin air.

However, the killer appeared on the streets again that night. At 2.55 a.m., a piece of Catherine Eddowes' apron was found at the entrance to 108–19 Wentworth Model Dwellings in Goulston Street, Whitechapel. It had not been there when Detective Constable Daniel Halse had searched the street at 2.20 a.m. Above it, scrawled in white chalk on the wall, were the words:

> *The Juwes are*
> *The men That*
> *Will not*
> *Be Blamed*
> *for nothing.*

At least, that's how it was taken down. Sir Charles Warren, commissioner of the Metropolitan Police, ordered it to be cleaned off before a photographer arrived, on the grounds that it might provoke anti-Jewish riots. However, what exactly the graffiti was supposed to mean is uncertain.

Walter had a few words to say about Jews. Like most of his class at that time, he was probably anti-Semitic. When Sarah gave birth to his child, Walter borrowed £50 from an unnamed Jew, promising to pay him £100 six months later – an extortionate rate of interest Jewesses also regularly procured for him.

There is a pattern to what happened on the night of 30 September – the night of the 'double event'. Men who appeared to be dressed like sailors or wearing deerstalkers were spotted with the victims near both murder scenes. They had moustaches. One of the suspects appeared in Church Lane, opposite the Gunmakers' Proofing House. Church Lane runs north towards Whitechapel. It is the street you would take to go to Mitre Square if you wanted to keep to the back streets. Again, Goulston Street is between Mitre Square and Commercial Road, where Walter's bolthole was located. The killer could have easily got himself around the various sites – Berner Street, Church Lane, Mitre Square and Goulston Street – and had time to stop off at the Gunmakers' Proofing House on the way.

Dr Frederick Gordon Brown, who saw the corpse of Catherine Eddowes in Mitre Square and wrote the report after the post-mortem in Golden Lane mortuary, noted that the piece of bloodstained apron found in Goulston Street corresponded exactly to the piece severed from the deceased's pinny. He also concluded that 'the perpetrator of the act must have had considerable knowledge of the position of organs in the abdominal cavity and the way of removing them . . . Such a knowledge might be possessed by someone in the habit of cutting up animals.' He also told a reporter from the *Star* that the murderer 'had some knowledge of how to use a knife'.

Dr George William Sequeira and Dr William Sedgwick Saunders, who also examined the corpse, backed Brown. Sequeira told the *Star* that the mutilation had been done 'by a man who was not altogether ignorant of the use of the knife'. Dr Phillips, police surgeon for H Division, went further. He said that 'as in the Metropolitan Police cases, the medical evidence showed that the murder could have been committed by a person who had been a hunter, a butcher, a slaughterman, as well as a student in surgery or a properly qualified surgeon'.

Dr Brown stuck to his opinion. In 1903, he told the Medico-Legal Society that the murderer had some knowledge of human anatomy, but used cuts suggestive of a butcher. Two years later, at a meeting of the Crimes Club in 1905 attended by Sir Arthur Conan Doyle, he repeated that opinion.

Again, Catherine Eddowes had a silk scarf around her neck, two pocket handkerchiefs, a comb, six pieces of soap, two clay pipes and, puzzlingly, a red leather cigarette case with white metal fittings. Walter, a cigar smoker, mentioned cigarettes several times, but in *My Secret Life* they were always smoked by Frenchwomen. What was Catherine Eddowes doing with a cigarette case when she seems to have been a pipe smoker?

It was only after the murder of Liz Stride and Catherine Eddowes that the press began calling the killer 'Jack the Ripper'. The name came from a letter delivered to the Central News Agency at 5 New Bridge Street on 27 September, three days before the murders took place. It was written in red ink by an educated hand and read:

> *Dear Boss,*
> *I keep on hearing the police have caught me but they wont fix me just yet. I have laughed when they look so clever and talk about being on the right track. That joke about Leather Apron gave me real fits. I am down on whores and I shant quit ripping them till I*

*do get buckled. Grand work the last job was. I gave
the lady no time to squeal. How can they catch me
now. I love my work and want to start again. You will
soon hear of me with my funny little games. I saved
some of the proper <u>red</u> stuff in a ginger beer bottle
over the last job to write with but it went thick like
glue and I cant use it. Red ink is fit enough I hope
<u>ha. ha</u>. The next job I do I shall clip the ladys ears off
and send to the police officers just for jolly wouldn't
you. Keep this letter back till I do a bit more work,
then give it out straight. My knife's so nice and sharp
I want to get to work right away if I get a chance.
Good Luck.*

Yours truly
Jack the Ripper

Dont mind me giving the trade name

Then, at the bottom of the page, written sideways, he added
a postscript:

*Wasnt good enough to post this before I got all the red
ink off my hands curse it No luck yet. They say I'm a
doctor now. ha ha*

It carried a London East Central postmark, dated 27 September.
However, the editor considered it a hoax and delayed two days
before he sent it to the police.

The text of the letter was published in the *Daily News* on
1 October and, in the first post that morning, Central News
received more correspondence. This time it was a postcard,
postmarked 'LONDON E.' and dated 1 October. It was in the
same hand and read:

*I was not codding dear old Boss when I gave you the
tip, you'll hear about Saucy Jacky's work tomorrow
double event this time number one squealed a bit
couldn't finish straight off. ha not the time to get ears*

for police. thanks for keeping last letter back till I got
to work again.

Jack the Ripper

Facsimiles of the letter and postcard appeared on posters outside every police station and were sent to the press, which published them on 4 October. From then on, the murderer was known as Jack the Ripper.

There were numerous other letters purporting to come from the Ripper, which were followed up but largely discounted. Only one of them was taken seriously. On 16 October, George Lusk, president of the Whitechapel Vigilance Committee, received in the post at his home a small cardboard box containing a kidney. It arrived shortly after it was announced that a shelter for 'outcast females' was to be opened at 34 Mile End Road. The Vigilance Committee had lent its support as the shelter would be a ready source of information on the virgin trade. The postmark was indecipherable but appeared to come from London. And as there was only one postmark, it was believed to have been posted in the same postal district as Lusk's home in Alderney Road – London East (otherwise there would have been two separate postmarks).

Lusk thought it was a cruel hoax, but at the next meeting of the Vigilance Committee, held in the Crown public house on Mile End Road two days later, he approached the treasurer, Joseph Aarons, in 'a state of considerable agitation'.

Aarons asked him what was the matter.

'I suppose you will laugh at what I am going to tell you,' Lusk said. 'But you must know that I had a little parcel come to me on Tuesday evening, and to my surprise it contains half a kidney and a letter from Jack the Ripper.'

Aarons laughed.

'It is no laughing matter to me,' said Lusk, visibly shaken.

The next morning, Aarons and other members of the Vigilance Committee went round to Lusk's home in Alderney Road. They opened the box. Inside was half a kidney, divided longitudinally. It stank. Subsequent medical examination concluded that it was a human kidney preserved in wine, but opinion was divided on whether it was Catherine Eddowes'.

The accompanying letter was again written in red, but this time in a more frenetic hand. It was headed 'From Hell' and said:

> *Mr Lusk,*
>   *Sor*
>   *I send you half the Kidne I took from one woman and prasarved it for you tother piece I fried and ate it was very nise. I may send you the bloody knif that took it out if you only wate a whil longer*
>
> > *signed*
> > *Catch me when you can Mishter Lusk*

Graphologists have concluded that this was not written by the same person who wrote the previous two missives to Central News.

Despite being written in a cod Irish accent – as in 'Sor', 'prasarved', 'Mishter – as handwriting experts observed, the writer also exhibited English characteristics, raising the 'r' in 'Mr' as was common in formal letters at the time. There is also the use of the dialect 'tother' and the misspellings. *My Secret Life* is full of examples of Walter reproducing – and lampooning – the speech of the working classes.

Long after the Ripper letters were first examined, the science of forensic linguistics was developed. In 1996, it was used to identify Theodore Kaczynski as the 'Unabomber' and, in 1998, to overturn the conviction of Derek Bentley, who was hanged in 1953.

Forensic linguistic comparison of the Lusk letter to *My Secret Life* gives surprising results. While it is plain entitling the letter 'From Hell' was a bookish flourish, a closer looks show Walter also favoured the word in his memoir, using 'hell' fourteen times in phrases such as 'see me in hell first'; 'Go the Hell and buggery' and 'hell if I've been fucked'.

Starting off 'Sor' – or 'Sir' – shows us the author knew how to craft a formal letter. Walter, a practiced correspondent, uses 'sir' more than 100 times in *My Secret Life*, mostly when feigning the phrasing of the poor. Walter wrote of his encounter with a servant:

> She opened the door . . . 'Oh! I'm her sister sir . . . I sleep here every night sir, Mrs W . . . pays me to do so sir. My sister is out sir.'

'Prasarved' or 'preserved' is used five times in *My Secret Life*. Fry comes up three times; 'nise' – or rather 'nice' – appears in 142 of the 184 chapters, often as 'very nice'. The kidney itself held meaning. Walter wrote of it as the organ most 'stimulated by champagne'. Finally, where Walter describes his lover's motto as 'Get money when you can', the Lusk letter writer signs off 'Catch me when you can'.

This word game shows Walter shared a distinct vocabulary with the writer of 'From Hell'. But his box held a more visceral clue. The posted kidney had been kept in medical ethanol – 'spirits of wine'. Why would a sex fanatic have such a chemical at hand? Spirits of wine was used to wash pubic lice, and Walter records buying 'crab remedy' to fix his infections. While this now raises the grim prospect of the diarist pickling innards in his own crab cure, far bleaker evidence that a man of Walter's tastes did commit the killings came out at the time.

On 8 October, Catherine Eddowes was buried in an unmarked grave. As the writer 'From Hell' posted off what he said was Catherine's kidney a week later, 'A Medical Man' wrote to the *Evening News* with a new notion: the culprit was enjoying a sex act, not committing plain murder.

> In the Whitechapel atrocities, we are brought face to face with . . . murder (and mutilation too) committed from purely voluptuous motives . . . This peculiar form of psychopathy is termed 'perversion of the sexual impulse' by von Krafft-Ebing, who . . . distinctly states that in all cases of murder with mutilation, in which

> *the bowels and genital organs have been either simply*
> *excised, or carried away . . . a 'Lustmord' has been*
> *committed.*

The Professor of Nervous Diseases at Vienna, Richard von Krafft-Ebing, had revolutionized thinking about sex killings – 'Lustmord' – with his 1886 book *Psychopathia Sexualis*. He had studied the confessions of such killers as the 'Girl-Stabber of Bozen', who would pierce the abdomens of women 'and take delight in the sight of the blood running from the knife'. He saw a pattern: 'Before he became a girl-stabber, he had satisfied his lust in the violation of immature girls.'

Krafft-Ebing realised stomach mutilation murders were committed by an astonishingly specific culprit – one with a fetish for raping virgins. He wrote:

> *The real meaning of the action consists in, to a certain*
> *extent, imitating, though perverted into a monstrous*
> *and ghastly form, the act of defloration . . . the victim*
> *has to be pierced, slit, even chopped up . . . The chief*
> *wounds are inflicted in the stomach region and, in*
> *many cases, the fatal cuts run from the vagina into the*
> *abdomen.*

Here was the message in the mark of the Ripper. 'I wanted to deflower her rather than to spend,' said Walter, 'and a desire to hurt her in doing it came into my mind.' Walter had both put motive more plainly and explained a mystery: why no ejaculate – 'spend' – was found at the Ripper crime scenes.

THE MURDER OF MARY JANE KELLY

By far the most gruesome of the Ripper killings was that of Mary Jane Kelly. Around 10.45 a.m. on Friday, 9 November 1888, rent-man Thomas Bowyer knocked on the door of 13 Miller's Court, Dorset Street, Spitalfields, the room Mary had rented with her boyfriend, Joseph Barnett, who had left after a row on 30 October. The rent was four shillings and sixpence a week. Mary was more than twenty-nine shillings in arrears and faced eviction. There was no answer to Bowyer's knocking. The door was locked, but Mary had broken a window pane when drunk. Bowyer reached through and pushed aside the old coat that was acting as a curtain. Inside he saw a horribly mutilated corpse. He ran back to the office to see his boss John McCarthy, owner of 'McCarthy's Rents', as Miller Court was known. McCarthy went to see for himself, then sent for the police.

At Commercial Street police station, Inspector Walter Beck was on duty. He and the young detective Walter Dew raced to Miller Court and witnessed the gruesome sight through the window, but they did not break down the door in case bloodhounds were going to be used. At around 1.30 p.m., news came that no dogs were available. A pickaxe was then taken to the door, though they need not have bothered. The door had a spring lock and the catch was within easy reach of the broken window pane.

Inside, the room was drenched in blood. The body of a young woman lay on the bed. Her throat had been cut and her face had been slashed so ferociously that she could only be identified by the colour of her hair and eyes. Again, the body had been cut open and the entrails removed. Her breasts had been cut off. One was found under her head with her uterus and kidneys; the other between her feet with her liver. Her intestines were to her right; her spleen to the left. Strips of flesh from her trunk and thighs – including her external sexual organs – were laid on the bedside table. The rumour circulated that she had been anally raped before she had been killed.

'This was about the worst of the murders,' said Chief Inspector Henry Moore, head of the Whitechapel murders investigation, when he reached Dorset Street. 'He cut the skeleton so clean of flesh that when I got here I could hardly tell whether it was a man or a woman. He hung the different parts of the body on nails and over the backs of chairs. It must have taken him an hour and a half in all.'

Mary Jane Kelly's heart was missing. The police raked through the ashes in the hearth in an attempt to find it. In the grate, they found burnt clothing, including the rim of a bonnet. Detective Dew said that Mary never wore a hat. Others who saw her immediately before her murder remarked that she was bareheaded. Why did the killer throw the clothes and the bonnet on the fire? Was he trying to hide something? Or did he want to create a blaze? Perhaps he needed more light to write by.

No one doubted that this was a Ripper murder. But why had he waited nearly six weeks to claim another victim after the double murder of Liz Stride and Catherine Eddowes? Perhaps he had been out of town. A story in *The Times* on 23 October noted: 'The sporting season in the Highlands is now nearly over, and the shooters, as the natives call them, are making up their registers preliminary to their departure to the south . . . '

The night before Mary Jane Kelly's murder, Bowyer had seen a man speaking to her who matched Matthew Packer's description of the man he had seen with Liz Stride. His appearance was smart and attention was drawn to him by his very white cuffs and rather long, white collar that came down over the front of his long black coat. He had a dark moustache. Detective Dew believed that the man Packer had seen with Liz Stride was her murderer.

On the night she died, Mary Jane Kelly spoke to Lizzie Albrook of 2 Miller's Court.

'About the last thing she said to me was, "Whatever you do don't you do wrong and turn out as I did,"' said Albrook. 'She had often spoken to me in this way and warned me against going on the street as she had done. She told me, too, that she was heartily sick of the life she was leading and wished she had money enough to go back to Ireland where her people lived. I do not believe she would have gone out as she did if she had not been obliged to do so to keep herself from starvation.'

Mary Jane Kelly had been born in Limerick, but brought up in Wales. At the age of sixteen, she had married a coal miner named Davies, who had been killed in an underground explosion two or three years later. She moved to Cardiff, where it is thought she worked as a prostitute. In 1884, she arrived in London, where she was known as 'Fair Emma' and 'Ginger'. It could have been Kelly who Walter referred to as 'a light-haired Irish bitch'.

'I never before saw an Irishwoman with that coloured hair,' he said. 'It was a peculiar, sandy red colour.'

However, Walter said the woman had just arrived from Dublin, not Cardiff. But there were other similarities. Both were attractive and had very pale skin. Mary Jane Kelly was known to be a 'quiet, pleasant girl' when sober but 'when in liquor she was very noisy' – in fact, abusive and quarrelsome, according to Mrs Elizabeth Phoenix who knew her in the East End.

When Walter had sex with his 'light-haired Irish bitch', he said: 'She burst out into such a torrent of baudy words, such obscenity, such ribald screeching, as I never heard before or since from a woman . . . "I hope I'll die a fucking." [she said] Is she mad or drunk, I thought?'

During another bout of sex, '"dams and bloodies" in end-less combinations she cried'. Then, after a brief conversation, Walter said: 'You've been drinking.' Her denial was followed by some choice blasphemy.

Walter also mentioned an 'Irish Kate'. The first time he had sex with her, she was drunk. She was very beautiful and worked out of a room lit by a single candle.

'The room was in disorder,' said Walter, 'the pot full, water in the basin, the bed unmade, the whole place the picture of disorderly, drunken, harlotry. A nightgown was lying on the floor, clean linen on a little table.'

The place was so miserable that Walter put down five shillings and made to leave.

'Come and fuck,' she said, rolling on the bed and pulling up her clothes.

She had a man, but he was neglecting her. After sex, they were disturbed by another woman who let herself in the front door. Despite her drunkenness, Irish Kate 'made a great impression on me. I was always, even quite early in life, taken with a crummy woman, quite as much as with a pretty face ... ' He sought her out again. They sat and talked on 'her little cane-bottomed chairs'. Afterwards he wanted to wash, but there was no soap. She remarked that the rent was due. He saw her for about a year, then he had to go abroad. When he returned, she had died of cholera, he said. However, the last major cholera epidemic in London was in 1866.

Mary Jane Kelly worked, at first, in a high-class brothel in the West End. According to the Press Association: 'It would appear that on her arrival in London she made the acquaintance of a Frenchwoman residing in the neighbourhood of Knightsbridge, who, she informed her friends, led her to pursue the degraded life which had now culminated in her untimely end. She made no secret of the fact that while she was with this woman she would drive about in a carriage and made several journeys to the French capital, and, in fact, led a life which is described as that "of a lady".'

Walter's French lover and procuress, Camille, went to Paris

to open a brothel, but returned to London and poverty when the enterprise failed.

In other accounts, Mary Jane Kelly went to Paris with a 'gentleman', but did not like it. On her return to London she went to stay with a Mrs Buki in St George's Street off Ratcliffe Highway, one of the roughest streets in the East End and famed for a series of vicious murders in 1811. By the time Mary moved there, the Central Vigilance Committee had been set up and would have taken an interest in Ratcliffe Highway. In April 1888, using their network of spies, they prosecuted two women – a brothel keeper and a prostitute – for procuring a girl under the age of sixteen.

From St George's Street, Mary and Mrs Buki 'went to the French lady's residence and demanded the box which contained numerous dresses of a costly description'. Walter's 'light-haired Irish bitch' also had a box, or rather two boxes. But she had left one in Birmingham when she had no money and ran away.

By 1886, Mary was living in Cooley's lodging house in Thrawl Street, where she met Joseph Barnett. They moved in together, taking lodgings in George Street, off Commercial Street. Later, they moved to Little Paternoster Row off Dorset Street, where they were evicted for not paying rent and for being drunk. Next, they moved to Brick Lane, then in the spring of 1888 to 13 Miller's Court. In August or early September, Barnett lost his job and Mary returned to the streets. She began allowing other prostitutes to stay in the room. Then, on the evening of 30 October, she and Barnett quarrelled and he moved out. However, they remained on good terms. He visited her frequently and, when he could, gave her money.

On the night she died, Barnett dropped by between 7.30 p.m. and 7.45 p.m. He said she was in the company of another woman from Miller's Court, probably Lizzie Albrook. Around 11 p.m., she was seen drinking with a young man with a dark moustache in the Britannia public house. Forty-five minutes later, Mary Ann Cox, another resident of Miller's Court, saw Mary Jane Kelly walking ahead of her down Dorset Street with another man – around thirty-five or thirty six and about five foot five inches tall. He was shabbily dressed in a long overcoat and a billycock hat. He had a blotchy face, small side whiskers, a carroty moustache and was carrying a pail of beer.

Another woman, a Mrs Kennedy, said she saw another man – respectably dressed with a dark moustache – with Mary Jane Kelly, later that night. The fact that a woman had been with other men would not have mattered to Walter. In later life, he began to relish having sex with a woman whose vagina had already been lubricated with another man's sperm. He developed a taste for 'buttered buns', he said.

'The cunts of the women when thus lubricated had seemed very delicious to me,' he said, and he would wonder 'if the enjoyment was increased by quickly entering a cunt after another man's journey there'. He began to believe that, that way, he could enjoy his forerunner's pleasure to enhance his own.

The most credible witness that night was George Hutchinson, a resident of the Victoria Working Men's Home on Commercial Street, who knew Mary Jane Kelly well. On Monday, 12 November, three days after the murder, he walked into Commercial Street police station and made a statement. He said that around 2 a.m. on the 9th, he had met Mary at the corner of Commercial Street and Flower and Dean Street.

'Can you lend me sixpence?' she asked.

'I can't,' said Hutchinson, 'I spent all my money going down to Romford.'

So she said: 'Good morning, I must go and find some money.'

Then she walked off in the direction of Thrawl Street. On the corner, she met a man Hutchinson had spotted earlier. The man put his hand on Mary's shoulder and said something that made both Mary and the man laugh. Hutchinson heard Mary say: 'All right.' And the man said: 'You will be all right for what I have told you.'

The man put his right hand around her shoulders and they began to walk towards Dorset Street. Hutchinson noticed that the man had a small parcel in his left hand with a strap around it.

Hutchinson stopped under a street light outside the Queen's Head public house in order to get a good look at the man. He told the police that the man had a pale complexion and a slight moustache turned up at the corners, although the following day he told the press that the man had a dark complexion and a heavy moustache. He wore a long dark coat trimmed in astrakhan, and a white collar with a black necktie fixed with a horseshoe pin. A large gold chain hung from his waistcoat. He was five feet six or five feet seven inches tall, about thirty-five or thirty-six years old and of Jewish or foreign appearance. However, this description must be treated with some scepticism. Hutchinson said the man kept his head down and had his hat pulled down over his eyes, and the lighting in Commercial Street was none too good. A local laundress named Sarah Lewis saw a man of similar description the previous night. At about 8 p.m., she had been on Bethnal Green Road with another woman when the gentleman concerned asked them to follow him. When they refused, he asked what they were frightened of and they ran away. She said he was about forty.

The relative youthfulness of Ripper suspects seen with their victims was discounted by Inspector Abberline.

'People who alleged that they saw Jack the Ripper at one time or another, state that he was a man about thirty-five or forty years of age,' he said. 'They, however, state that they only saw his back, and it is easy to misjudge age from a back view.'

In *My Secret Life*, Walter boasted about his youthful looks. On one occasion, when he was trying to have his way with a young hairdresser, she asked him his age.

'I told her one younger than I was,' he said, 'but she thought me ten years younger than that.'

Nor was he too old to be the Ripper. Police arrested Francis Tumblety for the killings aged 58. In 1889, a sixty-five-year-old man named John Rowley was convicted for stabbing a woman he had approached for sex in Whitechapel.

Hutchinson claimed in his statement he could identify the man if he saw him again.

'I could swear to the man anywhere,' he told the press.

However, he then said he thought he had seen him again that Sunday morning in Petticoat Lane, although he could not be certain.

After passing Hutchinson, Mary Jane Kelly and her companion turned down Dorset Street. Hutchinson followed them. They stopped outside Miller's Court and talked for about three minutes. Hutchinson heard Mary saying: 'All right, my dear. Come along. You will be comfortable.' The man put his arm around Mary who gave him a kiss. She said she had lost her handkerchief. He pulled one from his pocket and gave it to her. The couple then went into Miller's Court. Hutchinson followed them into the court. He waited for about three-quarters of an hour. They did not reappear. As the clock struck three, Hutchinson left.

Around 4 a.m., two neighbours in Miller's Court heard a woman scream: 'Murder!' But the cry of 'murder' in the Whitechapel area was not unusual and they ignored it. Mary Ann Cox, who lived at 5 Miller's Court, said she heard a door close at around 5.45 a.m. Then the situation becomes confused. Mrs Cox claimed to have seen Mary Jane Kelly – and even talked to her – at 8.30 a.m., and had seen her again half an hour later talking to a man outside the Britannia. Maurice Lewis, a tailor living in Dorset Street, told the newspapers that he had seen Mary in the Britannia at 10 a.m. However, when Dr Thomas Bond, police surgeon to A Division, examined the body around 2 p.m. on 9 November, it was cold and rigor mortis had already set in. He put the time of death at between 1 and 2 a.m., although Dr Phillips of H Division thought the body may have cooled more quickly because of the broken window pane, and said she had died between 5 and 6 a.m. But this may have put the time of death too late because of the blazing fire in the room. Whatever, she must have been long dead by the time Mrs Cox and Mr Lewis said they saw her and their evidence was discounted. But the evidence given by Hutchinson was not.

'I have interrogated him this evening,' Inspector Abberline wrote on 12 November, 'and I am of the opinion that his statement is true.'

So, in the early morning of 9 November, Hutchinson may well have caught a glimpse of the elusive Ripper and, perhaps, the elusive Walter.

On 19 November, Mary Jane Kelly was buried in a public grave at St Patrick's Roman Catholic Cemetery in Leytonstone under the name Marie Jeanette Kelly, the last memento of her trip to France. On her death certificate, though, her name is given as 'Marie Jeanette KELLY otherwise DAVIES'. Her boyfriend, Joseph Barnett, told the inquest that her husband's name was 'Davis or Davies'. We have seen a Mary Davis before. She was the girl Walter met after thinking of throwing himself in the canal. After having sex with her, he related in *My Secret Life* how he broke down.

> *The pleasure I had just had, the entrancement of the carnal pleasure contrasted so strongly with my misery at home, that I burst into tears and sobbed like a child. She rubbed her quim dry, then silently came up to me, put her hand on my shoulder and stood without uttering a word till my passion was over. 'Are you unhappy?' said she in a gentle tone. Yes I was. 'Never mind, I dare say it will be over some day – we have all got unhappiness.'*
>
> *Her kind voice and manner – she a gay woman who owed me no kindness – so contrasted with the coldness elsewhere, that it made me worse and again I sat sobbing and taking no notice of her; she still standing with her hand on my shoulder.*

Mary Jane Kelly lived in a single room. According to press reports, 'the only furniture was an oil stove, two rickety chairs and a tumble down. At the head of this bedstead was a piece of looking glass such as one buys in Petticoat Lane for a half penny.' This is how Walter described Mary Davis' room:

> *Her room was about twelve feet square. A large bed took up one-third of it, a table next the only window, two chairs (one easy), little cupboards in the recesses by*

the fireplace, on which stood china and glasses, a small
wash-hand stand, a chest of drawers, with slop-pail,
coal-scuttle, and looking-glass completed the furniture.

In both cases, their rooms were in buildings at the end of a
passage. The missing key to Mary Jane Kelly's room was,
perhaps, another clue. Several times, Walter took keys so that
women could not lock him out, or in.

Walter said that Mary Davis was twenty-five shillings
behind in the rent. Mary Jane Kelly was twenty-nine shillings
in arrears. Walter thought that he was to blame. He used her
exclusively for a week, during which time she could not see
her regular clients, who paid her rent. Barnett had been out
of her life – or at least her room – for over a month. Similarly,
Walter's description of Mary Davis as a good-looking woman
who could have made a lot more money working in the West
End matches that of Mary Ann Kelly.

Mary Davis' room was in a house kept by an old man and
woman. 'He used to fetch gin and beer for us,' Walter said.
Mary Jane Kelly's landlord, John McCarthy, and his wife lived
in rooms adjoining her apartment and had rooms upstairs.
They also ran a shop.

Walter said that Mary Davis' landlady procured a fourteen-
year-old girl for him, but Mary would have nothing to do with
it and prevented him going on with the 'seduction'. Even so,
after the passing of the Criminal Amendment Act, Mary would
have been a danger to him. She knew of his criminal interest
in young women and disapproved of it, having perhaps been
forced into prostitution that way herself. She could, of course,
be out to blackmail him. That is what W.T. Stead wanted her to
do. Press reports said that Whitechapel was 'overrun with spies'.
Inspector Moore said that there were 'half a hundred and at
times 200 unattached detectives, who pursue their respectable
or otherwise callings while they keep an alert eye and ear for
the faintest clue that may lead to the discovery of the invisible
murderer'. They were from the Vigilance Committee, and were
as eager to catch a man seeking a virgin as nab Jack the Ripper.

14

MORE MURDERS

The man charged with catching the Ripper, Metropolitan Police Commissioner Sir Charles Warren, was not a policeman. He was a soldier, imperialist, archaeologist and scholar. After serving in Palestine, he wrote three books about ancient Jerusalem. Wounded while commanding the Diamond Fields Horse in South Africa during the Kaffir War of 1877–8, he led the search for the missing expedition of Professor Edward Palmer in Egypt in 1882. He joined the expedition to relieve his close friend General Gordon at Khartoum in 1885. Then he was sent to Bechuanaland to restore order there.

In 1886, a demonstration against unemployment had turned into a riot with a mob smashing the windows of shops and clubs in Pall Mall, St James's and Oxford Street. Sir Edmund Henderson was Commissioner of the Metropolitan Police and Warren succeeded him. He did little better. The riots continued and Warren was derided by the press for his over-reaction to a rabies outbreak, when he ordered dogs muzzled and strays put down.

Warren also found himself pressured by the National Vigilance Association to crack down on prostitutes. On 28 June 1887, Elizabeth Cass, a respectable twenty-three-year-old milliner newly arrived from the north of England, was out shopping in Regent Street when she was arrested for soliciting. Although the case against her was dismissed, the magistrate insisted that she was a prostitute and cautioned her about her future conduct, observing that no respectable woman should be walking alone on Regent Street at 9 p.m. in the evening. Supported by her employer, Miss Cass protested her innocence and insisted she was merely on her way to purchase a pair of gloves. Stead took up the case in the pages of the *Pall Mall Gazette* and Warren had to issue an order prohibiting his officers from arresting streetwalkers unless a direct complaint had been made by a member of the public or there was corroborating evidence. The brothels were closed, but prostitutes were now free to roam the streets – easy targets when Jack the Ripper struck.

Following Bloody Sunday on 13 November 1887, Warren was, once more, in disfavour with Stead and the *Pall Mall Gazette*. By the following autumn – the Autumn of Terror – he was seen to be far more interested in catching Fenians than Jack the Ripper and, on 9 November 1888, the day Mary Jane Kelly's body was found, Warren resigned.

He was replaced by James Monro. In 1857, Monro joined the Indian Civil Service, rising to become Inspector-General of Police in Bengal. In 1884, he returned to England to become head of Scotland Yard's Criminal Investigation Department and, after a Fenian bombing campaign, head of Special Branch. There were even suggestions that the Ripper was a Fenian instigating a new terror campaign. When Monro took over, Scotland Yard was in disarray. Five horrific murders had taken place and the police were no nearer catching the killer. According to Detective Walter Dew: 'There were definite signs of panic among the populace.'

Children were afraid to go to school; women were petrified. The terror had set in long before the gruesome murder of Mary Jane Kelly.

'As soon as darkness set in on the night following Mary Ann Nichols' murder,' Dew said, 'hundreds of women locked themselves in their homes. Tradesmen made a rich harvest in making homes secure. Courts, which had hitherto remained in sinister darkness, were now illuminated by feeble lanterns.'

Vigilance committees were patrolling the streets. Hundreds of policemen of all ranks drafted into the area, searching for what Dew concluded was a 'sexual maniac'. Dr Barnardo was shipping vulnerable girls out to Canada; and the killer even seen taunting the police. On 2 October, construction workers building the Metropolitan Police's new headquarters, New Scotland Yard, on the Victoria Embankment found the torso of a woman in an unlocked vault. Her arms were later found dumped separately by the Thames. Dr Bond told the inquest that her uterus was also missing and his assistant, who examined the right arm, said it had been removed 'not by an anatomist, but by a person who knew the joints'. A piece of paper found near the remains was 'stained with the blood of an animal'. Bond also said that her hands were long and well-shaped – 'the hand of a person not used to manual labour'.

The press quickly attributed the killing to Jack the Ripper, although the police equally quickly dismissed it. No one wanted any more Ripper murders, least of all Queen Victoria, who seems to have been following the killings from the beginning. The day after the murder of Mary Jane Kelly in Miller's Court, she wrote to the Home Secretary saying: 'This new most ghastly murder shows the absolute necessity for some very decided action. All these courts must be lit, and our detectives improved. They are not what they should be.'

The man Monro called in to deal with the situation was Sir Melville Leslie Macnaghten, whom he had known out in India. Again, Macnaghten was no detective. The son of the last chairman of the East India Company, he had been the overseer of the family tea plantations. In 1881, he was attacked by Indian land rioters who, he said, 'assaulted me so badly that I was left senseless on the plain'. It was then that he met Monro. Macnaghten returned to England in 1887. Monro, by then Assistant Commissioner, wanted to take him on as Assistant Chief Constable, despite his lack of experience, but Warren blackballed him, saying Macnaghten was 'the only man in India who has been beaten by the Hindoos'. Nevertheless, Macnaghten took up the post under Monro in June 1889.

Macnaghten was the man who wrote the famous Macnaghten Memorandum. This ascribed to Jack the Ripper only five murders – those of Mary Ann Nichols, Annie Chapman, Elizabeth Stride, Catherine Eddowes and Mary Jane Kelly. Officially this was the complete list, even though, in an interview in the *Pall Mall Gazette* in November 1889, the man actually in charge of the investigation, Inspector Henry Moore, said that there were another five Ripper murders after the death of Mary Jane Kelly. The victims mentioned in Macnaghten's memorandum are now known as the canonical five.

In the memorandum, Macnaghten named just three suspects – Montague Druitt, a failed lawyer whose body was fished out of the Thames on 31 December 1888; Aaron Kosminski, a Jewish hairdresser who was confined to a mental asylum in March 1889; Michael Ostrog, a Russian conman and thief who, it seems, was jailed for theft in Paris on 18 November 1888. Macnaghten is thought to have favoured Druitt, who was last seen alive on 3 December 1888. Macnaghten had closed the case. He had drawn a line under the Jack the Ripper murders. According to the memorandum, there can have been no more victims after March 1889 at the latest – and after December 1888 in Macnaghten's estimation.

But the attacks continued. On the morning of 21 November, forty-one-year-old Annie Farmer picked up a 'shabby genteel' man in a suit at 7.30 a.m. and returned with him to Satchell's Lodging House, 19 George Street, Spitalfields. He paid for a bed for both of them. Two hours later, Annie screamed loudly. The man fled from the dosshouse, down George Street and into Thrawl Street. Passing two cokemen on the way, he cried 'What a ---- cow' and disappeared.

Annie's throat was cut and bleeding and she appeared distraught. She claimed that she had been attacked by Jack the Ripper. As Mary Jane Kelly had been buried only the day before, a crowd formed. It soon transpired that Annie had been trying to rob her client and, when she cried 'Murder!', given the fevered atmosphere at the time, he sensibly fled to escape being lynched.

At 4.30 p.m. on 20 December 1888, Police Sergeant Robert Golding found the body of Rose Mylett, a.k.a. 'Drunken Lizzie' Davis and 'Fair Alice' Downey, in Clarke's Yard between 184 and 186 Poplar High Street, less than two miles from the centre of the Ripper murders. She had been seen nearby with two sailors at 7.55 p.m. the previous evening and was heard to say 'no, no, no' to one of them. At 2.30 a.m., she had been seen outside the George public house on Commercial Road with two men, apparently drunk. But there was no mutilation and no obvious signs of injury. During the post-mortem, marks were noticed on her neck. Dr Phillips had noticed that there were signs of strangulation on Annie Chapman's neck and there was a theory that the other Ripper victims had been strangled to silence them before their throats were cut. However, Dr Bond could find no secondary signs of strangulation, such as a protruding tongue or clenched fists. He believed that Rose Mylett had fallen down drunk and been choked to death by her stiff velvet collar. But in the autumn of 1888, this was given no credence. The inquest jury found that she had been 'murdered by person or persons unknown'. However, Assistant Commissioner Robert Anderson refused to waste police time on the case. He later wrote in his memoirs that Rose Mylett's death was 'from natural causes, and but for the "Jack the Ripper" scare, no one would have thought of suggesting that it was a homicide'.

At 12.50 a.m. on 17 July 1889, the body of forty-year-old Alice McKenzie was found in Castle Alley off Whitechapel High Street. Earlier in the day, her boyfriend John McCormack had given her the rent money for their lodgings at Mr Tenpenny's lodging house at 54 Gun Street, Spitalfields, but she spent it on drink. They later had a row about it. Between 11.30 p.m. and midnight, she was seen rushing down Flower and Dean Street towards Brick Lane. She was not wearing a bonnet. There were regular patrols down the alley. PC Joseph Allen stopped there for a bite to eat at 12.15 a.m. and PC Walter Andrews walked through the alley at 12.20 a.m. He returned at 12.50 a.m. and found Alice's body. Blood was still flowing from the wounds on her throat. The pavement under the body was still dry, so she must have been killed before 12.45 a.m. when it began to rain in Whitechapel. Her skirt was pulled up, showing blood on her thighs and abdomen. There was a cut from her left breast to her navel. Seven or eight superficial cuts pointed from her navel down to the genitals and there was a small cut across her mons veneris. She was wearing odd stockings. Among her possessions were two clay pipes and a brass farthing, inviting comparison to the murder of Annie Chapman.

Dr Phillips said that the mutilations exhibited a degree of anatomical knowledge, but did not believe that they were the work of Jack the Ripper. Dr Bond disagreed. He believed that Alice McKenzie was another Ripper victim. So did Police Commissioner Monro. Macnaghten dismissed the case as Alice had been stabbed in the throat, rather than having her throat cut laterally, although the cause of death was the severance of the carotid artery, as in the other Ripper cases. A thief named William Wallace Brodie confessed to killing Alice McKenzie. In fact, he confessed to all the Whitechapel killings. However, he had been in South Africa from 6 September – two days before the murder of Annie Chapman – until 15 July 1889, two days before Alice McKenzie's body was found. He was dismissed as a lunatic and released, though immediately rearrested for fraud.

Then, at 5.15 a.m. on 10 September 1889, a woman's torso was found under some sacking in a railway arch in Pinchin Street, near the end of Berner Street where Liz Stride had been killed. It was covered by a chemise, and was already beginning to decompose. PC William Pennett, who discovered the body, was alerted by the smell. There was a paint works in Pinchin Street. Otherwise it was uninhabited. Later, some bloodstained clothing was found in Batty Street off Commercial Road, but nothing was made of it.

Walter, of course, had experience of railway arches. Prostitutes used to work out of the viaducts of the new railways that were springing up around London. Walter recorded often having 'letches' on the trains. In later life, he met two prostitutes at a station after visiting a relative.

> *After a time chatting, I gave the women a shilling apiece to feel their cunts, tho this was in the main road. Then said one, 'Why don't you have me? Let's go on the other side of the viaduct and nobody will see us, we are very often done there.' There I went with one, promising another shilling for an uninterrupted grope; it seemed a pleasant way of passing the time.*

Walter then offered to pay five shillings to watch a porter to fuck her. 'But I'll feel him first,' he said. After the next train had gone, she got a porter. Walter hid his face and the porter pulled his cap down over his face, too, while Walter felt his erect penis. 'My own prick then stiffened, throbbed sensuously, I longed to fuck her myself, and next to see him do it. The old letch for a lubricated cunt came – thrilling.'

He held the porter's testicles as he had sex with the woman in the railway arch. When the porter left, Walter gave her the five shillings and groped her again.

> *I now was trembling with lust. 'Oh I'd like to fuck you.' 'All right, put it in.' 'I'm frightened.' 'You need not be. I'm a married man.' 'So is he.' I wonder I restrained myself for my prick was throbbing with lust, but groping the lubricious receptacle, thinking of the solid prick which had spent in it, and God knows what other voluptuous reminiscences, I let her frig me, spent on the ground, and then pissed over my fingers to purify them.*

All his old perversions were in play. There was a house nearby where she sometimes took men if they were not in a hurry. Walter was interested and paid her another half a crown for a chat.

The abdominal region of the torso found in Pinchin Street was heavily mutilated, and it was reported that the handiwork was eerily reminiscent of the Ripper's work, although it was clear that she had not been murdered there. The slaying and dissection had been done somewhere more private. At least one account said that the womb was missing. Once she had been dissected, her torso had been brought there. There was no blood at the scene, except on the body itself. One cannot imagine that it would have been easy to carry a torso very far through the streets of Victorian London without being spotted. However, it would have been a relatively simple matter for Walter who had a lair just 400 yards away.

The chairman of the Whitechapel Vigilance Committee, Mr Albert Backert, said: 'From inquiries, I am confident that the murderer is a Whitechapel person, or at any point he is well acquainted with the back streets.' Walter certainly was, by his own account.

Walter recorded how he became obsessed with a part-time prostitute named Phoebe because of her hazel eyes. Phoebe taunted Walter, saying that he was not man enough to have her. So Walter took her to a hotel and paid for hot water to wash her. During their three-day stay in the hotel, Phoebe learned Walter's real name and address, information he usually guarded assiduously. She was 'not altogether a pleasant girl' and hinted she wanted regular money from him. Walter 'took her off at the railway terminus – and never heard or saw her since'. The woman taken to the railway arch had had her head cut off, like that of a trophy deer. Walter ended his description of Phoebe: 'Her face was lovely.' The head of the corpse in Pinchin Street was never found.

One newspaper named the victim as Lydia Hart, a prostitute who had been missing for some days. However, the identity of the corpse was never confirmed. The only clue was that her arms and hands were 'well formed and showed no signs of manual labour'. Nevertheless, the police came to the conclusion that the victim was a factory worker. Macnaghten's dismissal of the Pinchin Street murder was terse:

On 10 September 1889 the naked body, with arms, of a woman was found wrapped in some sacking under a railway arch in Pinchin St: the head & legs were never found nor was the woman ever identified. She had been killed at least twenty-four hours before the remains, (which had seemingly been brought from a distance) were discovered. The stomach was split up by a cut, and the head and legs had been severed in a manner identical with that of the woman whose remains were discovered in the Thames, in Battersea Park, & on the Chelsea Embankment on 4 June of the same year; and these murders had no connection whatever with the Whitechapel horrors. The Rainham mystery in 1887, & the Whitehall mystery (when portions of a woman's body were found under what is now New Scotland Yard) in 1888 were of a similar type to the Thames & Pinchin St crimes.

Inspector Henry Moore thought that the body in Pinchin Street was a Ripper victim. In November 1889, he told the *Pall Mall Gazette*, 'Once I had occasion to stand near the arch of Pinchin Street, Whitechapel, and I remarked to another officer, "This is just the place for Jack the Ripper" and sure enough, some few months later a "Ripper" body was found there in a sack.'

The other murders Macnaghten refers to were the so-called Thames Torso murders that were going on at the same time as the Ripper killings. Again, women were being murdered and the bodies mutilated, but the other murders did not take place in Whitechapel and, by and large, the victims were not identified.

On the morning of 11 May 1887, part of a woman's torso wrapped in sacking was pulled from the Thames at Rainham in Essex, downriver from London, by a lighterman. The arms, legs, head and chest were missing. The thighs had been pulled from their socket and the trunk had been sawn in two. The surrounding flesh had been cut with a sharp instrument.

'There was no jaggedness about any of the incisions,' said Dr Galloway, who had examined the corpse, 'showing that they had been done by an expert.'

He concluded that the victim had been dead for about two weeks.

'I am certain that whoever cut up this body had a thorough knowledge of surgery, for not only had the cutting-up been carried out in an exceedingly skilful manner, but the operation had been carried out on that part of the spine offering least resistance to separating, and that would only be done by a person having a very intimate knowledge of anatomy,' said Dr Galloway.

On 5 June, a second bundle containing a piece of thigh was found floating in the river at Temple Stairs, upriver beyond Whitechapel. It had not been in the water for very long. That same day, the upper parts of the body were found on the foreshore near Battersea Park piers. The condition of the body parts suggested the killer knew how to preserve them so that they would not decay. He did not mind running the risk of carrying them around, nor was he a poor man as he could afford some sort of transportation.

More remains were found in the Thames on 23 June and, on 30 June, the legs were found in Regent's Canal near St Pancras Lock at Chalk Farm. Walter often inhabited the canal system, particularly the Regent's Canal, and Chalk Farm was a hotspot for prostitutes after 1860. The victim was in her twenties or early thirties, but could not be identified. Her head was never discovered and it was thought that the weight of the skull would have prevented it floating. It was also impossible to determine the cause of death.

On 4 June 1889, two boys found a package in the water at St George's Stairs, Horselydown, Southwark. It contained body parts. Later, a thigh was found on the foreshore near Albert Bridge. It was wrapped in part of a coat. With it were part of a pair of drawers with the name L.E. Fisher written in black ink on a tape sewn into the band. The body parts had been in the river for less than forty-eight hours and,

The Times reported, 'the body had been dissected somewhat roughly by a person who must have had some knowledge of the joints of the human body'. Bruises seemingly from fingers on her thigh indicated that she had fought back against her attacker. There was also a small roll of linen inserted in the anus.

Two days later, the upper part of the trunk were found in Battersea Park, not far from where the thigh had been found. Some way from the river bank, it could not have floated there. It would have had to have been placed there in daylight as the park was locked at night, and it could not have been flung over the fence as it was 200 yards from the nearest entrance. After examining the torso, the police surgeon reported: 'The chest cavity was empty, but many internal organs, including the spleen, both kidneys and a portion of stomach intestines, were present. The lower six dorsal vertebra were in their place, but the five lower ribs are missing.'

Soon after, the neck, shoulder, liver and the first and second ribs were found off Copington's Wharf, Battersea. Over the next week, other parts of the same body were found down the river. One bundle was found in a waterside garden on the private estate of Sir Percy Shelley on Chelsea Embankment. It had either been thrown over the fence, or placed there by someone who had access to the garden. However, the head, neck and stomach were not found, and it was not possible to determine how she had died. It was possible that she had been killed in a botched abortion; the victim had been pregnant when she died. A foetus was found in a jar floating in the river, but the medical examiner did not think that it belonged to the dead woman. However, he did determine that the body had been cut up soon after death and there was a mark of a ring on her finger, which had been removed immediately before or shortly after death. In this case, though, details of parts of a coat and drawers found with the victim led to her identification. Her name was Elizabeth Jackson who, like several of Walter's victims, had been in domestic service before she turned to prostitution.

Curiously, Walter makes reference to this murder, although in *My Secret Life* there is never any mention of the Ripper or other Thames Torso murders. He said: 'The trunk of a young woman was found floating in the Thames, there was a peculiar scar below the bosom. I have often wondered if that was the end of Sarah.' He had seen Sarah again after she had gone to Paris with the *poses plastiques*. The business had not gone well. She had split up with her man, who had hit her and taken her children. When she threatened to go to a magistrate, he said that he would tell the court that he had kept the children because she was a whore and a drunkard. Walter says that years later he saw Sarah Mavis several times in the Euston Road and gave her money, but would not go with her.

There is a strange mismatch in Walter's recollection, though. The trunk was found in the park – it was the buttock and thighs that were found floating in the river. There is no mention of a scar on the torso in the newspaper reports – Walter was an avid reader of the newspapers – although Elizabeth Jackson had been identified by a scar on her wrist sustained in a childhood accident. What's more, three ribs had been removed at the very point where Walter said Sarah had the scar. That part of her body was never found.

There may also be something significant about the linen roll found up Elizabeth Jackson's anus. Walter tied a strip of linen torn from a handkerchief around his penis to stop it going too far into a tight orifice. He called this his 'linen stopper'. He wrote of 'plugging bumholes' and stuffing objects, such as a candle, into women.

The police made the connection between this murder and those at Rainham and Whitehall. Dr Bond told the inquest: 'The division of the parts showed skill and design; not, however, the anatomical skill of a surgeon, but the practical knowledge of the butcher or a knocker. There was a great similarity between the condition, as regarded cutting up of the remains and that of those found at Rainham, and at the new police building on the Thames Embankment.'

Elizabeth Jackson had been seen walking the streets in

Turk's Row, Chelsea, by her sister Annie. A former Grenadier Guard named John Faircloth took her to Colchester to look for work. Finding none, they returned to London, staying in a lodging house in Whitechapel. On 18 April 1889, they moved to Mrs Paine's Rooming House on Manila Road, Millwall. But Faircloth was violent and the couple split up. Elizabeth left Mrs Paine's owing a week's rent. She was seen walking the streets of Chelsea by a family friend who gave her thruppence to get something to eat and a coat, as Elizabeth said she was sleeping rough down by the river. At some point, she had bought some second-hand clothes with the name L.E. Fisher in them. The last time Annie saw her younger sister, Elizabeth was talking to a man who looked like a sailor.

Again, Walter had thoughts concerning death, perhaps even murder, near water. Once, in Switzerland, he went off with a young French-speaking woman.

> *She had told me where her lodging was and I agreed to follow her. She went away by a path I'd not traversed, crossed a wooden trembling bridge over the roaring rushing river, and was soon away from all street lights and human habitation as far as I could see. The road lay alongside the river, it was pitch dark, and at first I kept her just in sight, but as it was much further than I'd expected I got uncomfortable, as it was a spot where a knock on the head could very easily be given, and a body pitched into the river within a few yards of our path would have been thirty miles off before next morning, and had I screamed, the roar of the torrent would have drowned my voice, so I went up to her and said I could go no further. She said we were close by her dwelling and again we walked on.*

When the body was found in Pinchin Street on 10 September 1889, no one – least of all the police – wanted another Ripper murder, so the crime was ascribed to the Thames Torso killer, even though the body was more than 870 yards from the river.

The following day, Commissioner Monro dismissed any connection to the Ripper murders and wrote: 'I am inclined to the belief that, taking one thing with another, this is not the work of the Whitechapel murderer but of the hand which was concerned with murders which are known as the Rainham mystery – the new police buildings case – and the recent case in which portions of a female body (afterwards identified) were found in the Thames.'

The newspapers carried the headline that murder had returned to Whitechapel, though suggested that the Pinchin Street murder might be the work of the 'Chelsea Dissector'.

Dr Phillips believed that the victim had been killed by having her throat cut, but that could not be confirmed without the head and neck. He also said: 'I have no reason for thinking that the person who cut up the body had any human anatomical knowledge.' However, it was generally conceded that the killer had removed the head in a 'very skilled manner'.

The killings continued. At 2.20 a.m. on 13 February 1891, rookie Police Constable Ernest Thompson was out on his first beat alone when he heard the sound of footsteps retreating down Chamber Street, towards Mansell Street. Seconds later, he found a woman on the ground at the corner of Swallow Gardens. Blood was flowing profusely from a gash on her throat. Thompson saw her open and shut one eye. She was still alive, and police procedure dictated that he remain with her rather than chase the man he had heard leaving. She died before she reached hospital.

The victim was identified as Frances Coles, a.k.a. 'Carrotty Nell'. The daughter of a respectable family, she had worked as a packer for a wholesale chemist until she was eighteen, then she got a taste for drink and took to the streets. For eight years, she had managed to conceal this fact from her family, although her sister suspected. On 11 February, she met up with Thomas Sadler, a ship's fire stoker, who had just been discharged from the SS *Fez*. They spent the night together in Spitalfields Chambers, a common lodging house at 8 White's Row.

They spent the next day crawling the pubs in the area. Sadler had given her half a crown, which she spent on a new bonnet at a millinery shop in Bethnal Green. That evening, the couple had a row and split up. Frances went back to Spitalfields Chambers. Sadler was beaten up and robbed. He returned bleeding to the lodging house, but could not stay as he did not have his doss. Frances was so drunk she fell asleep on a bench. At around 1.30 a.m. she went to have three ha'pence-worth of mutton and bread to eat. Fifteen minutes later, she was ejected from the eating house. She then bumped into a fellow prostitute, who warned her against a violent former client who had given her a black eye. Frances solicited him anyway and they went off together towards the Minories and her death. The new bonnet was found beside her. Her old one was pinned under the dress.

The police quickly picked up Tom Sadler, who had returned to Spitalfields Chambers having once again been robbed on Ratcliffe Highway. That morning, he had sold a knife to a man for a shilling and a piece of tobacco. On 16 February, Sadler was charged with the murder of Frances Coles. However, witnesses said that between 1.15 and 1.50 a.m., he had got involved in a fight with dockworkers at the gates while he was trying to return to the SS *Fez* in St Katharine Dock. Sarah Fleming, the deputy at Spitalfields Chambers, said he was so drunk he could hardly speak coherently or stand up. The knife he sold was blunt and Dr Oxley, the first medical man on the scene of the crime, said that a man so drunk could hardly have caused the wounds he had seen with a blunt knife. Released, Sadler was cheered by a crowd as he left the court. However, Macnaghten continued to believe that he was guilty. In his memorandum he wrote: 'Frances Coles in Swallow Gardens, on 13 February 1891 – for which Thomas Sadler, a fireman, was arrested, and, after several remands, discharged. It was ascertained at the time that Sadler had sailed for the Baltic on 19 July 1889 and was in Whitechapel on the nights of 17 idem. He was a man of ungovernable temper and entirely addicted to drink, and the company of the lowest prostitutes.'

There were no further Ripper murders in London. However, the New York Police Department received a letter 'From Hell', signed by the Ripper and sent from London. Then, on the morning of 24 April 1891, the body of American prostitute Carrie Brown was found in a room in the East River Hotel on the waterfront of Manhattan. According to the night clerk who found her, her body was naked from the armpits down and had been mutilated. She had been strangled, but details of her injuries were played down although the press said that there were 'cuts and stab wounds all over her body'. Previously, the New York Police Department had boasted that Jack the Ripper would have been caught if he had committed his crimes in the US. However, Dr Jenkins, who had performed the autopsy, was said to have thought that the killer had attempted to completely gut his victim – like the Ripper. Walter recorded making a long sea voyage, probably to America.

An Algerian named Ameer Ben Ali was convicted of the crime and sentenced to life imprisonment. However, he was released eleven years later when it was shown that the blood-stains found in Ali's room – key evidence in the trial – had been carried there by the investigators.

There was one more killing that may have been linked. At 4 a.m. on the morning of 8 June 1902, the dismembered body of a young woman was found in Salamanca Alley in Lambeth, not far from the Albert Embankment. The body had been cut to pieces – even the torso had been cut in three. The parts had been arranged in a neat pile with the head on top. Some pieces seemed to be cooked, some charred. There was not a stitch of clothing with the pile and the face had been disfigured to render it unrecognizable. The teeth were in good condition and regular, although some were missing.

The corpse was never identified and the bizarre method of disposal remained a puzzle. Had the killer intended to throw the pieces in the river, but been prevented from doing so? However, the connection to the Thames Torso murders was made. The coroner, Dr Michael Taylor, said that the 'latest torso murder was on all fours [the same kind of murder in design and execution] as the murder of Elizabeth Jackson back in 1889'.

15

MY SECRET LIFE

Walter was a gambler. He played the stock market. In company, he would demand that ladies wager on the size of his prick.

'I'll bet,' said I, 'that if the ladies were to feel our pricks in the dark, they would not tell whose they each had hold of.' Roars of laughter followed.

He gambled on sex. He once lost badly when he bet a prostitute how many coins she could carry in her vagina.

Walter also believed in luck.

'I've always found three sovereigns a lucky number', he said. Three gold coins would invariably buy him sex if all else failed.

And he had faith in charm.

'The charm of talking baudily to a woman for the first time, is such that hours fly away just like minutes,' he would say. For Walter, time spent with a prostitute was 'the greatest charm of life'.

Walter clung to luck and charms because he had been tossed by fate from the day he was born. Although outwardly a wealthy man, Walter sailed troughs of poverty after maturing in the shadow of riches denied to him.

He came from a wealthy provincial family but his father lost most of his money and died when Walter was a lad. For much of his life, women would rule Walter by controlling his money. When he was a schoolboy, his religious-minded mother would give him next to nothing. He would make the hour's walk to the house of his rich aunt to beg for funds. His main male influence was a stern godfather, a retired army surgeon-major. Although his mother thought Walter was a quiet and well-behaved boy, she warned him not to offend the doctor. His death would bring Walter an inheritance. Alive, the doctor made Walter fear masturbation. There would be dire consequences if he was caught at it.

> *'No denial, sir, no lies, you have, sir,' he said, 'don't add lying to your bestiality, you've been at that filthy trick, I can see it in your face, you'll die in a mad-house, or of consumption, you shall never have a farthing more pocket-money from me, and I won't buy your commission, nor leave you any money at my death.'*

But Walter could not help himself. He had taken to masturbating over passages in the bible. When he moved from the Old Testament to the real thing, Walter had to borrow money from his aunt to get the farm girl Martha an abortion, and to have more sex. Then he got a job at the 'W. Office' and one of his uncles suggested to his mother that she give him a monthly allowance. He spent it on women.

> *I now found out that women of a superior class were to be had much cheaper than my great friends used to talk of; but at the time I write of, a sovereign would get any woman, and ten shillings as nice a one as you needed. Two good furnished rooms near the Clubs could be had by women for from fifteen to twenty shillings per week, a handsome silk dress for five or ten pounds, and other things in proportion.*

At twenty, Walter had to borrow money for the first time – from 'a Jew' – for an abortion.

At twenty-one, Walter came into his property. To the horror of his mother and family, he gave up his intended career as an officer, and resigned his commission although he had not yet been posted to a regiment. This cost him a lot of money. Walter was working, but still living with his mother, when he met Camille. The French prostitute made it her business to part Walter from his funds by expanding his sexual appetite. He had sixty or seventy of Camille's prostitutes before he was sated. 'Nearly a year ran away, and four thousand pounds, leaving me with infinite knowledge and a frame pretty well worn.'

His guardian remonstrated him for the rate at which he was spending. Walter 'left Camille and her bevy of women', and went to the seaside. When he came back to London, Camille had a new attraction. She asked Walter if he had ever had a virgin. Louise was produced, who, as already mentioned, cost him nearly £200.

'I am astonished now, that I was wheedled out of so much money for a French virgin,' wrote Walter. He was twenty-three.

Seducing Mrs Pender risked another £500. After spending £3 on a ten-year-old he met at Vauxhall Gardens, Walter went to Paris with his cousin Fred.

'Though short of money now, Fred and I at Paris took no heed, but rattled away as if our purses were inexhaustible.'

Fred told Walter not to worry because one of their relatives, who was childless, was going to leave Walter all his money. He had no one else to leave it to, even though he disapproved of Walter's behaviour. Again, with imminent death his saviour, Walter felt safe to party. But crisis awaited him across the Channel.

'Heaps of bills met me on my return. The thought of becoming bankrupt horrified me. I disposed of my remaining property, paid all, and was left with a few hundred pounds.'

Walter's economy drive exposed a strange compulsion – the less money he spent, the more his urge for sex.

I tried to retrench, but found it all but impossible. I spent five shillings for my dinner, where I used to spend twenty, went to live with my mother, put down my horses and carriage, and discharged my man and grooms. But as I diminished my amusements and extravagances generally, so I seemed more and more to need women. My cock stood all day, and half the night. Women I had by dozens. I tried to reduce their fees, and did to a little extent, but for some years I had been accustomed to a liberal expenditure in that article and though to a country girl I could give five shillings, to a Londoner I could only give gold, and never refused more if they pleased me, and were not satisfied . . .

Nevertheless, he went back to Paris for the 'theatres, excursions, high-feasting and unlimited whoring', making his 'acquaintance with six or eight of the best baudy houses'.

My remaining guardian and my mother had been always at me with advice, which I entirely disregarded, and flung away money in all directions. Had I only spent it on women it would have lasted years longer. That which women had I do not regret, they have been the greatest joy of my life, and are so to every true man, from infancy to old age. Copulation is the highest pleasure, both to the body and mind, and is worth all other human pleasures put together. A woman sleeping or waking is a paradise to a man, if he be happy with her, and he cannot spend his money on anything better, or so good.

All his inheritance had gone on his greatest pleasure. Once more, Walter found himself dependant on his mother. She upbraided him constantly. Then the relative he was counting on for his next legacy died leaving him nothing. He again went looking for the cheapest possible prostitutes.

'When I spent my first fortune, I took after longish continence, to visiting harlots who let me have them for five shillings, and would let a man do almost any thing.'

But then he began shelling out for sex with young girls, even a prostitute who kept a fourteen-year-old to service her.

By the time Walter was twenty-six, he was broke and living back with his nagging mother. The solution was a wealthy bride, but rather than ease his situation it gave him more problems.

> *My life was now utterly changed; married. I was quite*
> *needy, with a yearly income (and that not my own) not*
> *more than I used to spend in a month, sometimes in a*
> *fortnight. Every shilling I had to look at, walked miles*
> *where I used to ride, and to save a six pence, amuse-*
> *ments were beyond me, my food was the simplest, wine*
> *I scarcely tasted, all habits of luxury were gone, but*
> *worse than all I was utterly wretched.*

Walter had always loved women. Now his wife's penny-pinching bred a new fixation – hate. He hated his wife during the day. He loathed her in bed at night. He tried to do his duty, but it was impossible. He said he would rather masturbate in the streets, than have sex with his wife. Walter began to stalk the streets of the poorer areas of London with a few shillings in his pocket, looking for low-class prostitutes and young girls.

Eventually, Walter found a job. He was still poor and they only had one servant, but he lived in a 'small eight-roomed house', although he was pinched to keep up appearances. It was then that the housemaid Mary found Walter sobbing uncontrollably in the garden. She would be one of the few servants he did not rape. According to Walter's account, she surrendered willingly. When she left, he was still too poor for high-class prostitutes and found cheaper women in the Strand.

Some of Walter's money had been tied up in litigation. He won the case, and immediately went back to the better class of prostitute, until that money, too, was gone. Then, once more, death brought Walter great benefit – another inheritance, which he spent on 'nice women'.

With that money spent, Walter went back to pursuing serv-ants or cheap prostitutes. But now the realization he could not pay a better class of prostitute brought on a fit of violence. The dress-lodger's maid mocked Walter for having little money. He broke up the room and threatened to smash her with a poker.

He was still short of funds when he met actress-turned-streetwalker Sarah Mavis. His obsession with her drove him deep into debt.

'During the nine months I had known her she in fact ran me dry,' he wrote. 'I spent upon her more than I could have lived on for four years at the rate I lived at just before I met her.'

Then it drove him mad. Walter took to doodling sex pictures.

'I would pass hours sketching from recollection Sarah Mavis' limbs and form, her bum and cunt being the most favorite subjects.'

But the terror of masturbation, inflicted by his godfather, left Walter with no other outlet. His only shelter became his dreams.

'Then so randy that I did not know what to do with myself, I would rush out into the streets to prevent my frigging myself, – and erotic night-dreams were frequent.'

When Sarah Mavis left, he was reduced to doing the accounts at the J . . . s Street bawdy house.

His road to recovery was well trodden. He moved his activities out of the West End to find cheap prostitutes elsewhere. Then, when a woman he had impregnated asked him to leave his wife to be with her and their child, Walter had to admit to the woman his financial enslavement to his wife.

'I shall be all but a pauper without her money,' he said.

By this time, Walter was speculating on the stock market.

Then death came to his rescue once more. A Scottish relative left Walter his best legacy yet. He went abroad, only keeping in touch with his solicitors and bankers. Eventually, urgent legal business called him back to London. When he returned, he split from his wife, amicably although first he had to sack a footman and a housemaid who had been having sex.

'It would not have done to have passed over open fornication,' said Walter. 'Had I done so, the habit would have spread throughout the household.'

Naturally, Walter seized the opportunity to take the sacked housemaid, Lucy, to lunch in a private dining room where he seduced her. But then he lost money speculating and was reduced to having cheap prostitutes again.

Then suddenly, at forty-one, Walter stopped paying for sex – briefly. Once again, he thought he had found real love.

'For fifteen months, I have been contented with one woman; I love her devotedly, I would die to make her happy.'

But his fidelity came at a price. Despite his terror of it, he was driven to masturbation to quell his sex drive – the 'sensuous temperament' that he cannot conquer.

> *I have wept over this weakness, have punished myself in fines, giving heavily to charities the money which would have paid for other women. I have frigged myself to avoid leaving a woman whose beauty has tempted my lust. I have, when on the point of accosting a lovely frail one, jumped into a cab and frigged myself right off, tho unavoidably thinking of the charms I had not seen. I have avoided A*g**e and C**m***e, and any other place to which whores resort, for fear of being tempted. I have fucked at home with fury and repetition, so that no sperm should be left, to rise my prick to stiffness when away from home; fucked indeed till advised by my doctor that it was as bad for her as for me.*

He said that he gave 'all his sexual worship' to one woman because she was 'worthy of it'. But was it true love that had really turned Walter faithful? When Walter printed his book, he added bracket notes about the affair: 'This change in social life left me with a limited purse for free loves – I had generally not the money to enable me to have the high-priced strumpets of former days, tho at times I was seduced into such extravagances.' Lack of money made Walter faithful – almost.

When the love affair ended, Walter was driven to break the few sexual boundaries that remained to him. He began to crave anal sex, even though he was disgusted by it. Driven by a 'letch', he had to go to his club to borrow £3 for sodomy.

Irritation about his lack of money would drive Walter to his most disturbing acts. One afternoon, after Walter had been forced to make a costly settlement in a lawsuit, he picked up a drugged runaway, took her to a brothel and raped her repeatedly. He kept her in a lodging house for five days to make sure she did not escape. Walter called her Rosa W***e and said he thought she was 'sixteen and a half'. He describes Rosa's kidnap and his cover-up of her disappearance in great detail.

> *The girl's face was quite white, and dirty, the expression on it was stolid, dazed, almost like – that of one stupefied by a drug, or drink . . .*
>
> *'What's the matter with you, my girl,' I said kindly, and repeated it several times, without getting any reply. She stood breathing hard with her running, and staring at me. I saw she was handsome, pity came over me, and I told her she had better go to her home, where I had seen her followed by the woman a few minutes before. Then she broke out violently. 'I won't – I won't. I'll never go home again. I won't', and her eyes glared on me, but suddenly they altered again to their stupid expression . . .*
>
> *Side by side we walked to the larger thoroughfare. I hailed a cab, and held the door open, when with one of her feet on the step, 'You are going to take me back home,' said she, and stepped back from the cab. I told her I would not . . . She kept eyeing me in a strangely sullen, fixed, manner. Now I saw she was very handsome, and my prick tingled and rose up.*

Walter took her to a room in his regular J***s Street bawdy house where he had worked keeping the books. He described his first rape that night.

I put my hand rapidly up her clothes and touched her thighs. She firmly closed them and yelled out. 'Oh, now don't sir, pray. Oh, don't you.' 'Nonsense, my darling, I'm sure you've been fucked, now haven't you?' She struggled, but could not rise, for I had her down . . .

The next morning he left Rosa naked in the locked room.

I pulled off her petticoat (spite of her) and telling her on no account to open the door, nor to answer anyone, I left, after hearing the bolt of the door shot, and paying thirty shillings for the room. Taking a cab home, and saying I was going to stop with a friend, I brought away in a small portmanteau all the clothes needed.

During the next stage of her ordeal, Walter's plan was to show 'that I was master'. He raped Rosa again that night and forced her to strip naked in the morning.

Then I made her wash her cunt, setting her example by stripping naked, and washing my ballocks osten-tatiously. Then I would see her cunt, about which we again had a squabble, but it was done . . .

Rosa was suffering humiliations that Walter had practised before.

When a girl has been felt, fucked, her cunt has been looked at, and she has pissed and washed before me, she belongs to me entirely.

Walter's way was to isolate girls, terrify, shame and sexualize them. These were the actions of a sexual sadist. But it was done for a purpose. The recipe, followed vigorously, would produce for him a compliant sex slave. These were cheaper than prostitutes. Besides, Walter took an 'intense delight in destroying modesty in a virgin'. And still what he liked most was staring at the wound he had made in a girl's body.

'The contemplation of . . . the ragged edge left by the split of her virginity, drove me wild with lust.'

However, keeping Rosa in a West End bawdy house was proving too expensive. The madam wanted fifty shillings a day for the room. So Walter had to move his stupefied captive to cheaper parts.

> *We left next day. I hired two rooms for a week for two pounds, at a fairly respectable eating house, and paid down. They didn't seem to like my companion when they saw her. I got decent food there, and the girl was out of harm's way. My difficulty now was to know what to do with her.*

Walter had invented an alibi for himself to cover the time he was missing.

> *I was supposed to be in the country with a friend, and therefore kept mostly at the lodgings with her. I could not walk out with her either, and did not like her to go out alone, thinking she might disappear, for she was evidently a determined creature.*

After Rosa told Walter she would 'stick a knife' in the man who drugged and raped her, the end was near.

> *About the third day, I became uneasy about the ending of this affair. I could go out more freely from this house than from the baudy house, and went to my club for letters, but did not wish to be seen much.*

Walter made Rosa write letters to family to cover her disappearance.

> *The fifth day ended in her writing from my dictation*

to her relative at A*i**d*n. The letter was in some respects true, but all about what had taken place since her flight was a pack of lies. I thought out the whole thing.

It is not uncommon for killers to fake documentary evidence – a letter, say – to show that their victim is not dead, but has simply gone away.

I gave her envelopes, written with an address for me at a post office, and begged her to write to me, however short her letter was, and promised if she was in trouble still, to help her but I did not give her my real name.

Walter had already admitted dictating fake letters for Rosa to sign. He then said that he received one of these letters himself. 'About a week after, a letter reached me with "All right – Rosa" on it, and not a word more – I never heard of her again.'

Throughout the narrative he spoke of Rosa having been drugged, but by another man, although any drug administered before he met her would surely have worn off in three days. By then, she was no longer any use to him. 'I had now had all the pleasure the lass was capable of giving me.' Finally, Walter said he 'saw her to the station, and the train, with her, move off', although where she was going he did not say.

There is no proof a 'handsome' Rosa W***e was murdered, or indeed that she ever existed at all. Walter simply says he picked up a runaway 'one Tuesday towards the end of October'.

However, there is evidence that on 11 December 1884, a beautiful girl was found at an East End station. Her fate was detailed at length in *The Times*.

On the 11th of December a rough wooden case was left at a parcels receiving office at the Cambridge-heath-road, addressed to Mrs Green, 3 Abbey-road, St John's Wood. The box was taken for delivery by one of Messrs

Carter and Paterson's carmen, but as he could not find any such person at the address given, it was returned to the general office in Goswell-road, where it remained unnoticed until a disagreeable smell drew attention to it. The manager ordered it to be opened, and it was found to contain human remains. These were taken to the mortuary, where they were pronounced to be those of a girl between 13 and 14 years of age. The body was that of a fair-haired girl, good-looking, with well-formed teeth, but rather thin. It is said to resemble in many particulars that of one of the two girls who have been so long missing from West Ham, but their relatives failed to identify it. The opinion of the police is that both girls were taken to the Continent. Dr Yarrow, the police surgeon, made an examination of the body last night. He came to the conclusion that the cause of death was starvation and that the girl was of good parentage. He saw no reason to suppose that she had been poisoned or subjected to violence. The strongest proof that her parents did not belong to the lower classes is to be found in the state of her teeth. A careful examination showed that several of these were missing, having been extracted, not on account of premature decay, for those which remain are perfectly sound, but evidently solely for the purpose of preserving the regularity of the set, which would have been destroyed by overcrowding had those removed been allowed to remain. Her hair, which was fine, had been cut short all over the head. The inquest will be held this morning.

Rosa W***e, recalled Walter, had 'lovely teeth, and chestnut coloured, long, and silky hair'. Police immediately suspected the girl in the box had to do with forced prostitution. 'Taken to the Continent' was a euphemism for the raping of kidnapped girls uncovered by a series of prosecutions of Brussels brothel keepers from 1879 to 1881.

The girl in the box was not the only mystery in *The Times* that morning. There was news from Limehouse. Throat cuttings had begun.

> *Yesterday evening, information was forwarded to Sir John Humphreys, the coroner, of the death of a man unknown. It appeared that at about 2 p.m. a Mr Campion of Farrance Road was walking along the banks of the Lea, known as the Limehouse Cut, when he noticed something floating in the water. He at once called the attention of a constable, and a boat being procured, the two managed to bring ashore what proved to be the body of a middle-aged man, decently dressed. The body did not appear to have been in the water any length of time. The head was almost severed from the body, apparently by some sharp instrument. A shell was procured and the remains were conveyed to the Limehouse mortuary, where they were examined by Dr Matthew Brownfield, of the East India Dock-road, who was of the opinion that the injury to the throat had been inflicted before death. There was nothing at all in the pockets that is likely to lead to the identification of the remains.*

Throughout his life Walter suffered from bouts of 'the clap'. However, as he grew older a recurring pain brought on a change in his sexual behaviour.

> *The irritation in my gland about this time increased, and came on quite once or twice a week, in fact directly I wanted the love of woman. In coition then, a freshly washed cunt such as gay ladies like to prepare for their visitors, became to me more objectionable than ever. My first thrusts in the warm red avenues at the period of these visitations, were positively painful to me, and I thought incessantly of the pleasure I had, when the spermatic softness had just been given to the pudenda,*

by a pioneer on to the road which was open and ready
for me to enter.

Walter felt compelled to have sex in the semen other men had
left inside prostitutes. The soothing of his flesh created an
addiction in his mind. And, like many of his fetishes, Walter
was attracted to it because it had disgusted and scared him.

Strange it was however, that at that time, a dislike at the
idea of following another of my sex there, sometimes
came over me, a dislike mingled with fear. Foolish tho
it was for the time – a short time only – it restrained me
from giving myself the fullest pleasure.

The pain in his penis pushed Walter to obsess about lubrication.

'Lubrication, and even an excess of lubrication, of the right
sort, became absolutely needful to my pleasure.'

Walter was having sex with a married woman when he
found out that the right sort of lubrication could be blood.

'At the last spend she gave a scream, and began to sob,
uncunting my penis by a violent jerk, and there was blood on
it. I think some of it was mine. How often I spent that night I
never could tell.'

His partner, Mrs O*b***e, believed she was being
murdered. 'She kept begging me to stop after each of her
spends, and saying I should kill her . . . I fucked her till she
screamed, and so did I, with mixed pain and pleasure!' But,
afterwards, Walter was not pleased with his performance. He
feared that this sexual fury would drive him mad.

'Such a copulative fury had never occurred to me before. At
last I began to think that there was some ailment coming on.
I heard of such things, of men going mad through it, and got
alarmed.'

At a brothel in Paris, Walter suffered a 'violent pain in my
head' after sex and feared that he was losing his eyesight.
Nevertheless, he could not leave without having sex, even
though he felt no desire. The pain in his head got worse.

'I had pain as well as pleasure now, hollowed as I spent, and could not move afterwards. I had a splitting in my temples which alarmed me. I've had it at times lately.'

In the latter volumes of *My Secret Life*, Walter suffered a lengthy unspecified illness. This was quite different from bouts of gonorrhoea. It was 'an illness of quite a different class', he wrote. He took to home, and then a hotel. Walter wrote he was recovering from this different class of illness when, in 1888, he had his sex diary printed as a book.

The author wrestled with his ignorance of his own disease. He said his book would be 'for the good of others'. 'Have all men had the strange letches which late in life have enraptured me?' he wondered. 'I can never know this; my experience, if printed, may enable others to compare as I cannot.'

Reviewing the memoirs in 1966, *Time* magazine jeeringly diagnosed Walter as having satyriasis, an excessive, often uncontrollable sexual desire. This was stating the obvious. But Walter's manuscript itself suggests a deeper malady.

Writing such a monumental diary may be the clue to what plagued Walter. Such obsessive record-making is the mark of a psychiatric condition known as hypergraphia. Walter would write down his sex acts even when his partner was still in the room. Hypergraphia is considered a sign of epilepsy, manic depression or schizophrenia. Schizophrenics are not only significantly more likely to be prone to violence. Murders committed during bouts of schizophrenia may be bizarre and extreme.

He wrote of a controlling voice in his head – a common symptom of schizophrenia. As the child Pol was held on a bed so Walter could deflower her, a 'demon' spoke to him.

'The demon of desire said, "It's fresh, it's virgin, bore it, bung it, plug it; stretch it, split it, spunk in it", and I laid hold of her . . . '

Explaining his sex 'attacks', Walter spoke of a 'little devil' who 'took all control off of me' and 'fetched my lust up awfully'. This was more than a diarist's turn of phrase. In a bout of illness, Walter blamed himself for being 'too weak' to govern this persuasive imp.

'I never deliberately set to work to tempt them, but the lech when it took me seems to have overcome all my moral objections. Has the devil determined to tempt me in this direction? If so, am I to blame for not being gifted with control?'

Walter also showed symptoms of paranoia. After years of worshipping prostitutes, Walter came to believe they were tricking him.

> *A gay lady is almost by necessity a liar and trickster – money, money does it ... all women, modest or immodest, are liars, they will lie like a dentist to serve their turn. Trust them not, shall be my motto hence-forth.*

A compulsive drive to write also occurs as a symptom of fronto-temporal dementia, a degeneration of the front of the brain. This is an incurable genetic condition that often results in disinhibition, which shows itself as hypersexuality and aggressive outbursts. Describing his attempted rape of a soldier's wife in the East End, Walter said an irresistible sex urge brought on a brutal rage.

> *We struggled I don't know how long, and then breathless, fatigued, I got into a violent rage – a natural rage, not an artificial one – and it told as brutality often tells with a woman.*

His outburst was accompanied by another memory lapse. Walter accepted these outbursts of violence as part of the natural order of what he called 'cunt-hunting'.

'A man must first make himself agreeable, then successively familiar, endearing, coaxing, loose, bold, baudy, determined, then if needs be fierce, or even violent.'

Madness drove Walter by night. By day, he was driven by a need to make money.

As the 1880s approached, a shortage of funds sent him back to the stock market, then situated in Capel Court, but he did not seem to have had any more luck than he did before, although it was now easier for him to get to the City as more underground railway lines had opened up. The chance of bagging another rich wife seemed remote.

Walter's way out of his financial quagmire was to return to an old money-spinner he'd been too fearful to undertake a few years before. He would publish the sex diary he had slaved over. He would publish his own *Fanny Hill*, and he contacted Charles Carrington, the porn king of Paris, to help him. His motive was writ large on the front cover: 'Privately printed for subscribers'. Like-minded men would pay good money to read the story of his erotic life. At £20 a volume, Walter stood to make a killing. He would be rich again. Selling his memoirs could net 5,000 guineas with a print run of just twenty-five copies. It was enough to live well on for many years.

He could afford to make the volumes expensive. Gentlemen with similar tastes to his own tended to be rich. These were men who had been happy to fork out large sums to have sex with prepubescent girls – unfledged virgin cunt, as Walter called it. If they could no longer dare to indulge their perverted passion, they would at least pay to read about it – and there was no risk of any of his subscribers going to the police. This was, essentially, a paedophile ring and they were all in it.

There were great risks. The raw manuscript detailed 'abnormal eccentric tastes' – acts beyond even sodomy, rape and child sex. Those pages he must consign to the flames. 'Walter'– the false name to disguise his own identity – would emerge from the ashes. Then he would disguise the identity of anyone else who might still be alive, or anyone dead whose association with him might give the game away.

The greatest danger came from the women who had procured virgins and underage girls for him. Defloration, once considered a bit of fun for a wealthy gentleman, was now against the law. Since 1885, the vigilance committees were using madams as spies. Prostitutes had even been encouraged to use the new law as a blackmailer's charter. Anonymous letters had been sent to Walter's wife while she was alive. East End hags who sold virgins were now informing on the men who had bought girls. Walter had reason to fear blackmail, or worse. Whipping was back on the statute books for men like him. By 1888, Walter's old world of Georgian decadence had been swept away. For most of his life, London had provided an inexhaustible supply of prostitutes. Courtesans were celebrities and children were for sale. Now women were marching in the street against sex. Was he to be denied what he considered a birthright by class and natural desire? The Salvation Army was rescuing virgins from brothels to put on soapboxes. Reformed procuresses shouted out the crimes of men like Walter from the street corners. The Skeleton Army of pub men and brothel keepers had attacked the Salvationist women. They kicked Mrs Susannah Beatty to death in an alley for shaking a tambourine at their fun. But the Skeletons had blundered by attacking the whore-coddling Salvationists by day.

We propose Walter, the old stalker, adopted a new approach. He would come out at night. Blood lubricated his desires. The work would be a joy. He would silence women, as he silenced and gralloched deer. Those who would be a danger to him would know to keep their mouths shut. With the procuresses cowered by terror, he could sell *My Secret Life* in safety. He would then have money enough for his old age. And if he dropped hints that he was murdering the women who might blackmail him, so much the better. His readership would also be pleased to be rid of an ever-present threat. Besides, Walter – whoever he was – would have the added satisfaction of covertly bragging about his crimes. The confession – the braggadocio – would be there for anyone who could read it.

Walter had the means, motivation and opportunity to take his hunting knife to Whitechapel in 1888 – and, for that matter, leave a trail of Thames Torsos as well. For years he had loved prostitutes. Now, he must stop them betraying him. It had started as a boy when Walter looked up into the bum of a Whitechapel whore and he believed he saw the slit throat of a dog. It would end with a man looking down on a Whitechapel prostitute, her throat cut like a slain deer. Blood would flow from jagged slits. Walter would like what he saw.

16

WHO WAS WALTER?

If Walter was Jack the Ripper, then who was Walter? Academics have been puzzling over this for years. The most popular candidate is Henry Spencer Ashbee, the bibliophile and author who lived from 1834 to 1900. He was put forward by the author Gershon Legman in his introduction to the Grove Press edition of *My Secret Life* in 1966. He said that he had been told that Ashbee was the author by St George Best, himself an author, who in turn said he heard it from Charles Carrington. However, Carrington was a notoriously unreliable character who would have done anything to drum up customers for his 1902 edition of the book. Best smuggled Carrington's prohibited publications into the US and other countries, and would have gone along with anything Carrington said. Legman said he believed what he was told, as Carrington did not publicly advertise the sale of his presumably pirated editions of *My Secret Life* until 1902, after Ashbee had died. However, Legman himself found a handbill dating from 1894.

Ashbee was a wealthy bibliophile and collector of erotic books. His friend Sir Richard Burton, translator of the *Kama Sutra* and *The Perfumed Garden*, launched an attack on W.T. Stead and 'The Maiden Tribute of Modern Babylon' in 1889. When Ashbee died, his collection was bequeathed to the British Library, along with priceless material relating to Cervantes and a copy of *A Vision of Love Revealed In Sleep* by Simeon Solomon that had formerly belonged to Oscar Wilde.

However, the copy of *My Secret Life* in the British Library's Private Case is not Ashbee's. It was bequeathed to the library by another collector of erotica, Charles Reginald Dawes, in 1964.

Although very few dates are mentioned in *My Secret Life*, internal evidence indicates that Walter was born in 1820 or 1821, not 1834 like Ashbee. Walter was sixteen when his father died. Ashbee was thirty-three when he lost his. Ashbee's wife was still alive when he died, although he disinherited her after a row on the occasion of their silver wedding anniversary. Walter reported that his wife was dead. They had no children, while Ashbee and his wife had three. Ashbee lived at 46 Upper Bedford Street from 1865 to 1884, while Walter let it slip that for at least part of that time he lived at no. 34 in a street name that begins with the letter A.

Ashbee was a wealthy man whose financial situation did not fluctuate like Walter's. His main claim to fame was the three-volume *Bibliography of Prohibited Books* published under the pseudonym Pisanus Fraxi. Walter showed little interest in erotica. He seems to have had difficulties procuring relatively common books such as an illustrated copy of *Fanny Hill*, even saying that he thought it was written by a woman, although he may be being disingenuous. Ashbee was a noted linguist. Walter was fluent in French and knew some Italian, but was poor in German and Spanish. Both travelled widely, but Ashbee wintered in Spain for many years, while Walter only seems to have visited there once.

Legman suggested another candidate – Captain Edward Sellon. A sales catalogue of 1905 mentions that *My Secret Life* was 'the autobiography of an English captain who, day by day, noted his gallant prowesses since his youth'. But Sellon produced another autobiography called *The Ups and Downs*, which was published secretly in 1867. Why would anyone publish two anonymous autobiographies, especially when one of them was a million words long? Sellon committed suicide in 1866. In *My Secret Life*, the author refers to reading earlier volumes in print, so he must have been alive after 1888 and probably did not die until after 1894 when publication was complete.

Another suspect, in Legman's eyes, was Richard Monckton Milnes. The only thing that suggests him as a candidate is that he had three names – the same woman who said that Walter lived at 34 A– Street, also said: 'Your names begin with * * * and * * * * and * * * *.' Walter added: 'It was so exact that I started, but said, "No."' Milnes was another collector of erotica. Born in 1809, he died in 1885. He married at forty-two – not twenty-six like Walter – and his father died when Monckton Jr was forty-nine. Monckton's wife died in 1874, but she left him three children. Nothing seems to fit.

Gordon Stein, a literary detective who worked for the Center for Inquiry in Buffalo, New York, also investigated George Augustus Sala, a journalist friend of Charles Dickens. He died in 1895, which is about right, but he was born in 1828 – a little too late. His maternal grandfather had a plantation in British Guyana; Walter said his father went 'abroad to look after some plantations'. However, Walter was sixteen when his father died; Sala was still an infant. He had four siblings; Walter had three. He was married at the age of thirty-one in 1859. After his wife died in 1885, he married again six years later to a woman who survived him. Sala was another traveller. His financial situation, like Walter's, fluctuated. He spoke fluent French, learned from his mother, and wrote prolifically for the newspapers. He published his work anonymously on London's underworld, but his numerous poems and a book on flagellation appeared under his own name. Clearly, it was a practice he enjoyed. Walter observed flagellation, but it did not attract him unless blood was drawn. Overall, Sala is not a strong candidate for Walter.

Another Stein candidate was John Walter – born in 1818, died in 1894. The dates nearly fit, but those of his marriage do not. Although his surname is appealing, his father was the wealthy editor of *The Times*, so he never lived in penury. He was also said to be serious, retiring and scholarly, and the death of his eldest son in 1870 left him depressed.

Stein also suggested John Stephen Farmer, thought to be the author of the erotic work, *Suburban Souls*. Little is known about him, although he was probably born around 1845 and died in 1915, which puts him out of the running. William S. Potter, who wrote the four-volume pornographic novel, *Romance of Lust*, published between 1873 and 1876, falls at the same fence, having been born in 1805 and died in 1879. August John Cuthbert Hare, author of the six-volume, *The Story of My Life*, published in 1876, can also be ruled out. Born in 1834 in Rome, he died in 1903. He was raised in Sussex until he was eleven, when he was adopted by his godmother. He never married and lived in Italy where he wrote a number of travel books.

However, Stein spotted what he believe to be a telling clue in the text of *My Secret Life*. In Volume 2, Walter wrote:

> *Just at that time a case filled the public journals. It was a charge of rape on a married woman against a man lodging in the same house. She was the wife of a printer of the staff of a daily paper, who came home extremely late; she always went to bed leaving her door unlocked, so that her husband might get in directly when he came home. The lodger was a friend of her husband's, and knew the custom of leaving the door unlocked – in fact he was a fellow printer.*
>
> *She awakened in the night with the man between her thighs, had opened them readily, thinking it was her husband. It appears to have been her habit, and such her husband's custom on returning home, or so she said. The lodger had all but finished his fuck, before she awakened sufficiently to find out that it was not the legitimate prick which was probing her. Then she alarmed the house, and gave the man a charge for committing a rape. The papers delicately hinted that the operation was complete before the woman discovered the mistake – but of course it left much to the readers' imagination.*

Fred read this aloud. I knew more, for the counsel of the prisoner was my intimate friend. He had told me that the prisoner had had her twice; that she had spent with him; that he often said that he meant to go in and have her, that she had dared him to do it, and that she only made a row when she thought she heard her husband at the door on the landing, although it was two hours before his usual time of return . . .

Stein believed that this was the case of *Regina v. Richard Clarke*, which was tried at York Assizes on 16 July 1854. Vern L. Bullough, another literary detective who was Stein's collaborator, discovered that the men involved in that case were not printers, but clothiers – this is typical of the details Walter amends to avoid identification. The defendant's barrister was William Overend. Bullough discovered two friends of Overend who might qualify as Walter. One was Charles Stanley. Overend and Stanley were born in the same year, 1809, and possibly the same street – Church Street, Sheffield, where both their fathers lived. Overend and Stanley were in the real-estate business together in January 1883 and, when Overend died soon after, Stanley inherited a large part of his estate.

The other possibility was Overend's nephew, Thomas James Overend. Born in 1822, died in 1895, he had almost the same putative dates as Walter. However, he was married at twenty-three. He never lived in London for any length of time and, according to his death certificate, he was a 'silk weaver'.

Bullough plumped for Stanley, although his dates were not right. He was married at the age of forty-two in 1852, but Bullough reckoned this was a second marriage. According to his death certificate, this wife succeeded him. They lived at 9 Lancaster Gate in Bayswater, so it would have been easy to commute to central London, or even the East End, once the underground was in place. He appears to have been trained as a barrister, became custodian of the family bank and, latterly, a stockbroker. Bullough admits it is not a perfect fit, but Walter records that he made a long trip abroad around 1862 or 1863. A Charles H. Stanley was issued a passport on 24 March 1862. Walter said that his cousin Fred was a soldier who was sent abroad and was killed. David Stanley of the 17th Lancers was severely wounded at the Battle of Balaclava in 1854 and probably died of his wounds. According to Bullough, Stein was convinced he could unearth more collaborating evidence when he died in 1998. Bullough reckoned that, if Walter was not Ashbee, then Stanley was the best alternative.

However, in 2002, John Patrick Pattinson of the New Jersey Institute of Technology came up with an entirely new candidate. Pattinson used several clues in the book to work out that Walter was brought up in Camberwell, then a village separated from the sprawl of London by green fields. He then began to look for someone from Camberwell who, in later life, had the opportunity to travel and was in some way with the military. What he found was William Haywood, who was the son of William Haywood of Camberwell and was educated at Camberwell Grammar School. He was a prominent architect and civil engineer who was an officer in the City of London Rifle Brigade Volunteers from 1860, rising to become Lieutenant-Colonel in 1876. Haywood was responsible for covering the streets of London with asphalt, completing the Victoria Embankment and building the Holborn Viaduct. He was a Chevalier of the French Legion of Honour and, as Chief Engineer for the Commissioners of Sewers in the City of London, he travelled widely on the Continent and in north America to study advances made in his field there and lend his expertise.

Studying the records of the census for 1841, Pattinson found that there was a Haywood family in Vicarage Place, Camberwell, that matched Walter's. The father died when Haywood Jr was nearly sixteen, leaving them in reduced circumstances. Pattinson believes that the 'W** Office' that the young Walter worked in was not the War Office but the Works Office of the St Katharine Dock Company where William Haywood – listed in the census as an 'Arch' – is thought to have completed his apprenticeship. And the 'commission' he gave up when he came into his inheritance and 'lost much money by doing so' was not a commission in the Army, but an architectural commission.

When he 'went daily to the W** Office, returning at about half-past four', he said he returned one day to meet Charlotte, his first love, 'about half-a-mile from home'. The coach from the War Office, then in Pall Mall, would have stopped much closer to home, but the coach from Gracechurch Street, which he would have taken if he was returning from the Works Office in the City, would have dropped him nearly a mile from home.

After he inherited, Walter said: 'Nearly a year went by and 4,000 pound ... ' There is no record of Haywood working during that period, although when he later sought work he soon found clients and commissions. In 1845, Haywood became Assistant Surveyor to the Commissioners of Sewers for the City of London, as 'the young architect was too desirous of the security and other advantages of a secure income in quarterly payments to decline the post,' according to his obituary in *Civil Engineering*. He married on 16 October 1845, two weeks short of his twenty-fourth birthday.

The census of March 1851 puts Haywood and his wife living at 4 Isabella Place, Kennington, with one servant, fourteen-year-old Elizabeth. Walter said: 'It is difficult to narrate more without divulging my outer life. I would fain keep that hidden, but ... I was still poor, but had got into an employment, and was living in a small eight-roomed house. I kept one servant only.' This was Mary, with whom he had an affair.

In 1852, Haywood moved to 23 Albert Square, Kennington. Meanwhile, Walter said that he was much better off and 'now lived in a larger house with only three servants'. He referred to this as 'our new residence', telling someone that he lived 'the other side of the water', meaning south of the river.

After several years of a miserable marriage, Walter went abroad. Then he received news by messenger that his wife was dead. 'Death had done its work,' he said. 'Hurrah! I was free at last.' However, Pattinson could find no record of the death of Haywood's wife. He thinks they separated and the mention of her death was merely a way Walter 'mystified family affairs' as he warned in his preface. Afterwards, he enjoyed 'four years of freedom'.

Later, he told a different story. By 'two years after the Battle of Solferino' – that is 1861 – he renewed acquaintance with a young woman called Madeline S***h, who 'had worked at my house for years previously . . . I lost sight of her when I gave up that home as a freed man'.

If his wife had died, he would not have had to give up his home. So how, then, did he become a freed man? Divorce was difficult back then, but if he and his wife had made a private agreement to separate there would have been no public record. After hearing of his wife's 'death', Walter said: 'I travelled home night and day, hurriedly arranged affairs, gave carte blanche to solicitors, and agents, and with lighter heart than I had had for years, went abroad again.' Clearly some legal deal had been done.

He was certainly free one way or the other. Madeline S***h said 'she knew that I could do as I liked now'.

Haywood left Albert Square around 1858 and moved into lodgings in the Strand. Then he moved into a house near Regent's Park. The 1861 census showed him living at 7 Park Village East. He is listed as married, but living with two single women, aged twenty-five and twenty-six, who are listed as general servants.

In 1863, Haywood's father-in-law drew up a new will in favour of his daughter 'not withstanding her coverture' – her husband's legal authority over her and her property. The period between 1858 and 1863, Pattinson argued, corresponds to Walter's 'four years of freedom'. These are terminated by Winifred, whom he fell in love with. Walter says:

*[With Winifred terminated my four years of freedom.
I fell in love and was changed, yet my amorous frailty
clung to me. – I loved deeply, truly, shall love to my*

dying hour, and, spite of my infidelity, would at any time have slain any one of my paramours rather than give her pain.]

This paragraph appears in brackets. These bracketed paragraphs, Walter said, 'have been written since the manuscript of my life was finished, and have been added at this revision, when the narrative is put into form, revised, and much of the manuscript destroyed'. At that point, despite his infidelity, they still seemed to be together. He also referred to Winifred as 'the legitimate one'. Later, he referred to 'the one woman whom I adore' and of himself 'loving as I ever shall one woman to the end of my life'. He also mentioned, in brackets, that he did not stray so often 'having one voluptuous, lascivious beauty always available'. Walter, it seems, was having an ongoing relationship.

In the censuses of 1871 and 1881, Haywood was living at 56 Hamilton Terrace, Maida Vale with his wife Emma J. Both Haywood and Walter were 'married'. By 1891, they had five servants. Walter, too, seems to have moved a number of times between 1858 and 1871.

During his career, Haywood travelled abroad and received a number of awards from other countries. Walter mentioned no awards, but certainly travelled. Despite his achievement building the Holborn Viaduct, opened by Queen Victoria on 6 November 1869, Haywood never received a knighthood, unlike his colleague Sir Joseph Bazalgette, perhaps because Haywood was living with a woman who was not his wife.

Like Walter, Haywood was clubbable, a member of the Reform and the Gresham. While Haywood was working his way up through the ranks in the Volunteer London Rifle Brigade, Walter talked about visiting camp several times and said: 'All was I knew quite in the order of things, when a regiment was changing quarters.' He also mentioned seducing a woman on the train back from Aldershot. Haywood retired as Commandant in 1882 – while retaining the honorific of Colonel – giving him plenty of time to prepare and edit the manuscript of *My Secret Life*.

As Haywood grew older, his health began to fail and he was 'frequently required to seek the renewal of health abroad, where repose was complete and the climate less rigorous', while Walter said 'on my way to the sweet south, to get the sun in the months it's denied us here . . . Tired, worn out, ill, and alas getting older, I was nevertheless again at the lapunar [brothel] one night.'

Haywood died at his house in Hamilton Terrace on 13 April 1894, of chronic cystitis and asthenia, an abnormal lack of energy. He left £42,000, worth over £2.5 million at today's prices. He left his house and an income of £2,200 (£130,000 today) to 'my dear friend and companion Jemima Emma Haywood otherwise Jemima Emma Elbrow'. In other words, they were not married. Indeed, his first wife did not die until 1909.

Pattinson suggested that the underground catalogue *Paris Galante* of 1910 and 1912, which listed the 'Modern Casanova Memoirs' of the 'Well Known celebrated Col. W.', referred to Colonel W. Haywood. Despite his assiduous research, however, Pattinson still had not tied up all the loose ends. There was still the question of the nom de plume.

'But then, why "Walter"?' he concluded. 'Perhaps this we shall never know.'

However, the real problem is that William Haywood, with his relatively well ordered life, sounds nothing like the obsessive, tormented, sometimes demented Walter.

W.T. Stead had his own candidate for who Jack the Ripper might be – and he was a writer. In the April 1896 issue of the journal *Borderland*, which Stead, then a spiritualist, edited, he wrote in the foreword to an article: 'The writer . . . has been known to me for many years. He is one of the most remarkable persons I ever met. For more than a year I was under the impression that he was the veritable Jack the Ripper, an impression which I believe was shared by the police, who, at least once, had him under arrest; although as he completely satisfied them, they liberated him without bringing him into court.'

The writer in question was Robert Donston Stephenson, a.k.a. Dr Roslyn D'Onston, who had been a freelance journalist contributing articles on the Ripper murders to the *Pall Mall Gazette*. During the murders, Stephenson had checked himself into the London Hospital suffering from neurasthenia, or nervous exhaustion, a condition that could easily be faked. The theory was that he slipped out at night to do the murders – a man returning to his bed covered in blood would not attract attention in a hospital. It has even been suggested that the victim in the Rainham mystery was Stephenson's first wife. Stephenson himself claimed that the Ripper was an illiterate Frenchman, saying that 'Juwes' in the Goulston Street graffiti was actually 'Juives' – French for 'Jewesses'. He said that the geographical layout of the murders mapped out a Satanic symbol and that the missing body parts were used in black magic rituals. Stephenson himself was an occultist. He also accused one of the doctors at the London Hospital of being Jack the Ripper. This brought Stephenson to the attention of the police, who interviewed him on at least two occasions. Inspector Roots, who took Stephenson's statement and who had known him for twenty years, dismissed the idea that Stephenson was the Ripper, describing him as: 'One who has led a bohemian life, drinks very heavily, perpetually fuddled and who always carries drugs to sober him and stave off delirium tremens.'

Nevertheless, in later life, others who knew Stephenson continued to suspect he was the Ripper. Stories circulated that he had a collection of bloodstained neckties that had once been used to conceal the victims' stolen body parts. In the 1920s, the ties supposedly came into the hands of the satanist Aleister Crowley, who said that they had belonged to Jack the Ripper and he had received them from Stephenson after his death. Crowley also had a copy of *My Secret Life*. Unfortunately, Stephenson was born in 1841, which is too late to be Walter.

On the night of 14 April 1912, W.T. Stead took his suspicions with him to the bottom of the Atlantic. He'd been asked to address a peace conference in New York and chose to sail there on the maiden voyage of the *Titanic*. The man who'd risked his freedom to save virgins from the London Minotaur, was last seen holding back male passengers out to steal the places of women and children on the final lifeboats being lowered into the abyss.

ACKNOWLEDGEMENTS AND ENDNOTES

Researchers Andy James and Lizzie Toms contributed much effort, mileage and hard thought in archive and document research. Alison Cooke's transcription and deciphering of copperplate handwriting is much appreciated. Staff at the Salvation Army Heritage Centre and the University of Liverpool Josephine Butler Collections were kind and helpful. Any book about Jack the Ripper rests on a bed of hard work done by dedicated researchers before them. Special thanks must be made to the scholars who have put together invaluable reference works: Paul Begg, Martin Fido, authors of *The Jack the Ripper A-Z*, and Stewart P. Evans and Keith Skinner, authors of *The Ultimate Jack the Ripper Sourcebook*, both of which have been an invaluable reference. Special thanks to Stephen P. Ryder, editor of the website *Casebook: Jack the Ripper*, and to his many contributors, for providing both raw information and a healthy new enquiry into an old tragedy. Chris Oxley of Laurel Productions had the initial faith to support the research into *Walter – Secret Life of a Victorian Pornographer*, the Channel 4 documentary that was the springboard to this book. Paul A. Woods and Sondra London shared personal insights into the confession tactics and literary styles of modern serial killers.

Please note that the numbers next to the entries denote the page reference in the text.

Introduction

1   'Classic of Victorian pornography': Wilson and Seaman are among the few reviewers who have failed to see Walter as a master of erotica. They

point to *My Secret Life* as a milestone of a culture shift in pornography that ushers in the modern serial killing phenomenon. Wilson, Colin; Seaman, Donald. *The Serial Killers* (W.H. Allen, 1990).

1 'Koh-i-noor of . . .': Sutherland, John. *Offensive Literature: Decensorship in Britain 1960-1982* (Rowman & Littlefield, 1983: p. 90).

1 'Comes in eleven volumes': A 12th volume may exist. No copy has resurfaced but bibliographer Peter Mendes believes it is an index, with the Introduction and Prefaces possibly printed in Paris after 1894. Mendes, Peter. *Clandestine Erotic Fiction in English 1800-1930* (Scolar Press, 1993).

1 'Printed secretly in Amsterdam': Type ornaments at the beginning of chapters can be traced to a print shop used by Auguste Brancart, who operated largely from Amsterdam but also Brussels and France. Bullough, Vern L. 'Who Wrote My Secret Life?' (*Sexuality & Culture*, 4/1, March 2000).

1 'Six copies': MSL Vol. 1, Chapter 1.

1 'At least twenty sets': Twelve complete sets had been traced in 2000, printed from the same setting of type, as well as copies of a number of broken sets. Stein estimated twenty-five sets were originally published. Bullough, Vern L. 'Who Wrote My Secret Life?' (*Sexuality & Culture*, 4/1, March 2000).

1 'The Dawn of Sensuality': Legman, Gershon, *The horn book: studies in erotic folklore and bibliography* (University Books, 1964: p. 28).

1 'Go between who': Gibson, Ian. *The Erotomaniac: the secret life of Henry Spencer Ashbee* (Perseus Books Group, 2001: p. 169).

1 'The manuscript': My Secret Life claims to be rewritten from the daily diary of the author, Walter. He includes raw extracts to demonstrate his technique. 'Here from my manuscript are two extracts illustrative of my notes as written almost day by day at that period – many and many a page there was of them . . . 21 January.' 'A funny little bitch about four feet six high, thin.' 'A modest looking juvenile cunt.' 'One of the smallest I ever put into – quite tight as I pushed my penis up it – hurt me as I pulled prick out quite stiff – I'd spent, tho I feared – washed.' '"You're in a hurry,' said she light-haired, squinny face. 23 March' 'A hairy arsed, low, she.' 'Wonder I poked her, glad to get away – ten and six – dirty rooms.' (MSL, Vol. 7, Chapter 6). Walter also wrote essays on such subjects as 'cunts' and 'copulation', written as factual descriptions. These fed into political opinions on sex such as 'The philosophy of fucking virgins and juveniles' and 'Fornication philosophy of the poor'. Walter finally announced his own 'philosophy of fornication': 'There can be no indecency, or impropriety in women or men amusing themselves any way they like in private'. (MSL Vol. 10, Chapter 7). Among other purposes, Walter intended his work to be appreciated as a political tract relevant to its time.

1 'He was selling': Marcus, Steven. *The Other Victorians: a study of sexuality and pornography in mid-nineteenth-century England* (Basic Books, 1966: p. 79).

2   'Sold at auction': Christie's' sale of a copy of MSL took place in Paris on 27 April 2006. The catalogue described the provenance as 'the small but exquisite erotica collection of the Amsterdam banker and celebrated children's book collector, the late C.F. van Veen (1912–1982)'.

2   'In 1932': An imitation of *My Secret Life* appeared as the 'Lord Roxboro' series by Robert Sewall. See Cornog, Martha. *Libraries, Erotica and Pornography* (Oryx Press, 1991). Sewall was in truth Lupton Wilkinson, film publicist and emissary for Hollywood's chief censor, Will Hays of the Motion Picture Producers and Distributors Association, lending weight to the *allegation* that censors themselves were covert producers of pornography. Brulotte, Gaétan; Phillips, John. *Encyclopedia of Erotic Literature* (CRC Press, 2006).

2   'Professional purveyor of filth': Tribe, David H. *Questions of Censorship* (Allen & Unwin, 1973: p. 260).

2   'Various abridged': reviewer Maya Mirsky pointed out the Wordsworth Classic Erotica series cut 'the original 2,360 pages of hardcore to a mere 624'. *Critique Magazine*, internet only (http://www.critiquemagazine. com), publisher Katherine Arline. See http://www.critiquemagazine.com/article/mysecretlife.html.

3   'Oldest friend . . . psychology': MSL, Vol. 1, Introduction.

4   'I have one fear . . . malice to gratify': MSL, Vol. 1, Preface.

4   'Shall it be burnt': MSL, Vol. 1, Second Preface.

4   'Two volumes': MSL, Vol. 3, Chapter 2.

4   'These details also gave studies of character': MSL, Vol. 3, Chapter 2.

5   'What has been described as': '*My Secret Life* is by far the most famous and the longest sexual autobiography written in the nineteenth century. Its eleven fat volumes contain invaluable material for social and cultural historians, literary scholars, students of manners and morals – and I believe it has more of what we might call "encounters" than any narrative ever penned. Since the book's publication around 1902 (sic), this astounding document – narrated by the otherwise anonymous "Walter" – has been notorious as an energetic, entertaining narrative of one man's tireless sexual activity. Since only scholars and the mentally tangled could read the original in its entirety, nearly everyone who knows *My Secret Life* has read it in an abridged form. The abridgements have generally taken care to present a somewhat expurgated and sanitized image of Walter.' Kincaid, James Russell and Tithecott, Richard. *My Secret Life: An Erotic Diary of Victorian London*, (Signet Classic, 1996: p. v).

5   'Parade of genitalia': Maya Mirsky. *Critique Magazine*, http://www.critiquemagazine.com/article/mysecretlife.html.

5   'A split gaping': MSL, Vol. 1, Chapter 8.

5   'Shooting at a rabbit': MSL, Vol. 2, Chapter 11.

5   'Hunting clothes': Walter describes hunting 'Quay women' in Dundee where he 'felt cunts at a shilling a piece, I was clad in a well worn shooting suit'. Vol. 6, Chapter 15.

5   'The most evil thing you have ever read': the prosecution in the Dobson trial asked every defence witness if Walter's violation of the ten-year-old girl was the most evil thing they had ever read. Historian Steven Marcus responded: 'Do you mean that literally?'. Sutherland, John. Ibid., p. 94.

5   'Small beer for a serial killer': British general practitioner Dr Harold Shipman was convicted of fifteen murders in January 2000. After his trial, the Shipman Enquiry, led by Dame Janet Smith, suggested he had killed 250 of his patients, with 218 positively identified. In 2007, Moscow supermarket worker, Alexander Pichushkin, the so-called 'chess killer', was convicted of forty-eight murders.

6   'Write about his victims?': After compiling the writings of thirty-seven killers, Brian King observed: 'The murderers need to express themselves through an outlet other than murder. They have attempted to decipher their psychopathic actions, their writings and artefacts are genuinely human documents of sadism, guilt, delusion and madness, filtered through various forms of explanation, fabrication and exculpation. Some had such a need to express themselves that their words and images led to their capture, conviction and execution.' *Lustmord: The Writings and Artifacts of Murderers* (Bloat, 1996).

Chapter 1 – A Maniac on the Loose

8   'The affair ... complete mystery': London had a series of unsolved killings, known as 'mysteries', four years before where a prostitute was the victim. The series culminated with the death of Mary Ann Yates, nineteen, on 9 March 1884. She was found on her bed in her lodging room at 12 Burton Crescent, Camden Town. She had been hit about the head and had a towel tied around her nose and mouth. Death was by strangulation. Police had difficulty identifying the body. Mary had been abandoned as a five-year-old in Regent Street, brought up in an Industrial School and sent into service as a maid. She had 'turned bad' at sixteen and was taking men she met in Tottenham Court Road to her room. The coroner said the case was 'one of a series of mysteries which had occurred in the immediate neighbourhood and of the highest importance it should be sifted to the very bottom' (*The Times*, 20 March 1884). No killer was found. Six years before in Burton Crescent, the lodger of aged widow Rachael Samuel found her battered to death with the fragment of a hat rail. The pocket of her dress had been cut off and a pair of boots was missing, but no other property was missing. Griffiths, Arthur George Frederick. *Mysteries of Police and Crime*, Vol. 1 (Cassel, 1898: p. 42).

9   '*The Pall Mall Gazette*': Clarke, Bob. *From Grub Street to Fleet Street: an illustrated history of English newspapers to 1899* (Ashgate, 2004).

10   'The woman who was murdered': *Pall Mall Gazette*, 1 September 1888.

10   'A bonnet and parasol': MSL, Vol. 8, Chapter 7.

10   'A parasol to Sarah': MSL, Vol. 8, Chapter 8.

10 'I'll give you a bonnet': MSL, Vol. 3, Chapter 11.

10 'My fate to have sisters': MSL, Vol. 2, Chapter 3.

10 'Buying a bonnet': MSL, Vol. 2, Chapter 3.

11 'In Switzerland': MSL, Vol. 5, Chapter 15.

12 'Absorbed by her clothing': Inspector Helson, J Division, gave a description of the deceased's clothing. The back of the bodice of the dress, he
said, had absorbed a large quantity of blood. Report of Nichol's inquest,
Manchester Guardian, 4 September 1888.

13 'Similarity with the murders of the two other women': another newspaper
compared the killing to an earlier death, that of Lucy Clark. She had
been found with her throat cut in the premises above her Marylebone
dress shop in January 1888 (*The Times*, 28 January 1888). The press had
trouble with the conclusion that Clark's unsolved death was motiveless
slaughter by a 'homicidal maniac'. 'The revelations in connection with
the late Marylebone murder have, however, given the police a plausible
pretext for the theory . . . human beings . . . utterly callous to all feelings would deliberately slay their fellow men without the incentive of
gain, without the at least comprehensible pretext of enmity . . . Second
thoughts showed them that even homicidal maniacs must be caught.'
Evening News, London, 1 September 1888.

13 'Old Nichol gang': there is no contemporary record of the police's
suspicions. Former Navy intelligence officer turned spy writer, Donald
McCormick, was the first to link a gang called Old Nichol to the murder
in 1959. 'PC Haine [sic – Thain] cut this unproductive conversation short
by suggesting the murder was the work of the Old Nichol Gang, who
were known to blackmail prostitutes.' McCormick, Donald. *The Identity
of Jack the Ripper* (Jarrolds, 1959: p. 26). The espionage expert argued
a Russian anarchist, Dr Pedachenko, was the killer. In 1998, respected
author Melvin Harris revealed that McCormick had invented quotes
and bogus documents. Harris, Melvin. *The Maybrick Hoax: Donald
McCormick's Legacy, 1998 Dissertation Casebook: Jack The Ripper*.
This information was published on the web. See http://www.casebook.
org/dissertations/maybrick_diary/mb-mc.html.

13 'Something about Emma': Dew, Walter. *I Caught Crippen: Memoirs of
Ex-Chief Inspector Walter Dew CID* (Blackie, 1938).
'Her legs were open': Walter described in some detail his method of spreading
legs when having sex outdoors with streetwalkers: 'the uprighter'; 'she
was a shortish girl, and I stretched out both legs, and twisted my body,
to get to fuck her as she stood with her back against the wall.' MSL,
Vol. 6, Chapter 14. Ripper victims Annie Chapman and Catherine
Eddowes were similarly found outdoors, by a fence and wall respectively,
with legs splayed.

15 'W--- Office': MSL, Vol. 1, Chapter 10. It is possible young Walter's first
job was a messenger boy in the labyrinthine halls of the old War Office
then in St James, known as Horse Guards. The building housed the

administration for the British Army and had been extended during the Napoleonic Wars. After 1858, the War Office moved to the south side of Pall Mall, where out of 958 officials, 164 were employed as messengers. *History of the Old War Office* (Ministry of Defence, 2001).

15   'From a penknife': Walter used his boot to make a penknife into a more effective weapon for sexual voyeurism. 'With my penknife I pointed a piece of wood, applied it to the plug, and taking off my boot to lessen the noise, hit it hard with the heel, and at length out tumbled the plug.' MSL, Vol. 4, Chapter 16.

15   'Like most men': Folding pocket knives were called 'pen knives' after their popular use for sharpening goose-feather quills. British schoolchildren learned the skill and carried their own knives in schools until about 1850. It is most likely Walter, a diary-keeper from the age of twenty-five, would have begun his memoir with a feather and knife. The introduction of metal pen tips thirty years before 1888 erased the ubiquity of penknives. However, new marketing of double-bladed pocket knifes helped revive interest. Moore, Simon. *Penknives and Other Folding Knives* (Osprey, 1988).

16   'Had it been servants': MSL, Vol. 2, Chapter 12.
        'carried a gimlet': Walter bought his first gimlet at the age of about twenty-two to fix a shaving mirror to a Paris hotel room. MSL, Vol. 5, Chapter 2.

16   'Piercer': Walter used violent imagery to describe his penis. He spoke of 'impaling' ('Lifting her clothes I tried to impale her as she stood.' Vol. 2, Chapter 5) and to inflicting pain with his 'cunt rammer' ('A vigorous hard rammer of even six inches hurts many women', Vol. 10, Chapter 14).

16   'Home Office files says': MEPO 3/140.

16   Colonel Francis Hughes-Hallett (1838–1903), MP for Rochester, 1885–1889.

16   'Caught committing adultery': the intrigue was apparently discovered when Hughes-Hallett and twenty-two-year-old Miss Beatrice Eugenie Selwyn were staying in the house of Mr Henry Smith. Smith's account of the MP and the maiden in the upstairs bedroom was published in the *Pall Mall Gazette* of 27 September 1887: 'The only words which I uttered were these. They were strong words, no doubt, but I record the fact: "You damned blackguard, I have long suspected this: you shall leave this room and my house instantly."' Hughes-Hallet attempted to ride out the affair, until finally resigning his seat in March 1889. He then embarked on a protracted court battle to keep hold of some of his American wife's fortune (*New York Times*, 7 February 1893).

17   'Told the American press': the *Atlanta Constitution* of 7 October 1888 ran the headline 'A MANIA FOR BLOOD – COLONEL HUGHES-HALLETT ON THE WHITECHAPEL FIEND – The Murderer Evidently a Gentleman With High education'.

18   'Brought on a stricture': MSL, Vol. 2, Chapter 4.

22   'Shield such a monster': Dew, Walter. Ibid.

Chapter 2 – The Ripper's Lair

23 'I had a friend': MSL, Vol. 1, Chapter 8.

23 'Gun factory': Walter had reason to call the proof-house a 'factory'. In 1824, 100,000 guns a year were being fired and branded within its walls (*Newsletter of the Worshipful Company of Gunmakers*, Issue 18, Autumn 2007). Gun-proofing is a two-stage business. First the gun is fired with an extra dose of powder to make sure it doesn't blow up. Surviving guns are marked with a 'proof', a symbol hammered into the stock. Anvils, powder rooms and stamping machines gave the proof-house the noise, look and smell of a factory. The London Proof House marked its guns with four different stamps. Definitive Proof, the most common, showed the gun had passed; Nitro Proof showed the gun had been proofed with new, smokeless, 'nitro' gunpowder rather than black powder; Provisional, given to partially worked barrels; Reproof, for barrels proofed after modification; Choke Reproof, proofing of the removal interior tube of the shotgun alone. The Whitechapel proof marks were a crown, a lion and, most interestingly for Walter's later obsessions, an arm with a sword. See: http://www.gunmakers.org/proofhouse.html (last accessed on 19 August 2009).

'Matched this description': It is possible Walter's 'gun factory' was the Baker rifle factory at 24 Whitechapel Road. Ezekiel Baker made guns for the East India Company. In 1805, Baker set up a manufactory at Whitechapel to make rifles that would take on Napoleon in Europe. A warehouse was converted to fit barrels to stocks. Baker also designed bayonets on the site and had his own proof-house. He died in 1832. The firm was carried on under the name of E. Baker & Son from 1833 to 1853, a circumstance that differs from Walter's description of his friend Henry. A smaller concern near Liverpool Street, run by John Squire, made guns until 1886. Finally, two Johns of the famous Wednesbury gun-making clan, the Spittles, made gunlocks in Whitechapel between 1836 and 1861. Blackmore, Howard L. *Gunmakers of London Supplement 1350–1850* (Canada: Museum Restoration Service, 1999).

24 'James Purdey, the patriarch': details of the Purdey family and their involvement with the Whitechapel proofing house can be found at: http://www.purdey.com/history/history-of-purdey/.

24 'At one end . . . we heard at times': MSL, Vol. 1, Chapter 8.

41 'I put a pillow under her head': the stalking and half-murder of Mrs Smith is told in MSL, Vol. 1, Chapter 9.

41 'In about three weeks': MSL, Vol. 1, Chapter 9.

Chapter 3 – In the Mortuary

43 'Performed with anatomical knowledge': inquest of Nichols, quoted from the *Morning Advertiser*, 24 September 1888.

43 'An unmarked white handkerchief': 'PC Neil said Inspector Spratley came to the mortuary, and while taking a description of the deceased examined her clothes ... No money was found, but an unmarked white handkerchief was found in her pocket.' *Lloyd's Weekly*, 2 September 1888. The presence of the distinctive handkerchief was considered remarkable enough for the *Police Illustrated News* of 22 September 1888 to run an illustration of Annie Chapman's unusual possession.

44 'Make it two': MSL, Vol. 1, Chapter 9.

44 'I think now of the Exquisite delight': MSL, Vol. 1, Chapter 9.

45 'When with but . . . prig it?': MSL, Vol. 1, Chapter 9.

45 'A piece of comb': inquest of Nichols, reported in *Lloyd's Weekly*, 2 September 1888.

45 'Stole combs': MSL, Vol. 3, Chapter 12.

45 'The hair interested me': MSL Vol. 6, Chapter 9.

46 'There was a good five . . . went to bed.': MSL, Vol. 5, Chapter 12.

46 'J***s Street had looking-glasses': MSL, Vol. 4, Chapter 9.

47 'One day I wished': MSL, Vol. 10, Chapter 5.

47 'I stirred the fire': MSL, Vol. 5, Chapter 11.

47 'Glasses in profusion': MSL, Vol. 7, Chapter 7.

48 'We used to attitudinize': MSL, Vol. 8, Chapter 1.

48 'One muddy night in the Strand': MSL, Vol. 3, Chapter 2.

48 'Dress-lodger': social reformer James Greenwood also went eye to eye with a dress-lodger in 1869. 'They are bound hand and foot to the harpies who are their keepers. They are infinitely worse off than the female slaves on a nigger-plantation, . . . these slaves of the London pavement may boast of neither soul nor body, nor the gaudy skirts and laces and ribbons with which they are festooned. They belong utterly and entirely to the devil in human shape who owns the den that the wretched harlot learns to call her "home". You would never dream of the deplorable depth of her destitution, if you met her in her gay attire. Splendid from her tasselled boots to the full-blown and flowery hat or bonnet that crowns her guilty head, she is absolutely poorer than the meanest beggar that ever whined for a crust. These women are known as "dress-lodgers".' Greenwood, James. *The Seven Curses of London* (Fields, Osgood & Co, 1869: Chapter XVII).

50 'A woman came in': Walter encountered the young dress-lodger's keeper; 'the bawd, – she looked like a bilious Jewess'. Greenwood noted the role of the bawd as a minder who makes sure the dress-lodger always returns to the house. 'There's always a "watcher". Sometimes it's a woman – an old woman, who isn't fit for anything else . . . watches you always, walking behind you, or on the opposite side of the way.' Greenwood, James. Ibid.

56 'The owner of the house was transported': if Walter is correct, this dates the incident before 1867. The punishment of transportation – banishment

to the Australian prison colonies – was formally abolished in 1857, but continued until as late as 1867.

56 'The same man who was called Bill': if Walter is correct, the incident may have occurred in 1887. William McEllicott, known as Billy Mac, was indicted in the Old Bailey on 25 July 1887 for the manslaughter of James Driscoll after an altercation above the stairs of a Drury Lane boarding house. However, no evidence was offered on the manslaughter charge.

Chapter 4 – The Devil At Large

58 'Practised hand': *The Lancet*, 29 September 1888.

59 'Great anatomical knowledge': Dr Phillips would refine his opinion as the murders continued. After seeing Elizabeth Stride's injuries in October, Dr Phillips told her inquest: 'The more he examined the body the more he thought that the throat was cut by somebody who knew about throat-cutting.' *East London Advertiser*, 13 October 1888.

    'His godfather': MSL, Vol. 1, Chapter 2.

59 'Surgeon-major in the Army': Walter's godfather had surgical instruments, and Walter would inherit from him. In the early nineteenth century, all British army surgeons kept their own surgery kit. The set had dental instruments, amputation knives, scalpels and cylinder-bladed trephines. The surgeon had to buy these himself, but by the end of the Napoleonic Wars (1799–1815) the War Department bought them for the surgeon. Crumplin, M.K.H. The Myles Gibson military lecture: 'Surgery in the Napoleonic Wars'. This lecture was published in *The Journal of the Royal College of Surgeons of Edinburgh*, 47/3, 01/07/2002: pp. 566–78.

59 'Surgeon with a crack regiment': MSL, Vol. 4, Chapter 14.

59 'Had a suspicious fit': MSL, Vol. 2, Chapter 1.

60 'Bought medical books': MSL, Vol. 8, Chapter 8.

60 'I shouldn't hurt you': MSL, Vol. 7, Chapter 5.

61 'I sent her five pounds': MSL, Vol. 7, Chapter 5.

62 'Jews were attacked': 'Bodies of young roughs raised cries against the Jews and many of the disreputable and jabbering women sided with them. This state of things caused several stand-up fights, thus putting a further and serious strain on the police, many of whom began to express their fears of rioting.' *Lloyds Weekly*, 9 September 1888.

62 'Belonged to her son': *Daily Telegraph*, 13 September 1888.

63 'Pint of beer': *Daily Telegraph*, 11 September 1888.

63 'I haven't sufficient . . . don't let the bed': *Daily Telegraph*, 10 September 1888.

63 'Polished farthings': *The Star*, 10 September 1888.

63 'Placed there in order': *Daily Telegraph*, 14 September 1888,

64 'Two pills . . . Spitalfields': Joseph Chandler, Inspector of H Division, Metropolitan Police, found the pills in the yard after Chapman's body had been taken away. *Daily Telegraph*, 14 September 1888.

64 'Another lodger . . . kitchen floor': evidence of William Stevens at the Chapman inquest. *Daily Telegraph*, 20 September 1888.

64 'Desire for a youthful . . . gratify it': the rape of the virgin Emma takes up all of MSL, Vol. 7, Chapter 12.

69 'Drank shrub': shrub was a rum- or sometimes gin-based cocktail of water, sugar, lime or lemon juice with flavours such as honey. *Blackwoods* magazine of 1826 reported: 'Shrub is decidedly a pleasant drink, particularly in the morning. It is however, expensive.' Walter used it to seduce children: 'I have always found young girls will take shrub, it warms the stomach, rises to the brain, makes the cunt heat and tingle.' MSL, Vol. 7, Chapter 12.

70 'Common aperients': an aperient is a purgative or laxative.

Chapter 5 – Defloration Mania

77 'Defloration mania': German sex researcher Magnus Hirschfield would devote a chapter to the dark meaning of the Victorian pleasure. 'The so-called defloration mania is closely related to rape. The sadistic stimuli are similar to those that operate in assaults on children.' Hirschfeld, Magnus. *Sexual Anomalies: The Origins, Nature and Treatment of Sexual Disorders* (Emerson Books, 1948).

79 'Pain became an essential . . . of the house': Edholm, C. The Women's Temperance Publishing Association, 1893.

79 'Crispin Street': Ryan, Michael. *Prostitution in London, with a comparative view of that of Paris and New York* (London: H. Balliere, 1839: p. 109).

79 'Pornological clubs': Bloch, Ivan. *A History of English Sexual Morals* (London: Francis Aldor, 1936: p. 179).

79 'Every evening': Pearsall, Ronald. *The worm in the Bud: the world of Victorian sexuality* (Macmillan, 1969: p. 350).

79 'London Female Mission': Bartley, Paula. *Prostitution: prevention and reform in England 1860-1914* (Routledge, 2000: p. 35).

80 'Many girls . . . out of her': Ellis, Havelock. *Sex in Relation to Society* (F.A. Davis, 1910: p. 210).

80 'Maids, as you call them . . . young children': *Pall Mall Gazette*, 6 July 1885.

86 'Unutterable disgust': *Pall Mall Gazette*, 7 July 1885.

87 'Benjamin Tarnowsky': The Russian forensic psychiatrist and syphilis specialist Tarnowksy (born in 1838) was the author of *Anthropological, Legal and Medical Studies on Pederasty in Europe*, published in 1933. The translation of his 1898 work, *The Sexual Instinct and its Morbid Manifestations*, was published in Paris by Charles Carrington. Carrington was thought to be involved in the printing of *My Secret Life*.

87 'Mrs Travers': Petrie, Glen. *A Singular Iniquity: the campaigns of Josephine Butler* (Viking Press, 1971: p. 239).

87 'Vamped up virgins': *Pall Mall Gazette*, 7 July 1885.

88 'Charlotte Hayes': Bloch, Ivan and Forstern, William H. *Sexual life in England, Past and Present* (F. Aldor, 1938: p. 190).

88 'Normal female parts': Ibid., p. 189.

88 'I one night talked about virgins': MSL, Vol. 1, Chapter 14.

89 'Then although she knew every incident . . . friends home': MSL, Vol. 1, Chapter 14.

90 'French girl called Louise': Walter's rape of Louise is told in MSL, Vol. 2 Chapters 1 and 2.

98 'A funny episode': MSL, Vol. 2, Chapter 2.

99 'value to "psychology"': MSL, Vol. 1, Introduction.

100 'Wrote to Louise': MSL, Vol. 2, Chapter 3.

100 'My illness . . . served me right': MSL, Vol. 2, Chapter 3.

101 'I never heard of': MSL, Vol. 2, Chapter 3.

101 'Law then said': in 1875, the British Parliament passed the Offences Against the Person Act, raising the age of consent from twelve to thirteen after outrage over child sex in brothels.

101 'Dozen little ones': MSL, Vol. 6, Chapter 6.

101 'Virgin named Molly': the rape of the virgin Molly is detailed in MSL, Vol. 6, Chapter 7.

106 'Jemima Smith': MSL, Vol. 5, Chapter 16.

106 'Yet I met . . . I'm afraid': MSL, Vol. 5, Chapter 17.

107 'Jemmy laid down': MSL, Vol. 5, Chapter 17.

108 'Girls all under sixteen': MSL, Vol. 5, Chapter 17.

108 'All circumstances . . . anatomy matters': MSL, Vol. 10, Chapter 8.

111 'H was impecunious . . . was remarkable': MSL, Vol. 10, Chapter 8. Impecunious here means lacking money, penniless.

111 'I'll swear': MSL, Vol. 10, Chapter 8.

111 'I had had none of that sensuous': MSL, Vol. 2, Chapter 8.

112 "In bed, thinking" MSL Vol. 2 Chapter 8.

112 'Oh don't': women utter the phrase eighty-four times in Walter's life story, from the innocent (Servant Jenny's cries of 'for God's sake don't tickle" in MSL, Vol. 3, Chapter 18) to recounting the wartime gang rape of Gertrude ('Oh, don't anymore do it. Oh, you'll kill me' in MSL, Vol. 6, Chapter 16).

112 'Get into bed': MSL, Vol. 8, Chapter 7.

112 'Unconsciously she wanted': MSL, Vol. 8, Chapter 1. Walter assumed the identity of Mr F*z* r in his plan to get sixteen-year-old Harriet 'from the outer suburbs' drunk and then rape her.

112 'Spell of the prick': MSL, Vol. 8, Chapter 7.

112 'How I gloried': MSL, Vol. 8, Chapter 7.

113 'Mutual spasms':– MSL, Vol. 8, Chapter 7.

113 'Divine function': MSL, Vol. 8, Chapter 7.

113 'Whatever their struggles': MSL, Vol. 9, Chapter 4.

113 'Willing virgin': MSL, Vol. 9, Chapter 5.

113 'Women I think . . . did': MSL, Vol. 10, Chapter 4.

114 'Fourteen-year-old named Pol': MSL, Vol. 3, Chapter 4.

114 'A poor girl's ruin': MSL, Vol. 3, Chapter 18.

114 'Sixteen-year-old Carry': Carry is one of several girls Walter raped after luring into a horse-drawn cab hailed for the purpose. 'The cabman I am sure knew my game, for he grinned.' MSL, Vol. 8, Chapter 12. Walter penned a short essay, 'On the fornicating facilities of four wheel cabs . . . I have fucked in them, as they rumbled along with a discreet cabman, and the profit that it gets him, the profit of ambulating brothels.'

114 The 'Great Eastern', Walter's Brunelian child procuress, weighed twenty stone. 'She was quite six feet high, had chestnut coloured hair, lovely soft dark hazel eyes, chestnut coloured cunt thatch and armpits, was big, fleshy, almost heavy, from neck to ankle. Yet she was a grand woman, was beautifully formed, indeed a lovely voluptuous figure.' He called her 'the roly poly big cunt in the huge arse', MSL, Vol. 8, Chapter 13.

114 'Even got the mother': Walter's fixation was Betsy, 'fifteen and a half', the eldest of a carpenter's wife who lived downstairs from 'the twenty-stone whore', MSL, Vol. 8, Chapter 13.

114 'Pretext that he was a doctor': Walter had an interest in seeing inside of women, so went further. 'Miss Great Eastern had said I was a surgeon, so would I look at the child. I indulged in the sham.' MSL, Vol. 8, Chapter 13.

114 'After getting married': Walter never said who he married, writing only of an unnamed wife. However, his marriage came after a 'fairly regular' relationship with Mabel (MSL, Vol. 2, Chapter 15), an educated twenty-one-year-old from Plymouth who had been introduced to Walter by his cousin Fred's wife, Laura.

115 'East End groping': MSL, Vol. 2, Chapter 15.

115 'Girl whose mother just died': Walter had offered the landlady of Mary Davis 'money to get me a girl of about fourteen years of age, a virgin'. MSL, Vol. 2, Chapter 16.

115 'Virgin in the back of a cab': Walter kidnapped the girl by a roadside after desiring 'a little hairless quim'. 'It was lighter than usual and some man passing the main road shouted out "Leave that girl alone." I went further up the turning.' He hailed a passing cab, and continued the attack with the girl inside: '"Cabman, cabman, let me out," she yelled . . . The driver if he heard took no notice, but she got so vociferous that I stopped the cab. She got out, ran off, not waiting for her gift, and in a second was lost in the darkness. A little further on I stopped near a footbridge, paid the cabman liberally, and went off. I never saw the girl afterwards, for the scene of my amatory doings was not near my home.' MSL, Vol. 7, Chapter 11.

115 'Virginities of these poor': MSL, Vol. 7, Chapter 11.

115 'Desired a little one': MSL, Vol. 7, Chapter 11.

124 'British court in 1969': the trial at Leeds Assizes of Arthur Dobson,

thirty-one, bookseller and printer of Fagley Road, Bradford, for possessing obscene articles for publication for gain concerning volumes one and two of *My Secret Life* by Walter (The Guardian, 30 January 1969). The trial is described in some detail in Sutherland, John. *Offensive Literature: Decensorship in Britain 1960-1982* (Rowman & Littlefield, 1983: p. 93) and in Grove, Valerie. *A Voyage Round John Mortimer* (Viking, 2007: p. 223). The year Dobson was jailed for obscene articles in Leeds, a US court found *My Secret Life* was not obscene. On 30 October 1969, the Michigan Court of Appeals decided on an application by Billingsley, Schort and Bloss against their convictions of sale and possession for sale of obscene literature. The charge concerned three books, *Pleasures and Follies*, *Les Enfants Terribles*, and *My Secret Life*. The trial judge found that *My Secret Life* was not obscene and limited the jury's consideration to the other two.

124 'Narrative of some adventures': MSL, Vol. 6, Chapter 12.
125 'More manuscript must be destroyed': MSL, Vol. 9, Chapter 8.

Chapter 6 – The London Minotaur

128 'As in the labyrinth . . . to inflict on his kind': *Pall Mall Gazette*, 8 July 1885.
129 'The Minotaur is a man': Journals of Regy Brett, 15 July 1885. Quoted in Kaplan Morris B. *Sodom on the Thames* (Cornell University Press, 2005: p. 174).
129 'Learned erotomaniac . . . are his passion': Hart-Davis, Rupert. *The Letters of Oscar Wilde* (Harcourt, Brace & World, 1962: p. 630), quoted in Dowson, Ernest Christopher; Flower, Desmond; Maas, Henry. *The Letters of Ernest Dowson* (Fairleigh Dickinson University Press, 1968).
129 'An expert in flagellation': MSL, Vol. 11, Chapter 2. Walter, with his usual eye for bloodshed, observed her patrons 'all paid very handsomely for bleeding a fair pair of buttocks'.
129 'Being bandied about': the Minotaur was named as different politicians. A Canadian gossip columnist made reference to Sir Charles Dilke (*Daily Colonist*, 2 September 1889), Laura Ormiston Chant's Gospel Purity Association named Cavendish Bentinck, MP for Whitehaven (*Te Aroha News*, 26 September 1885). More alarmingly for Walter, in July 1885, W.T. Stead threatened to 'subpoena as witnesses all those alluded to in our enquiries . . . down to the minotaur of London' (*Pall Mall Gazette*, 11 July 1885). The previous day Cardinal Manning had accepted Stead's offer to see 'complete proof of all its revelations, including every name' (*Toronto Word*, 11 July 1885).
129 'The abbess': Walter used the term generally on two occasions, describing a Continental brothel keeper as 'Abbess of this open-thighed nunnery' (MSL, Vol. 6, Chapter 10). In a typical example of his jumbled chronology, Walter introduced readers to this specific London madam in

his final volume: 'The abbess, as I shall call her, we ascertained would procure us every pleasure' (MSL, Vol. 11, Chapter 2). Two volumes previously, this abbess was quoted as witness to an 'interesting controversy' that Walter insisted was 'astonishing' – an expression of wind from the vagina, which he called a 'cunt fart'.

130 'Flogging or birching': Terrot, Charles Hugh. *Traffic in Innocents: the Shocking Story of White Slavery in England* (Dutton, 1959: p. 54).

130 'Leopold II, King of Belgium': in the Armstrong trial of 1885, W.T. Stead said Mrs Jeffries 'admitted to one of my staff that she had taken at least one English girl to the King of the Belgians for lustful purposes' (*Brisbane Courier*, 21 November 1885). A servant of the brothel keeper went much further, testifying in a later trial of Mrs Jeffries that Leopold, Queen Victoria's cousin, had purchased as many as 100 underage English virgins a year, paying £800 a month for the supply. *The Truth about the Armstrong Case and the Salvation Army* (Salvation Army Book Stores, 1885).

130 'Inspector Minahan': the Inspector's frustration made it to Parliament, with MP Edward Sheil baiting the Home Secretary with Minahan's testimony in Jeffries' 1885 trial. 'That he had reported to his superintendent respecting the defendant's houses, but was laughed at, and told he had better be careful what he was saying. He was laughed at for refusing to accept gold as a bribe.' House of Commons debates, HC Deb, 16 April 1885, fol. 296, cc 1852–3.

130 'In 1880': Dyer's ally Josephine Butler spelt out the trade in a pamphlet of 1 May 1880. 'In certain of the infamous houses in Brussels there are immured little children, English girls of from ten to fourteen years of age, who have been stolen, kidnapped, betrayed, carried off . . . The presence of these children is secretly known only to the wealthy men who are able to pay large sums of money for the sacrifice of these innocents.' Butler, Josephine. *Personal Reminiscences of a Great Crusade* (Horace Marshall & Son 1910). The same year Dyer had produced a twopenny report, 'The European Slave Trade in English Girls – A Narrative of Facts', and distributed it to parliamentarians. He detailed girl-snatching by London-based kidnappers Jean Deroo and Jean Sallecartes. Dyer then described his mission to help English youngsters escape from Brussel's brothels and reported that Continental pimps ('slave-owners') had attacked 'the friends of outraged maidenhood'. Dyer's Committee issued two more extensive reports into the Belgian child sex industry, in 1881 and 1882. Dyer's remarkable reports were the template for Stead's Maiden Tribute articles.

131 'Patrons from exposure': *Pall Mall Gazette*, 8 July 1885.

131 'Rebecca Jarrett': Jarrett's life story is told in a handwritten account, written before her death in 1929 (*Rebecca Jarrett's Narrative* (c. 1928), Salvation Army Heritage Centre) and in the book *Rebecca Jarrett* by Josephine Butler (Morgan & Scott, 1886).

131 'Brothels in Manchester, Bristol and Marylebone': Armstrong case testimony, proceedings of the Central Criminal Court, Twelfth Session October 31, 1885 (Stevens and Sons, 1885) p. 989.

132 'Rescue Home in Hanbury Street': Opened on 22 May 1884. Immediately there was violence and murder threats against women out to stop Whitechapel's child sex trade. Mrs Elizabeth Cottrill, a baker's wife, converted to Salvationism in about 1875. She took in child prostitutes and was attacked outside the Hanbury Street shelter. 'Some of the men who were after the girls I'd got would wait for me, and get hold of my bonnet and drag it off; or they'd throw me into a passage; or kick me in the shins, and when a man is wearing butcher boots they can give a bad kick. My husband used to say, 'I shall have you killed one of these days . . . ' *The Deliverer*, May 1921, p 37. Quoted from Sandall, Robert, 'The History of The Salvation Army', Vol. III, 1955: pp. 14–18.

132 'Skeleton Army': Salvation Army bands faced mobs of up to 7,000 during a decade of street conflicts known as the Salvation Riots. As Booth's Methodist splinter group installed females as lead officers, the riots had the look of a bloody war on women. Reports of attacks can be seen in *The Times* – Shepton Mallet: 'seized their musical instruments', 5 April 1882: p. 8; Yeovil: 'females . . . brutally hustled', 4 October 1882: p. 12; 'female Salvationists savagely assaulted', 7 February 1883: p. 7; Bethnal Green: 'threw stones', 13 February 1883; Gravesend: 'blood ran copiously', 16 October 1883.

132 'Own banners and publications': Skeleton Army flags bore a skull and crossbones, varied by the addition of two coffins and the motto 'blood and thunder'. Others had a devil, monkeys or rats. A yellow banner with three Bs – beef, beer and 'bacca – was also used. The news sheet *The Skeleton* was published in Honiton in December 1882 (Salvation Army International Heritage Centre).

132 'Threats against Jarrett's life': Butler wrote to her second son and political confidante Stanley Butler of 'four brutal brothel keepers' out to 'kill Rebecca'. The murder mission against the whistle-blowing procuress is alluded to in Stead's editorial in the *Pall Mall Gazette* of 11 July 1885 as 'much more serious menaces of personal violence'. Letter to Stanley, London, Friday [date unknown], July 1885. Ref No. JB 1/1 /1885/07/00(II), Josephine Butler Memorial House Archive, University of Liverpool.

132 'The despised Negro': Butler, Josephine. *Personal Reminiscences of a Great Crusade* (Horace Marshall, 1911: p. 26).

133 'At Colchester': the murderous violence in Colchester forged a new political vision: that English prostitutes controlled by state laws were akin to chained slaves. Butler wrote: 'Our opponents may laugh at the formation of a new party (supporting prostitutes), just as their prototypes in America were filled with derision when a "nigger party" was

first organized in that country. This new party here is to the cause of insulted and downtrodden woman.'

133 'Mrs. Booth had been touched': her husband, William, started his movement's new crusade against London's child sex predators in Whitechapel seven years after giving up soup kitchens. 'The story begins in the Rescue Home in Hanbury Street, Whitechapel, where the Director, Mrs Bramwell Booth, newly the mother of a girl, and, therefore, exceptionally sensitive to stories of moral misfortune among young women, heard from young harlots, tales of . . . male debauchery which deeply distressed her.' Ervine, St John Greer. *God's soldier: General William Booth* (Macmillan, 1935).

134 'Fourth was Rebecca': Josephine Butler sent Jarrett to the *Pall Mall Gazette* office to meet the editor. Seven months later, recounting their first meeting to Stead himself at the Old Bailey trial, she said: 'I brought a letter from Mrs Butler who told me to answer all the questions you might put to me – to make a clean breast of it. I told you I had kept a house of evil repute, and had procured young girls of thirteen or fourteen . . . The girls, I told you, were brought to these houses, not knowing what they were, and drugged and violated . . . (bursts into tears)'. The Old Bailey, 30 October 1885. Quoted in Plowden, Alison. *The Case of Eliza Armstrong: A Child of 13 Bought for £5* (British Broadcasting Corporation, 1974).

134 'I do not know': Stead, Estelle W. *My Father: Personal & Spiritual Reminiscences* (W. Heineman, 1913: pp. 140–152).

134 'Among its members': Stead unveiled the members on the fourth day of his newspaper revelations under the headline 'The Truth about our Secret Commission', *Pall Mall Gazette*, 9 July 1885.

136 'Valuable introductions . . . investigations closed': Waugh, Benjamin and Stead, William T. *A Life for the People* (London: H. Vickers, 1885: Chapter III).

136 'Persuaded Rebecca Jarrett': the strategy of buying a girl did not come from Josephine Butler or the Salvation Army. The idea struck W.T. Stead at his first meeting with the procuress at his paper's office on 25 May 1885. Stead then kept the recovering alcoholic away from the Salvationists so he could turn her into his undercover agent. Jarrett described how Stead hatched the scheme at her Old Bailey trial on 29 October 1885: 'I went to Mr Stead's office in Northumberland Street . . . Mr Stead said that he would supply me with money to buy the child. I told him I must speak to Mrs Butler about it first. I was unwilling, but he insisted on it, as I had led a bad life, to atone for what I had done.' When Jarrett said she wanted to speak with Josephine Butler, Stead physically stopped her. 'Mr. Stead then said he would not let me go home, but would write down to Mrs Butler and tell her what he had asked me to do.' Plowden, Alison. *The Case of Eliza Armstrong: A Child of 13 Bought for £5* (British Broadcasting Corporation, 1974).

137 'Poor little thing': W.T. Stead, *Pall Mall Gazette*, 6 July 1885.

Chapter 7 – The Maiden Tribute of Modern Babylon

140 'Deliberately evoked ... the Minotaur': Stead's evocation of the Minotaur inspired artist George Frederick Watts (1817–1904) to paint an image of Stead's defiler captioned 'artist's representation of the greed and lust associated with modern civilisations'.

140 'For days and nights ... fruitless': W.T. Stead, *Pall Mall Gazette*, 6 July 1885.

140 'Mesdames X. and Z': W.T. Stead, *Pall Mall Gazette*, 7 July 1885.

141 'Stirred up Hell ... fine on him': W.T. Stead, *Pall Mall Gazette*, 8 July 1885.

141 'In the final part': headlined 'The Truth about our Secret Commission', *Pall Mall Gazette*, 9 July 1885.

143 'No such abrupt': *Pall Mall Gazette*, 8 July 1885.

143 'American journals reprinted': on 7 July 1885, the *Boston Daily Globe* ran five pages headlined 'Piccadilly Minotaur Horrible Disclosures of Vice in High London Society'.

143 '*The Times* mentioned': the letters page deplored the Maiden Tribute series as 'this new apocalypse of evil' harmful 'for women whose brains become heated by the horrors of which they read', *The Times*, 4 August 1885.

143 'Cavendish Bentinck': the second reading of the Criminal Law Amendment Bill began on 9 July, as Stead's fourth instalment of the Maiden Tribute series hit the news-stands. Tory MP Bentinck used multiple tactics to stifle the bill. On 30 July, he demanded parliament protect the 'male sex' from 'extortion by women'. Stead was publishing a pamphlet instructing young girls to use the new law to do just that. Bentinck worked behind the scenes to have Stead and other secret commissioners charged for the Eliza Armstrong purchase: the MP had a secret motive in watering down age of consent laws. Bentinck was named to the police as a client of the notorious underage brothel in Cleveland Street in 1889. Kaplan, Morris B. *Sodom on the Thames* (Cornell University Press, 2005: p. 173).

144 'The Bill': the anodyne Criminal Law Amendment Bill bore the racier subtitle 'An Act to make Further Provision for the Protection of Women and Girls, the Suppression of Brothels, and Other Purposes'.

144 'Saunterer in the Labyrinth': the London correspondent to the *New York Times*, Harold Frederic, is one of those named as the caddish correspondent, 'the Saunterer'. Hapke, Laura. *Girls Who Went Wrong: prostitutes in American fiction 1885–1917* (Popular Press, 1989: p. 71–73). Others have suggested Stead himself wrote the letters.

144 'Believed that Labouchere': *Te Aroha News*, 26 September 1885.

144 'Shame Shame Horror': Bristow, Edward J. *Vice and Vigilance: purity movements in Britain since 1700* (Macmillan, 1977: p. 113).

145 'Great ladies': Walkowitz, Judith R. *City of Dreadful Delight: narratives*

296   *David Monaghan & Nigel Cawthorne*

of sexual danger in late-Victorian London (University of Chicago Press, 1992: p. 104).

145 'That the people': Pearson, Michael. *The Age of Consent: Victorian prostitution and its enemies* (David and Charles, 1972).

146 'Pamphlet called Vigilance Committee': Stead's undated pamphlet was published between the passing of the Criminal Law Amendment Bill on 15 August and its supporters' conference of 22 August 1885.

148 'Came to the sitting room': MSL, Vol. 10, Chapter 12.

148 '*Lloyd's Weekly News* picked up': by 12 August, the paper reported 'Mrs Armstrong . . . is grieving over the sad fate which she has heard has befallen her unfortunate child'. Eliza Armstrong, meanwhile, was in Paris, happily sewing buttons under the care of her Salvation Army keeper, twenty-three-year-old Mrs Coomb. Eliza wrote 'I am a good girl. does all that Fanny tells me to[.] my coton dress is finished and I keeps it very nice and clean.' Plowden, Alison. *The Case of Eliza Armstrong: A Child of 13 Bought for £5* (British Broadcasting Corporation, 1974).

149 'Her Lost Child': what to do with Eliza Armstrong once they'd bought her split Stead's secret commissioners. In an undated letter apparently written at the start of August, Rebecca Jarrett wrote to Bramwell Booth's wife Catherine, urging her to return Eliza to her mother: 'Mrs Bramwell I cannot keep the child I did not buy her as a slave.'

149 'Appeared at Bow Street': *The Times*, 3 September 1885.

149 'Tried to overturn': Jarrett, Rebecca. *Narrative of Rebecca Jarrett's Life* (approx. 1928).

149 'an assassin squad': 'four brutal brothel keepers came down from London to kill Rebecca. I shut up the cottage! It was touching to see Rebecca's bible and hymns and writing all about showing her love . . . and she herself a fugitive for her life.' Letter to Stanley, London, Friday [date unknown], July 1885. Ref No JB 1/1 /1885/07/00(II) Josephine Butler Collection, University of Liverpool.

149 'Hunting the Hanbury Street prostitute': the Butler letters and subsequent documents detailing the plot to kill the whistle-blowing procuress from Whitechapel were ignored by police seeking a motive for the murders of Whitechapel prostitutes three years later. As the Metropolitan police had been pressured to convict Jarrett, Stead and the Salvation Army for the Maiden Tribute revelations, exploration of this alternative motive was compromised.

150 'The London public': MSL, Vol. 6, Chapter 6.

151 'Brothels in France': see 'The Traffic in White Slaves Not Confined to London', *Te Aroha News*, 26 September 1885.

151 'Taken over by William Alexander Coote': Ditmore, Melissa Hope. *Encyclopedia of Prostitution and Sex Work* (Greenwood Publishing Group, 2006).

151 'Butler split with the movement': Butler and the Salvation Army faction favoured a women-led movement accepting of prostitutes as fallen sisters,

only to find Coote a puritan keen on suppression of sex as immorality. The Booths accepted fornication and acted against exploitation. 'It was not the immorality that stung us so much, horrible as it was; it was the deliberate scheming and planning whereby mere children were bought and sold as irrevocably as in a slave-market.' Booth, William Bramwell. *Echoes and Memories* (Hodder and Stoughton, 1925: p. 123).

151 '200 brothels': Haggard, Robert F. 'Jack the Ripper as the Threat of Outcast London' in *Essays in History Vol. 33* (University of Virginia, 1993).

152 'Intensely stupid man': Shaw, George Bernard. *The Collected Works of Bernard Shaw* (W.H. Wise & Co., 1931: p. 31).

Chapter 8 – Blood Sports

153 'She attempted . . . her quieting me': MSL, Vol. 1, Chapter 1.

154 'Filthy creature': MSL Vol. 1, Chapter 1.

154 'Until he was sixteen': MSL, Vol. 1, Chapter 1. Walter said that until he was twenty-two his mother had 'implicit belief in my virtue' until she found he was keeping 'a French harlot'.

154 'Obsessed with blood': Walter described making twenty different women bleed in his book, referring to blood or bleeding eighty-one times. See Chapter 11 for an extensive examination of his blood fetish.

155 'The next thing . . . sensitive': MSL, Vol. 1, Chapter 1.

155 'One day Fred and I': MSL, Vol. 1, Chapter 1.

156 'Pushed me away': MSL, Vol. 1, Chapter 4.

156 'In the root-shed': MSL, Vol. 2, Chapter 8.

156 'Persuasion, kisses, promises': MSL, Vol. 2, Chapter 10.

158 'Gave a whole chapter': Walter's recital of the gang rape of Gertrude made plain his interest in the killing of women during sex. His pornographic description suggests imminent death intensifies orgasm: 'You're murdering my sister,' she cried . . . 'Oh, you'll kill me,' said she. Meanwhile a voluptuous sensation crept thro her cunt . . . He pushed her back and put his prick in her. 'Oh, you're killing me,' she cried, 'I wish I was dead.' 'You'll have a lot more of it before you die, love,' and he finished fucking. MSL, Vol. 6, Chapter 16.

158 'Rabbit with my prick': MSL, Vol. 2, Chapter 11.

158 'Hunting in Darlington': Darlington is one of three northern towns where Walter said he had relatives, the others being Sheffield and Bradford. For instance: 'On my way back from my uncle in the North I stopped at B***f**d'. See Bullough, p. 44.

158 'Deer-hunting': other than rabbits (and cunt), Walter did not say what he was hunting. However, tactics used indicate rabbits were side game to the main quarry of grouse, pheasant or, more likely, deer. Walter hunted in invited shooting parties, with quarry driven from woods by beaters (MSL, Vol. 2, Chapter 11). However, while grouse hunting begins on

12 August and ends on 10 December, Walter and Fred went shooting 'towards the end of November' (MSL, Vol. 2, Chapter 12) after the 1 November start of the season for hunting female deer. Elsewhere, Walter playfully called a friend an 'old buck' – the sports term for an adult male deer (MSL, Vol. 7, Chapter 9).

158 'Hunting manuals': 'the rule is for the huntsman to go in as soon as he can, or dare, and cut the deer's throat with his knife'. Walsh, John Henry. *Manual of British Rural Sports* (O. Routledoe & Co., 1856).

158 'Gralloching': the ritual was a staple of hunting literature: 'Ah, that plunging of your man's long knife into his chest, which is followed by such a stream of blood, is a very kind one indeed.' The deer, after having been thus bled, was opened and gralloched. 'Eli, look to the white-puddings, sir, and see till the fat in his brisket and inside, and just pass your hand over his haunches. Lord, what a deer!' Scrope, William. *The Art of Deer-stalking* (J. Murray, 1839: p. 68).

158 'Sweet meats were kept': deer-stalkers such as Walter were expected to know the placement of internal organs to extract treats for their dogs; 'sportsmen are accustomed to give their dogs portions of the deer's liver when he is gralloched'. Ibid., p. 319.

159 'On a hunting trip': MSL, Vol. 3, Chapter 20.

159 'Vulgar females revived': MSL, Vol. 6, Chapter 14.

159 'Well worn shooting suit': MSL, Vol. 6, Chapter 15.

159 'In France': MSL, Vol. 11, Chapter 10.

159 'Thro a cut I made': MSL, Vol. 8, Chapter 1.

159 'Sex and hunting': Walter's term 'cunt hunt' crystallises how he links blood sports and women. At first, Walter used general pursuit metaphors ('I went to stay with my mother to be nearer my game, and nightly I hunted the girl', Vol. 4, Chapter 15) but graduated to a self-description as a cunt hunter: Walter pondered his hunt as a near mystical idea; 'I wonder at the amatory course . . . when I am cunt hunting, as I term it' (Vol. 7, Chapter 2). But more often he saw it as brutal practicality; 'there was difficulty in getting at the girl unobserved, but nothing stood in my way when cunt-hunting'.

161 'Vicar of St. Jude's': Stead quoted Barnett from *The Times*, 19 September 1888.

Chapter 9 – The Murder of 'Long Liz' Stride

164 'During the three years': *Daily Telegraph*, 6 October 1888, p. 3.

164 'Accustomed to live entirely without control': *Daily News*, October 1888. The *Daily News* reporter won details of who would appear to be Elizabeth Stride; 'a very touching case of a woman who seemed sincerely desirous of amending'. But as the *Daily News* published before formal identification of Stride as the Berner Street victim, the paper ran the circuitous story of a bookish but uncontrollable prostitute. The reporter, however, made clear the missionary knew

Stride, saying 'the missionary made mention of another associate of the Berner-street victim'. At the very least, the story indicates that at the time of her death, Elizabeth was in reach of the Whitechapel missionaries who would turn a procuress into a whistle-blower.

165 'Been to a meeting': Bernardo said he met Stride at her lodgings four days before her murder. 'I put before them the scheme which had suggested itself to my mind, by which children at all events could be saved from the contamination of the common lodging houses and the streets, and so to some extent cut off the supply which feeds the vast ocean of misery in this great city' (*The Times*, 9 October 1888). Barnardo wanted a 'shelter of young children of the casual or tramp class, something between the casual wards of the workhouse and the lodging house itself – places where only young people under sixteen would be admitted' (*The City Press*, 13 October 1888). Barnardo already had a shelter that snatched children from the arms of pimps. The Rescue Home for Young Girls in Special Danger operated from a secret East End address. Batt, John Herridge. *Dr. Barnardo: The Foster-Father of 'Nobody's Children': A Record and Interpretation* (S.W. Partridge, 1905: p. 125).

165 'Identified her body': *East London Advertiser*, 13 October 1888.

165 'Was a political struggle': the feminists convinced the Salvation Army leaders to use madams as spearheads for a new crusade against child sex. 'May we not . . . send forth the saved . . . to save others. For example old keepers of bad houses transformed' (Butler to Florence Booth, 26 March 1885.) This was new. The rescue society run by Ellice Hopkins had middle-class churchgoers meet brothel girls. Rescued prostitutes had been made powerless and shut into workhouses, and industrial schools barely discernible from prisons.

165 'Best and John Gardner': *Evening News*, 1 October 1888.

165 'Carrying a parcel': *The Times* [London], 6 October 1888. A parcel would feature in Walter's street pick-ups: 'I met her in O**f*d St. walking fast, and carrying a large parcel. I stopped her, induced her into H*n*v*r S****e, where we kissed, then I felt her cunt and then with much difficulty got her to a neighbouring brothel.' 'Only to have a talk,' said I. MSL, Vol. 9, Chapter 4.

166 'Your prayers': *East London Advertiser*, 13 October 1888. Walter associated prayers with his joy in sadistic rape. Recalling his rape of the sixteen-year-old boarding-house servant Sally, he wrote: 'Her prayers (asking me) "not to do it any more" I shall recollect to the last day of my life . . . I never had more pleasure in baudiness than I had in hurting her.' MSL, Vol. 4, Chapter 10.

166 'Friend knew sailors . . . and gas.': MSL, Vol. 6, Chapter 13.

167 'Bunch of grapes', MSL, Vol. 2, Chapter 14.

168 'The knife employed': Walter described a sword, a razor and a knife in connection with murder or threats of murder. But he put the knife in female hands. '"If I get near him, I'll stick a knife in him, kill him," said

she savagely and with a look in her eyes, which made me think that she would if she got the chance.' Vol. 6, Chapter 5. Walter went so far as to claim his most virulent accomplice in procuring children, the prostitute Sarah F**z*r , had murdered – 'served out' – an old lover. 'Furiously she said, "If he were here, I would knife him. I'd fuck before his damned eyes. I'd murder him." Then after a short pause, "But I have served him out." "Who?" "Nobody you know," she said sullenly – and no more could I get out of her.' MSL, Vol. 7, Chapter 7.

168 'Disembowelling the slaughtered': *The Times*, 23 October 1878.
169 'Same shabby things': MSL, Vol. 6, Chapter 13.
169 'I recollect': MSL, Vol. 2, Chapter 12.
170 'Baudiest old rascal': MSL, Vol. 3, Chapter 17.
171 'About three days': MSL, Vol. 3, Chapter 17.
172 'Thus I talked . . . leave off': MSL, Vol. 3, Chapter 17.
173 'Had a moustache': Walter had been proud of his face hair since he was a lad. 'I was about sixteen years old, tall, with slight whiskers and moustache.' MSL, Vol. 1, Chapter 5. By the final volume of his memoirs, Walter was still discussing sex 'with moustache dripping', MSL, Vol. 11, Chapter 3.
173 'As Schwartz has': Sugden, Philip. *The Complete History of Jack the Ripper* (Carroll & Graf, 2002: p. 217).

Chapter 10 – The Young Walter

176 'One afternoon after . . . by myself': MSL, Vol. 1, Chapter 4.
178 Walter's first attacks on the maid, Charlotte, are told in MSL Vol. 1, Chapter 5.
180 'Mary the cook': Walter's seduction of Mary is told in MSL, Vol. 1, Chapter 6. Of all the women he had, this was the kitchen hand who had made him feel inferior 'in manner, conversation, and general behaviour, I always felt as if she were a superior person to me.'
182 'Kiss and grope': MSL, Vol. 1, Chapter 7.
182 'Saw blood': Walter was eighteen when he realised blood excited him. 'My spunk was slowly oozing out, streaked with blood . . . the sight took effect . . . I pulled her on to her back and got on to her.' MSL, Vol. 1, Chapter 7.
183 'Meanwhile there was either no servant': MSL, Vol. 1, Chapter 8.
183 'Feel for a silk': MSL, Vol. 1, Chapter 9.
183 'Long promised appointment': MSL, Vol. 1, Chapter 9.
184 'Fell on her knees': MSL, Vol. 1, Chapter 10.
184 'Never saw Charlotte again': MSL, Vol. 1, Chapter 10.
184 'Devilskin': MSL, Vol. 1, Chapter 10.
186 'Waterloo Road': the prostitutes of Waterloo Road were an international attraction. In 1840, French journalist Flora Tristan toured there 'accompanied by two friends armed with canes'. 'The girls were at the

windows or were seated before their doorways, laughing and joking with their pimps. Half-dressed, several bare to the waist, they were shocking and disgusting.' *Promenades in London* (London: W. Jeffs, 1840). Walter, then nineteen, toured at about the same time: 'Each woman had generally but one room, but two or three used to sit together in the front room in their chemises . . . one lolled out of the window, showing her breasts, and if you gave such a one a shilling, she would stoop so that you could see right down past her belly to her knees, and have a glimpse of her cunt-fringe. Sometimes one would pull up her garter, or another sit down and piddle, or pretend to do so, or have recourse to other exciting devices when men peeped in.' MSL, Vol. 1, Chapter 11.

186 'Offered a shilling': MSL, Vol. 1, Chapter 11.

186 'Anal sex': the prostitute who lured Walter into sodomy at Waterloo Road left him a friction of shame and fascination that would spark into violence years later. 'I pulled it out with an indescribable horror of myself . . . I scarcely slept that night for horror of myself, never went up the street again for years, and never passed its end without shuddering, have no recollection of having had pleasure, or of any sensation whatever; all was dread to me. And so ended that debauch; one I was deliberately led into by that woman.' MSL, Vol. 1, Chapter 11.

186 'Sarah and her sister Susan' MSL, Vol. 1, Chapter 12.

186 'A pretty fortune': MSL, Vol. 1, Chapter 12.

186 'Waterloo Place': Walter's new pick-up place was a universe away from Waterloo Road. The latter is on the south bank of the Thames, stretching from a grubby milestone at St George's Circus, Camberwell, to the riverside. Waterloo Place off Pall Mall was a vast open square dominated by the white marble colonnade of the Opera House on the north side of the river.

186 'Camille': Walter's choice of name for his first French prostitute would lend him an air of literary elegance to the reader of 1888. In 1848, Alexandre Dumas the Younger's novel, *The Lady of the Camelias*, about Camille, a courtesan with a golden heart, was a bestseller. *Camille*, as it was known, went on to be a hit play and an opera, sung by Adelina Patti in London in 1878.

187 'Six altogether . . . this high': MSL, Vol. 1, Chapter 13.

187 'Girl nor her manner': MSL, Vol. 2, Chapter 6.

187 'Curtsy to me': MSL, Vol. 2, Chapter 5.

188 'Twelve years of age': MSL, Vol. 2, Chapter 8.

188 'Virgin offering': MSL, Vol. 2, Chapter 10.

188 'Vauxhall Pleasure Gardens': MSL, Vol. 2, Chapter 9. The glory of Vauxhall's Pleasure Gardens was long faded when Walter visited. It shut for good in 1859. The seediness of the summer dress show was mocked in verse: 'Know ye the scene where the clerks and the tailors / Are deck'd out in costume both dirty and fine / Where till-robbing shop-boys, as soldiers and sailors / Now stoop down to beer-now ascend up

to wine?' Forrester, Alfred Henry. *The Vauxhall Papers* (John Andrews, 1841).

188 'Females fell to me': MSL, Vol. 2, Chapter 11. Walter listed his winning ways as a rural attack rapist: 'suddenness and impetuosity with which I made at times my advances, and the boldness with which I proceeded to baudy extremities . . . baudy, rapid assaults, lustful cunning and an innate power of stirring up voluptuous sensations in women when once I spoke, got me them more than anything else. When in the country, I was thinking of nothing else, and had nothing else to do but to hunt down cunts, and feed myself up for fucking them. When in London the game was different'.

189 'Modest as a whore': MSL, Vol. 2, Chapter 11.

189 'German Jewess': MSL, Vol. 8, Chapter 11.

189 'In the Argyle Rooms': MSL, Vol. 9, Chapter 7.

Chapter 11 – *The Huntsman*

191 'Terrace house': Walter described it as in ' the very quarter of London where I first lived after I had run thro my first fortune'. MSL, Vol. 5, Chapter 13.

191 'Black stockings': MSL, Vol. 2, Chapter 12. Walter's impotent horrors at a glimpse of dark tights would dog him for decades. 'You've got black stockings,' said I, noticing them for the first time, as I once did with Mabel years ago. MSL, Vol. 4, Chapter 19.

192 'Ugly and middle-aged . . . her': MSL, Vol. 1, Chapter 7.

192 'Amazed and wondered': MSL, Vol. 2, Chapter 13.

192 'Another fellow's doodle': MSL, Vol. 2, Chapter 13. Later in life, Walter's violence erupted as he wrestled with his latent homosexuality. He had an urge to kick a man to death after anal sex and raped his wife after fondling a sailor's genitals in a 'bloody spree'.

192 'Erotic engravings': MSL, Vol. 2, Chapter 13. Walter learned a lesson about the shock power of public display from Fred. The cousins argued over how best to excite the schoolgirls with pornographic prints. Walter wanted to post them to one girl. Fred convinced him: 'better be seen by several, they would tell each other, and thus all see them.' Fred laid the prints of naked bodies 'in a long building, half-shed half-summerhouse'. As Walter peeped the girls reacted. Walter revelled in the result: 'dare say their cunts are as hot as fire'. Years later, W.T. Stead would observe the Whitechapel deaths as 'murder as advertisement', a 'psychological moment . . . printed in letters of gore'. *Pall Mall Gazette*, 19 September 1888.

192 'Letter from a lawyer': MSL, Vol. 2, Chapter 14.

194 'Before this . . . of England': MSL, Vol. 2, Chapter 14.

194 'I had fits': MSL, Vol. 2, Chapter 14.

195 'Hateful in day': MSL, Vol. 2, Chapter 16.

195 'Mary Davis'. Walter told of his relationship with Mary Davis in MSL, Vol. 2, Chapter 16. He would stand 'in the shadow of the carts "to listen out for prostitutes having street sex", then "rush into Mary Davis' or Kate's to get a relief for my excited ballocks."' The Whitechapel murders would claim both a Mary Davis (Mary Jane Kelly's married name) and a Kate, Catherine 'Kate' Eddowes, who offered sexual services within yards of each other.

196 'Seven surrounding streets': Walter gives contradictory clues to the location of Mary Davis' one-room bordello. It is quite likely, but not certainly, in Whitechapel. Walter spoke of 'streets about seven in number' around Mary's place, an apparent hint to Seven Dials, the notorious slum of seven radiating alleys below Covent Garden in West London. However, Walter began in an area of gay women 'I had known in my early youth'. This indicates the East End and the 'gun factory' at Commercial Road, Whitechapel, where he had watched streetwalkers copulating above a street grating. He then said he met Mary when he 'found out other poor quarters . . . a spot where women of a somewhat better class lived in its centre, and on its outskirts very poor harlots' – a puzzling description that could apply to areas of East or West London.

196 'Cry of pain': MSL, Vol. 2, Chapter 18.

196 'Small eight-roomed house': MSL, Vol. 2, Chapter 19.

196 'Worked at my occupation': MSL, Vol. 2, Chapter 19.

197 'Kind, sympathetic association': MSL, Vol. 3, Chapter 1.

197 'Indiscriminate cheap whoring': MSL, Vol. 3, Chapter 1.

197 'Neighbours had two daughters': Walter's fixation with the girls next door is insightful to his public and psychosexual fixation. After being drawn to acts that disgusted him, Walter told of how he found healing in violence against women. He reflected that the neighbours' girls 'used to say (I am told), that I was a strange man, for I always stared at them as if I had never seen a woman before.' Walter was stalking the sisters to the lavatory wracked with symptoms – 'randy almost to pain' – of a fantasy of seeing women's insides extruding out. To live his whim he negotiated a cesspit, maintaining silence by holding open his own 'arsehole to lessen the noise of my trumpet'. He was fixed on seeing what revolted him: the neighbour's girls shitting 'their wax as it fell to the bottom . . . the paper with which they wiped their bums, and could hear them fart.' Walter masturbated but his climax brought a crisis – 'sorrow always came over me as I saw (my semen) spilling it on the privy-floor'. Walter ended the chapter 'cunt-hunting' on the Strand, abusing a prostitute by flinging his sperm, swapping the sorrow of the privy floor for gratified rage of seeing a defiled woman's face. MSL, Vol. 3, Chapter 1.

198 'You cheating whore': MSL, Vol. 3, Chapter 1.

198 'Scoured the area': Walter described a stalking pattern in the Strand so extreme a prostitute had to 'beg him' not to follow her. He was unable to buy sex as he was in debt, so he entered a trawling phase. Violence to

women in his memoir of the Strand pursuits indicates he may have been tailing women to rape. First, Walter trawled: 'Would walk backwards and forwards . . . for hours, looking at the women, thinking which I should like, and whether I could afford one. Sometimes I would follow the same woman, stop when she stopped if a man spoke to her, cross over, and wait till she moved off by herself. This pleased me much.' Then he would strike: 'If intending to have a poke I waited for a girl known by sight.'

198 'Open my piss-pipe': MSL, Vol. 3, Chapter 1.

198 'Brighton Bessie': the plump twenty-one-year-old brothel worker was one of the more complex of Walter's paramours. She succumbed to drink after she fell in love with Walter, keeping with him even though she was disgusted by his paedophilia. 'All such young bitches should be sent to prison, and the men who had them ought to be punished', she said when he told her of his sex with the prepubescent Kitty (MSL, Vol. 3, Chapter 6). There is some indication his decade-long relationship with Bessie continued into 1888, when he was reviewing the printed volumes of his memoirs. MSL, Vol. 3, Chapter 2.

198 'How the cat jumped': MSL, Vol. 6, Chapter 15.

199 'Two young girls': Walter's rape of the child, Pol, with her friend Kitty was told in MSL, Vol. 3, Chapter 3.

201 'I saw . . . plugged daily in handy': this dates Walter's rape of Pol to prior to 1875, when Parliament passed the Offences Against the Person Act 1875, making sexual relations with a girl between the ages of twelve and thirteen a crime punishable by two years' imprisonment. The law change had been brought on by Josephine Butler's campaign against child prostitutes in English and Continental brothels. Butler's success was the first improvement in laws protecting girls from men in 600 years, since the Statute of Westminster in 1275 set the age forbidding 'ravishing of maidens' at twelve years. Temkin, Jennifer. *Rape and the Legal Process* (Oxford University Press, 2002: p. 139).

202 'The greatest fun': MSL, Vol. 3, Chapter 8.

202 'Two artist friends': MSL, Vol. 3, Chapter 12.

202 'Interlude with Sarah Mavis': Walter began his affair in MSL, Vol. 3, Chapter 12, ending with his 'wonder' of a corpse found floating in the Thames, MSL, Vol. 4, Chapter 1.

205 'She sank back': MSL, Vol. 3, Chapter 16.

206 'Death had done its work' MSL, Vol. 6, Chapter 9.

206 'Long voyage across the sea': MSL, Vol. 6, Chapter 11.

206 'Winifred terminated': MSL, Vol. 7, Chapter 6.

207 'Why with this feeling': MSL, Vol. 7, Chapter 6.

207 'A man to bugger': MSL, Vol. 8, Chapter 3.

207 'My brain whirled': Walter used the phrase 'brain whirl' to describe points of transgression throughout his life, particularly associated with anal sex. 'I discharged a week's reserve up her rectum. My brain whirled';

'my brain whirled with strange desire, fear, dislike, yet with intention.' Walter's murder urge after buggering the man had its roots in his first 'brain whirl' during the buggery of a Waterloo Road prostitute when he was nineteen (see MSL, Vol. 1, Chapter 11).

208 'The idea of catching': MSL, Vol. 4, Chapter 3.

209 'With a glove': MSL, Vol. 8, Chapter 10.

209 'Two vaginas': MSL, Vol. 11, Chapter 2.

209 'Hooks and ropes': MSL, Vol. 8, Chapter 3.

209 'Piercer': MSL, Vol. 3, Chapter 4.

209 'Drink her piss': MSL, Vol. 10, Chapter 10.

210 'Hurt her': MSL, Vol. 2, Chapter 9.

'Patches of blood': MSL, Vol. 2, Chapter 2.

'Blood on my handkerchief': MSL, Vol. 5, Chapter 16.

'Made me bleed': MSL, Vol. 9 Chapter 4.

'Smeared with blood': MSL, Vol. 8, Chapter 7.

'Blood on my finger': MSL, Vol. 4 Chapter 8.

'Red stream followed,: MSL, Vol. 3, Chapter 6.

'Violent jerk': MSL, Vol. 4, Chapter 15.

'Satisfaction of finding': MSL, Vol. 8, Chapter 13.

'Mass of blood': MSL, Vol. 7, Chapter 12.

'Pouring down blood': MSL, Vol. 1, Chapter 6.

'The jagging seemed': MSL, Vol. 4, Chapter 9.

'Shemmy bloody': a shemmy is a long shirt. MSL, Vol. 3, Chapter 4.

'Bloody bitch': MSL, Vol. 3, Chapter 2.

'She'll bleed': MSL, Vol. 11, Chapter 1.

210 'The link between blood fetish, sex and murder': The link had been noted by the German researcher, Richard von Krafft-Ebing, when he described the fantasies that drove the killer, 'Case 25 Mr X': 'Imagining representations of blood and scenes of blood . . . Without the assistance of this idea, no erection was possible. Death followed imagining 'Injury to Women' (Stabbing, Flagellation etc.) Following lust-murder and violation of corpses, come cases closely allied to the former, in which injury of the victim of lust and sight of the victim's blood are a delight and pleasure.' Krafft-Ebing Dr R. von. *Pyschopathia Sexualis* (Stuttgart, Ferdinand Enke 1886: p. 72).

'Oh joy, that blood': Walter's joy might today be diagnosed as haematolagnia, the sexual attraction to blood. The fetish has figured in notorious crimes. Candice A. Skrapec's studies of Peter Kurten's blood fetish were published in 'Defining Serial Murder: A call for a return to the original Lustmörd', *Journal of Police and Criminal Psychology*, 16/2 (June 2001). Jeffrey Dahmer's crimes and related blood fetish are detailed in Purcell, Catherine E. and Arrigo, Bruce A. *The psychology of Lust Murder: paraphilia, sexual killing, and serial homicide* (Academic Press, 2006: pp. 77, 82, 109).

212 'Around sixty-seven': Bullough, Vern L. 'Who Wrote My Secret Life?'

(*Sexuality & Culture*, 4/1, March 2000: pp.46–47). Bullough used the following references made in MSL to date Walter's age: railway (London to Brighton), 1841; cholera epidemic in London, 1849; opening of the Argyle Rooms, 1850; railway (Paris to Avignon), 1851; Great Exhibition of London, 1851; crinolines first appear, 1857, Crystal Palace opening, 1873–1874; Battle of Solferino, 1859; the Great Eastern Steamboat, 1859; first railway sleeping cars, 1873–1874.

Chapter 12 – The Murder of Catherine Eddowes

213 'I think I know him': 'An Extraordinary Incident: A reporter gleaned some curious information from the Casual Ward Superintendent of Mile End, regarding Kate Eddowes, the Mitre-Square victim. She was formerly well known in the casual wards – part of a workhouse for the accommodation of the poor – there, but had disappeared for a considerable time until the Friday preceding her murder. Asking the woman where she had been in the interval, the superintendent was met with the reply, that she had been in the country "hopping". "But," added the woman, "I have come back to earn the reward offered for the apprehension of the Whitechapel murderer. I think I know him." "Mind he doesn't murder you too," replied the superintendent jocularly. "Oh, no fear of that," was the remark made by Kate Eddowes as she left. Within four-and-twenty hours afterward she was a mutilated corpse.' *East London Observer*, 13 October 1888.

213 '*East London Observer*': the same article aired more suspects. Jenny, a prostitute, fingered a blackmailing foreigner; Dodge, a seaman, named a Malay. Most interesting was a professional informant: 'a well-known medical man in east London has communicated information regarding a former assistant of his, who, he is equally convinced, is the man needed. He spent all his money amongst loose women in Whitechapel, and eventually contracted a disease, which utterly ruined his prospects and sent him mad. Ever since that time he has cherished the most intense hatred of these women, and has repeatedly declared his intention of revenging himself upon them.' Walter fits the bill with lost money, Whitechapel women, sex disease and hatred ('Ten years ago, I would have fucked each of them twice. I am paying penalty today . . . how unfit I feel, (I) almost hate cunt.' MSL, Vol. 9, Chapter 12). Moreover, Walter's old school chum was an assistant surgeon who told him the hymen of poor women could be seen by an 'assistant' in a staged examination. So Walter, already a practised medical imposter, played assistant in an internal examination on a private patient. 'I asked him to explain (a virginity) to me on a woman, and he gave me a full lecture. It was an odd sight to see him explaining the situation of a virginity, I holding a candle to see better. One of the girls roared with laughter, the others fancied they had some ailments . . . We did not fuck either of the women.' MSL, Vol. 2, Chapter 1.

214 'Shan't fall into his hands': the quote comes from an interview that John Kelly, Eddowes' boyfriend of seven years, gave to *The Star* newspaper on the morning of 3 October 1888, at Cooney's lodging house at 55 Flower & Dean. Kelly broke down in tears during the dialogue, which ended when police collected him to locate Catherine's two daughters.

216 'Borrowed £50': MSL, Vol. 1, Chapter 12.

216 'Jewesses regularly procured': Madame S***k*n*us, a German Jewess and dressmaker, ran an establishment near Leicester Square that supplied Walter with teenage sisters, Nellie and Sophie. MSL, Vol. 8, Chapter 11.

217 'The perpetrator of the act': Dr. Brown's post-mortem on Catherine Eddowes, from a handwritten copy made by Coroner Langham at the Corporation of London Records. Quoted from *Jack the Ripper A-Z* by Paul Begg, Martin Fido and Keith Skinner (Headline, 1996).

217 'Had some knowledge': *The Star*, 1 October 1888.

217 'Not altogether ignorant': Ibid.

217 'A hunter, a butcher, a slaughterman': Begg, Paul. *Jack the Ripper: The Uncensored Facts* (London, 1988: p. 124).

217 'Cigarette case': 'the following articles were in the pockets of her dress: a short clay pipe and an old cigarette case; a matchbox, an old pocket handkerchief, a knife which bore no traces of blood, and a small packet of tea and sugar.' *The Star*, 1 October 1888.

217 'Clay pipes': Catherine Eddowes' two clay pipes were an unusual possession among English prostitutes. Walter describes only one experience with a pipe smoker in a Continental brothel: a Muslim Armenian 'dark-eyed lady smoking a *chibouque*, with something like lemonade in a glass beside her'. MSL, Vol. 7, Chapter 5.

217 'A cigar smoker': Walter makes more than a dozen references to his cigar habit, even noting his cigar supplier: a shop run by two women 'with a big sofa in a back parlour, one keeping shop whilst the other fucked'. MSL, Vol. 2, Chapter 3.

219 'Committee had lent its support': Six months before the Kelly murder, Douglas Norman of the Central Vigilance Committee prosecuted prostitute and madam team, Louisa Pears, 27, and Bertha Christopherson, 31, in Thames Court. The charge was taking underage girl, Dorethea Dahloff, into the Pennington Street brothel in Stepney to work as a prostitute (*The Times*, 13 April 1888). Local vigilance committees would pass cases of underage sex to the Central Vigilance Committee for prosecution, in a system set up by W.T. Stead to enforce the new age of consent law. A Stepney vigilance committee – most likely Lusk's or its predecessor – would have informed on Bertha's underage brothel in Pennington Street. It is of interest that both Stead's vigilance men and Walter targeted a Bertha in the East End. Walter's Bertha was a fruiteress and he had began an affair with her when she was eighteen. Uncharacteristically, Walter burned the final diary entries about Bertha as a 'regretful' situation arose that was still affecting him in 1888. Walter

wrote: 'Here I break off purposely. I have given her a name not even pho-netically resembling her own, and have avoided giving such description of (Bertha) as would lead to identification. For the same reason I burn the rest of my narrative relating to her. The liaison so began, was fruitful in events that both regret, and the consequences of which affect me still. She is still living.'(MSL, Vol. 7, Chapter 4). Walter took the trouble to tell this East End woman was not among the dead after unnamed 'regretful events'. There is no certainty the persecution of Bertha's brothel by Lusk's vigilantes sparked Walter's crisis and an Autumn of Terror in 1888. What is certain is that W.T. Stead had instructed his vigilance com-mittees to school prostitutes in using the 1885 age of consent laws to blackmail paedophiles. Walter told us the prostitute Mary Davis – Mary Kelly's married name – refused to procure underage girls for him (MSL, Vol. 2, Chapter 16). Mary Jane Kelly was linked to Bertha's Pennington Street brothel. She worked there, or at a brothel in the same street. Kelly's partner, Joseph Barnett, said when she had returned from France, Kelly went to the Ratcliffe Highway 'to Pennington-street, a bad house, where she stayed' (*Daily Telegraph*, 13 November 1888).

219 'Shelter for "outcast females"': 'A shelter for outcast females will be opened in a few days at Harlow House, 34 Mile-end-road. Such poor creatures who are without home, food, friends, or money will be given a warm shelter, with a supper of a pint of coffee and bread . . . if a little assistance is given us we will soon erect a large iron or other building on the site, which is close to the scene of one of the late brutal murders . . . Members of the Vigilance Committee have offered their help, as they have found in the courts, alleys, passages, carts, vans, &c., countless poor creatures crouching away and in abject fear.' R.H. Winter, J.L. Dale, Hon. Secs. Office, 94, Mile-end-road, E. (*Morning Advertiser*, 13 October 1888.)

221 'Spirits of wine': *Morning Advertiser*, 19 October 1888.

221 'Used to wash pubic lice': 'For lice on the pubes . . . the nits can be dislodged by washing the hairs with spirits of wine' Ringer, Sydney *A Handbook of Therapeutics* (W. Wood and Co. 1888). We know Walter used liquid cure for pubic lice from MSL, Vol. 4, Chapter 19 'crabs . . . defied anything but chemical solutions.'

221 'Get money when': MSL, Vol. 8, Chapter 6.

221 'Eddowes was buried': *St James Gazette* of 8 October 1888 reported 'Thousands of people lined the streets' of the procession to Ilford Cemetary, including 'women whose attire was far from appropriate to the occasion.'

221 'A Medical Man': *Evening News*, 15 October 1888.

221 'By von Krafft-Ebing': Professor Richard von Krafft-Ebing reported on the 'Girl-Stabber of Bozen' as Case 26 in the 1894 translation of *Psychopathia Sexualis* (Rebman Company, New York, 1894), alongside such cases of sexual sadism as 'The Girl-Cutter of Augsburg'. However,

Krafft-Ebings views on the 'ghastly' connection of mutilation murder to virgin taking was not published in English until much later editions of *Psychopathia Sexualis*, such as that by Thomas, New York, in 1959 (reprinted as *Aberrations of Sexual Life*) p. 214.

222 'Revolutionized thinking about sex killings': Correspondence from ex-Chief Inspector John Littlechild in 1913 shows police who had hunted the Ripper came to accept Krafft-Ebing's analysis of sex killers. Littlechild thought the suspect Tumbelty 'although a "Sycopathia Sexualis" subject, he was not known as a Sadist (which the murderer unquestionably was)'. Begg, Paul. *Jack the Ripper: The Definitive History* (Longman, London, 2002: p. 345)

222 'I wanted to deflower her': MSL, Vol. 10, Chapter 4.

222 'Why no spend': At the inquest of Martha Tabram, Dr Timothy Robert Keeling 'stated positively that there were no signs of there having been recent connexion' (*East London Advertiser*, 11 August 1888). Dr Frederick Gordon Brown reported 'no indications of connexion' in his autopsy report on the body of Catherine Eddowes. Evans, Stewart P. and Skinner, Keith. *The Ultimate Jack the Ripper Companion* (Basic Books, London, 2001: p. 231)

Chapter 13 – The Murder of Mary Jane Kelly

224 'Could only be identified': the mutilations on Mary Jane Kelly were so extreme Dr Bond, police surgeon for A Division, Westminster, contributed a paper on them as a tough case of determining the sex of a corpse. 'In the particular illustrative instance, the woman was murdered in a bedroom. The body was naked when found. The eyebrows, eyelids, ears, nose, lips and chin had been cut off, and the face gashed by numerous knife-cuts. The breasts had been cut off, and the whole abdominal parietes, together with the external organs of generation, had been removed. The skin and much of the muscular tissue, not, however, exposing the bone, had been slashed away from the anterior aspect of the thighs as far as the knees. The abdominal viscera and pelvic viscera, including bladder, vagina, and uterus with appendages, had been torn from their cavities and in fact there was no sign of sex except the long hair upon the head, and, as is well known, that alone is not positive sign, inasmuch as in some nations the hair is worn long by men. The fact the whole bladder had been removed did away with the help that might have been afforded by the presence of the prostate gland. In this case, to be sure, all the organs except the heart were found scattered around the room, and showed the sex without doubt. But if all the organs and parts had been taken away or the body exposed to the effects of decomposition, a careful preparation of the skeleton would have been imperative to decide that the body was that of a woman. It might further be stated that in this case, in consequence of the hacking of the features, the presence or absence of

a beard could not be stated, and if the hair had been designedly cut off there would have been absolutely no sign by which sex could have been determined. The hair on the pubes had been removed in this case, and the difference in the growth of the pubic hair tapering up towards the umbilicus in the male, and simply surrounding the organs of generation in the female, could not be availed as an indication of sex.' Hamilton, Allan McLane and Godkin, Lawrence. *A System of Legal Medicine Vol. 1* (E.B. Treat, New York, 1894: pp. 62–3).

224 'Anally raped': the rumour of Kelly's defilement appears to have come from correspondence between editor W.T. Stead and journalist (and Ripper suspect) Roslyn D'Onston Stephenson. Stead published Stephenson's fanciful theory on the occult origins of the murders in the *Pall Mall Gazette* of 1 December 1888 under his pseudonym, 'One Who Thinks He Knows'. Theorising the Whitechapel women were sodomised, whether true or not, would propel Stephenson's new theory of a devilish hand. The idea that satanists were sodomisers had been around for centuries (see Naudé Gabriel and Davies John, *The History of Magick* (J. Streater, 1657: p. 145)). Latterly, the missing autopsy notes of Dr Bond (MEPO 3/3153, ff. 10–18) have fuelled speculation that more odious details of the Kelly murder were suppressed. However, Dr Bond failed to mention sodomy in his contribution to Hamilton's *A System of Legal Medicine* (see previous endnote). The forensic textbook, which describes the use of sticks to widen the orifice of a child for rape, is unlikely to have shied away from such detail.

224 'More light to write by': Walter wrote details of his rape and sadistic abuse of the drugged and kidnapped girl Rosa W. by his side in MSL, Vol. 6, Chapter 5.

224 'Season in the Highlands': *The Times*, 23 October 1878: p. 4. Walter was very keen on Scottish sports. He had the urge to shoot while in France and travelled to Glasgow to hunt. 'I came back by way of Paris, mainly to see if a lady whom I had loved had gone away, and then straight to London. Then with my gun I went to Scotland for some shooting. There my lust for the common, coarse, vulgar females revived.' MSL, Vol. 6, Chapter 14.

224 'Parts of the body on nails': Chief Inspector Henry Moore told Philadelphia journalist R. Harding Davis the details on or about 3 September 1889 during a walk around the Ripper murder sites. Harding's story was syndicated in America and run by W.T. Stead in the *Pall Mall Gazette* on 4 November 1889. Moore may have added a significant and suppressed behaviour of the killer's ritual or simply misremembered. The press had reported the killer had simply 'placed the pieces of flesh and strips of skin on a table' (*Echo*, 9 November 1888). Inspector Moore added another startling idea unremarked at the time – that the Ripper had accidentally locked himself in the room with his victim and had to smash his way out 'through the larger of those two windows'.

Police surgeon Dr Bagster had told the Mary Jane Kelly inquest the year before that the bigger window was intact and 'two panes in the lesser window were broken.' *Daily Telegraph*, Tuesday, 13 November 1888.

225 'Light-haired Irish bitch': MSL, Vol. 8, Chapter 10.

226 "Irish Kate" Walter tells of this relationship in MSL Vol. 2 Chapter xvii.

226 'Camille went to Paris': 'She had been away from England two years or so, having saved money, with which in her native country she had either bought or set up a licensed house for whoring. It had not succeeded, she had lost all, and had come back here to harlotry. She cried as she told me about her losses, then began to smoke a cigarette.' Walter began this chapter describing sex with the 'light-haired Irish bitch'. He ended it with details of an Irish woman in a French brothel. 'Once since, at a French brothel, I found an Irish woman, who certainly was more highly obscene than her sisters there. One French woman said she was the greatest '*cochonne*' in the house, and all the women were afraid of her.' MSL, Vol. 8, Chapter 10.

227 'Also had a box': MSL, Vol. 8, Chapter 10. Walter met the Irish prostitute in Coventry Street. She had a trunk in the West End. 'Irish Kate' took him to 'a house and a comfortable room with a good fire'. Walter reported 'a large trunk was on the floor'. The packing was of great significance to this Irish girl. She told Walter, 'I've left one of my boxes at Birmingham. I ran away. I'd no money. I would not stay to be ill thraited, but the first money I get I'll be after it. I pawned me watch to pay my week's lodgings here this very day, sure and I hadn't enough money to pay me cabman. Pay down the first week, says the landlady, or it's no good yer leaving your box here. Wait a minute, ma'am, where's a pawn-broker's? and me and me box and the carman went to pawn me watch.'

228 'Buttered buns': MSL, Vol. 8, Chapter 12. Walter's obsession was to do with the homoerotic image of another man's penis. 'I thought fucking after a man, a dirty trick, yet my prick stood at times, as at the idea of its having been in the same sheath directly after another.' As with anal sex, the tug between Walter's attraction and repulsion of the act brought out violent urges.

229 'Easy to misjudge age': *Pall Mall Gazette*, 24 March 1903.

229 'Thought me ten years younger': MSL, Vol. 10, Chapter 12.

229 'Nor was he too old': Royal surgeon, Sir William Gull, Stephen Knight's famous Ripper suspect, was five years older than Walter in 1888. Although past seventy, Gull lured four Whitechapel victims into a carriage where he murdered them with the help of coachman John Netley. Knight, Stephen. *Jack the Ripper: The Final Solution* (George G. Harrap & Co Ltd, 1976).

229 'Tumblety . . . aged 58': Gordon, R. Michael. *The American Murders of Jack the Ripper* (Greenwood Press, Buckinghamshire, 2003: p. 10).

229 'A sixty-five-year-old man': on 16 September 1889, John Rowley (sixty-five) was sentenced at the Old Bailey to twenty months' hard labour for feloniously wounding Mary Ann Potts, with intent to do her grievous bodily harm on 2 September 1889. Besley, Edward T.E. Central Criminal Court sessions paper, Eleventh Session, held on 10 September 1889. Minutes of evidence (London: Stevens and Sons, 1889: p. 1110).

231 'The pleasure I had just had': MSL, Vol. 2, Chapter 16.

232 'Room was about twelve feet . . . the furniture': MSL, Vol. 2, Chapter 16.

232 'Walter took keys': the fate of Mary Jane Kelly's key is a subject of debate. It was widely reported the killer stole it: 'The lock of the door was a spring one, and the murderer apparently took the key away with him when he left'. *Pall Mall Gazette*, 10 November 1888. Walter was a key stealer. 'It was a key almost as big as a shovel; she never noticed that I had taken it away.' MSL, Vol. 3, Chapter 16.

232 'Good-looking woman': Walter described Mary Jane Kelly as 'a short woman about nineteen years old, plump without fat, but as nicely covered as any woman I ever saw; had a big bum, large thighs . . . soft, kind face, beautiful grey eyes, nearly black hair which draped naturally, and was altogether as nice a little woman as one could have wanted.' MSL, Vol. 2, Chapter 16.

232 'More money working in the West End': there are several indications in *My Secret Life* that Walter worked part time in London's sex business. His offer to put Mary Davis to work in a better locale is telling. 'I have wondered often how she could have settled down in a neighbourhood of costermongers, and taken five shillings for her person, when she might as well have been a two-sovereign woman, had she tried elsewhere. I put her up to trying at a future day, but she never would.' MSL, Vol. 2, Chapter 16. Walter kept the accounts of the 'baudy house' in J***s Street for Hannah (MSL, Vol. 3, Chapter 14 and Vol. 4, Chapter 1).

232 'Used to fetch gin': MSL, Vol. 2, Chapter 16.

232 'Would have been a danger to him': London Central Court records from 1885 and 1887 show just how much of a danger the new laws were for Walter. Men were being hit hard for sex with girls between the ages of thirteen and sixteen. On 14 September 1885, in one of the first convictions under the new law, William Brace, forty-five, got ten years for four indictments of feloniously carnally knowing and abusing Elizabeth Brace, under sixteen years of age. The crackdown on sex with younger girls was even harder. Meshac Lee, twenty-nine, was jailed for life on 23 May 1887 for carnally knowing Laura Lily Linstead, a girl under thirteen.

232 'Overrun with spies': *Pall Mall Gazette*, 4 November 1889.

Chapter 14 – More Murders

233 'Archaeologist and scholar': Sir Charles' interest in the ancient mysteries

of the Middle East were making news as late as 1887. The *Saturday Review* reported in April 1887 that 'Captain Conder has found out all about the Hittites, and has told Sir Charles Warren.'

233 'Overreaction to a rabies outbreak': Sir Charles Warren later acknowledged his dog killing did not stop the London rabies outbreak. 'I think it was the muzzling that stopped it.' House of Lords debates, 27 June 1889, vol. 337 cc.858–65.

233 'Elizabeth Cass': the Cass case and court scandal that followed was covered by the *Pall Mall Gazette* in 'The Police Outrage in Regent Street' on 4 July, with further coverage on 12 and 22 July. By the next month, it was Miss Cass who had PC Endacott in court for inferring she was a prostitute. Cass was rocketed into a feminist celebrity, the glove-maker's picture alongside W.T. Stead's under the headline 'Wronged Women in Queen Victoria's Jubilee' (*The Penny Illustrated*, 20 August 1887).

234 'Warren had to issue': the triumph of the streetwalkers following the Cass case was mocked by columnist Codlin: 'Exit Warren limping! London no longer a rabbit-Warren! Miss Cass avenged! But, my goodness, at what a price! Regent-street is almost impassable after nightfall.' *The Penny Illustrated*, 24 November 1887.

234 'More interested in catching Fenians': the machinations of Sir Charles Warren and Scotland Yard in Irish terror plots are excellently described in Christy Campbell's *Fenian Fire: The British Government Plot to Assassinate Queen Victoria* (Harper Collins, 2003).

234 'Ripper was a Fenian': Novelist Henry James observed how the Whitechapel murder joined with Fenian politics. Writing from Geneva on 29 October 1888, James said 'the Continent gives one a refreshing sense of getting away – away from Whitechapel and Parnell and a hundred other constantly thickening heavinesses'. James, Henry and Horne, Phillip. *Henry James: A Life in Letters* (Penguin Press, 1999: p. 212). In September 1888, a commission into forged letters smearing Irish political leader, Charles Parnell, had begun.

'Signs of panic': Dew, Walter. *I Caught Crippen: Memoirs of Ex-Chief Inspector Walter Dew* CID (Blackie, 1938).

235 'Sexual maniac': Melville MacNaghten, who joined Scotland Yard on 1 June 1889, would use this term to describe the Ripper. 'The man, of course, was a sexual maniac, but such madness takes Protean forms . . . Sexual murders are the most difficult of all for police to bring home to the perpetrators, for "motives" there are none; only a lust for blood and in many cases a hatred of woman as woman. Not infrequently the maniac possesses a diseased body and this was probably so in the case of the Whitechapel murderer.' Macnaghten, Sir Melville. *Days of My Years* (London, Edward Arnold, 1914: p. 62).

235 'The torso of a woman': a representative of the *Daily Telegraph*, who saw the remains within half an hour of their discovery, stated that 'the body, placed on its back, was wrapped in a skirt of some stuff like black

mohair, and the steel dress improver was included in the parcel. The flesh had a dark reddish hue, as if it had been plentifully sprinkled with antiseptic, such as Condy's fluid.' *Daily Telegraph*, 3 October 1888. The same story had the authorities backpedalling on a previous cover-up of a severed arm 'with clutched fingers' found by a shoeblack in Southwark, two days before the Stride and Eddowes murders. The police, who had denied initial reports an arm had been found at all, were now looking in the Blind School. 'As to the second arm found near the Blind School, in the Lambeth-road, on the 28th ult., the authorities are quite positive that it was not amputated recently, and in fact they have received some assurances as to the source from which the bones in question were derived.'

235 'Shipping vulnerable girls': on 20 September 1888, Dr Barnardo sent ninety girls aged six to nineteen for adoption in Montreal on the steamship *Parisian*. The girls had been 'rescued from absolute destitution, or worse'. *Evening News*, 25 September 1888.

235 'The police equally quickly dismissed it': while police pooh-poohed links among the torsos by the river, the medical men examining them concluded the killings were the work of the Ripper. In 1894, Dr Charles A. Hebbert, assistant to the Westminster Divisional Police Surgeon, contributed lengthy material on the Whitechapel murder to Allan McLane Hamilton's textbook, *A System of Legal Medicine*. Hebbert 'lately associated with Mr Bond, the Coroner of London, England . . . in conjunction with Dr F.A. Harris, presented for the first time . . . the records of the Whitechapel murder cases, and the deductions therefrom'. Hebbert deduced 'in the years 1887–89 . . . nine women were murdered and mutilated by an unknown assassin.' Hebbert did not name the nine, but said the killer continued his work into 1889. In 1888, Hebbert, with Dr Bond, had attended the autopsies of Mary Jane Kelly, Rose Mylett and the Whitehall torso and in 1889 the Pinchin Street and Thames Torso discoveries.

235 'No one wanted any more Ripper murders': police attempts to stop new murders being linked to the Whitechapel chain began in December 1888 when Assistant Police Commissioner Robert Anderson pressured Dr Thomas Bond to change his findings on the death of Rose Mylett. MEPO 3/143, ff. E–J.

236 'Annie Farmer': *The Star*, 21 November 1888.

237 'Rose Mylett': the Ripper and Rose Mylett were linked in a gruesome newspaper scoop on Christmas Eve 1888. *The Star* spoke to Dr Matthew Brownfield, divisional police surgeon of Poplar after he gave evidence at the inquest on Mylett's first post-mortem. 'I have no doubt at all that death was caused by strangulation, of which the mark round the neck of the body is the evidence', he said. Brownfield had done his own experiments on what type of thin cord was used. He concluded the Ripper would strangle or partially strangle his victims first and then cut their

throats. The doctor said the Ripper had obliterated traces of strangulation by cutting along the line left by his 'strangler's cord'. Brownfield
went on to explain why this was likely. 'If his object is mutilation . . .
he could cut their throats so much more cleanly and deliberately. And
this would explain, too, how the murderer would be able to do his work
without getting covered with blood.' *The Star*, 24 December 1888.

237 'After a time chatting': MSL, Vol. 10, Chapter 8.

240 'Walter certainly was': Walter had intimate knowledge of London's
streets because of a urine fetish. He would seek out hidden places women
used and pay prostitutes to piss on his hand. 'I often times when out
late, gave women a trifle to feel their cunts, and then if they were able
to accomplish it, a further gift if they would piddle over my fingers. It
always delighted me to feel the sherry tinted jet strike on my fingers,
fresh and warm as it issued from the cunt' (MSL, Vol. 5, Chapter 17).
Walter hunted back streets and dark corners to indulge his fetish. 'I used
to prowl about to see the girls pissing, and when I had cheek enough,
stand and piss by the side of them. That delighted me much.' MSL,
Vol. 3, Chapter 1. The Ripper's street victims were found in dark spots
dangerous for copulation but ideal for urination. For a killer to lure a
victim with payment to pass water, then urinate to wash evidence from
his hands, was a psychosexual tactic uncontemplated in 1888.

240 'Lydia Hart': concerns about Lydia were abated by an interview con-
firming she was alive and well in *The New York Herald*, of 11 September
1889. A further suspicion the torso was that of Emily Barker was
brought to light in Stewart Evan's illuminating book about Whitechapel
detective, Edmund Reid. (Evans, Stewart P. *The Man Who Hunted Jack
the Ripper*, Cambridge: Rupert Books, 2000: pp. 88–89). Reid concluded
the Whitechapel killer met his victims in pubs and, after closing time, he
was lead by them to locations for sex where 'his mania came upon him'.

240 'Victim was a factory worker': ' . . . the arms were intact. The latter
were not developed muscularly, and the hands, long and slender, with
filbert-shaped nails, showed no signs of recent hard work. No ring marks
were detected, and nothing was noted which would indicate the woman's
position in life, or her calling, although an opinion was expressed that
she might have been a factory hand or rope-worker'. *Walthamstow and
Leyton Guardian*, 14 September 1889.

241 'On 10th Sept. '89 . . . Pinchin St crimes': Macnaghten Memo, 23
February 1894, National Archives MEPO 3/141.

241 'Once I had occasion': *Pall Mall Gazette*, 4 November 1889.

241 'There was no jaggedness': Gordon, R. Michael. *The Thames Torso
Murders of Victorian London* (McFarland, 2002: pp 33–47).

242 'Prostitutes after 1860': Barr, A. 'Primrose Hill, an urban village examined: with lessons for brownfield developments', *Urban Design Studies*,
Vol. 1999: p. 9.

242 'Inhabited the canal system': of Walter's six direct references to canals,

three are about throwing women into, or committing suicide by, London's waterways. MSL, Vol. 8, Chapter 11; Vol. 9, Chapter 8; and Vol. 9, Chapter 1. 'It would kill the old people. If I don't get on better soon I'll drown myself. I go and look at the canal sometimes'.

243 'The body had been dissected': *The Times*, 5 June 1889.

243 'Roll of linen inserted': Walter used a device he called 'a linen stopper'. He tied it to his penis for sex in a small orifice. He would convince a victim he would insert himself only to that point, before thrusting beyond. The stopper brought out bloodlust and sadism. 'I lifted her back on to the bed, and rolled the strip of handkerchief round the stem again; but I longed to hurt her, to make her cry with the pain my tool caused her, I would have made her bleed if I could; so wrapped it round in such a manner, that with a tug I could unroll it' (MSL, Vol. 2, Chapter 9). A stopper used in anal sex would bring up homosexual associations for Walter, which provoked homicidal urges. MSL, Vol. 8, Chapter 3.

244 'Linen stopper': Walter even devoted a chapter heading in MSL, Vol. 2, Chapter 9 to his invention: 'A juvenile Harlot – A linen stopper'.

244 'Plugging bumholes': MSL, Vol. 8, Chapter 5.

244 'Such as a candle': MSL 5, Vol. 8, Chapter 4.

245 'She had told me where': MSL, Vol. 10, Chapter 2.

246 'Not the work of the Whitechapel murderer': National Archives HO 144/221/A49301K.

246 'Murder had returned': The *Galveston Daily News*, which picked up the PA story, listed the Pinchin Street corpse as the twelfth victim in the Whitechapel series, under the headline 'War on Lewd Women'. A Press Association report of 11 September 1888 was headlined 'Murder Sits Enthroned Again at Whitechapel'.

246 'Chelsea dissector': 'If the Chelsea dissector is still at work, and his motives were never made clear, he must, it is thought, have purposely removed his quarters to the East-end, or have conveyed the body which he wished to get rid of thither.' *Walthamstow and Leyton Guardian*, Saturday, 14 September 1889.

246 'Human anatomical knowledge': Dr Phillips told the coroner he thought the dissector knew how to cut up animals. 'I believe the mutilation to have been subsequent to death, that the mutilations were effected by someone accustomed to cut up animals or to see them cut up, and that the incisions were effected by a strong knife 8in. or more long.' *The Times*, 12 September 1889.

246 'Carotty Nell': Frances Coles' nickname may refer to W.S. Gilbert's popular 1869 ditty, *Sir Barnaby Bampton Boo*. In it, Carrotty Nell is 'the prettier, p'raps, of my gals, But, oh! she's a wayward chit; She dresses herself in her showy fal-lals, And doesn't read TUPPER a bit!' Martin Farquhar Tupper (1810–1889) was an English author of moral and religious poetry.

247 'Dr Oxley': 'The wound could not have been inflicted by a man who

was incapably drunk, and that the knife purchased by Campbell could hardly have produced so large and clean a cut'. *East London Advertiser*, 28 February 1891.

247 'Macnaghten continued to believe': Macnaghten's poor grasp of the evidence of Sadler's innocence given at the Cole inquest is one reason his key canon on the Whitechapel murders – that there were "five victims – and five victims only" – should be doubted. In making his case for five victims, Macnaghten appears to have relied on the report by Dr Thomas Bond to the head of London CID, Robert Anderson, dated 10 November 1888 and made the day after the killing of Mary Jane Kelly. Had Macnaghten relied on later deductions by doctors who examined suspected victims, he would have canonized nine murders, the total Bond's colleague Dr Hebbert attributed to the Ripper in the 1894 forensic textbook, *A System of Legal Medicine*.

248 'Probably to America': Walter was coy about what would appear to be a sojourn to the United States. In Vol. 8, Chapter 5 of *My Secret Life*, Walter went to 'the other side of the ocean' where he encountered a 'white woman (who) was American' in a brothel. He was repulsed watching a Negro and Negress have sex, but then joined them. He said: 'I must for reasons give not much account of my doings there, they were written but I have destroyed most of the narrative.' Unlike other episodes, Walter prefaced the incidents apparently written or at least annotated during his preparation of the manuscript as 'two years back', potentially dating it as late as 1892.

'Details of her injuries': new light has been thrown on the injuries done to Carrie Brown since 2003. Researcher Michael Conlon discovered mortuary photographs and Wolf Vanderlinden the autopsy report. Vanderlinden concluded that while there were elements of the Ripper's signature in the New York attack, there were dissimilarities in wounds, body position and organization of the crime. *Ripperologist* No. 46, May 2003; *Ripper Notes: America Looks At Jack The Ripper*, June 2004.

248 'One more killing': Gordon, R. Michael. *The Thames Torso Murders of Victorian London* (McFarland 2002: pp. 201–210).

Chapter 15 – My Secret Life

249 'I'll bet': MSL, Vol. 2, Chapter 14.

249 'How many coins': Nelly won the eighty-four shillings she held in her 'cuntal purse'. Walter, once again, had been scanning the paper for dirty stories when he was inspired to wager. 'Talking with her about a woman who had been taken up for robbing a man, and had kept the stolen trinket in her cunt for two days before it was found there. (This was told in obscure language in the newspapers.) I doubted the possibility. Nelly averred that it was easy, and it ended in my going out to get the silver, putting forty shillings up her cunt, and seeing her walk up and

down the room naked, holding the money in that feminine receptacle. Then she squatted over a pot, and the money dropped out.' MSL, Vol. 9, Chapter 9.

repeatedly recruited young girls to rape then monitored their progress to professional prostitutes. He called it 'delight in destroying modesty'. MSL, Vol. 6, Chapter 5.

254 'But a pauper': MSL, Vol. 4, Chapter 6.

254 'Stock market': MSL, Vol. 4, Chapter 13.
'Open fornication': MSL, Vol. 5, Chapter 3.

255 'For fifteen months . . . wept over this weakness': MSL, Vol. 7, Chapter 6.
'This change in social life': MSL, Vol. 7, Chapter 6.

256 'Rosa's kidnap': Walter detailed his dealings with the girl 'Rosa W * * * e' in MSL, Vol. 6, Chapters 4 and 5. There was another Rosa, whom he called Rosa B. Walter paid to watch the 'middle sized, haggard woman' have lesbian sex – 'flat fucking' – with Nelly. The 'drunkard, lascivious' Rosa farted dildoed and screamed her way through a threesome. 'This evening terminated my ultra erotic amusements this year, to be resumed early in the year following.' Then Walter added without explanation: 'Rosa B. died two years after.' Oddly, Walter highlighted 'Rosa's death' as the headline to this chapter. MSL, Vol. 9, Chapter 7.

259 'Killers to fake documentary evidence': from 1987 to 1992, Gloucester serial killer Fred West manufactured telephone messages from Heather, the sixteen-year-old daughter he had murdered, to cover her disappearance from his other children. West had buried her under a back-garden patio.

259 'Girl was found at an East End station': *The Times*, 20 January, 1883.

260 'The inquest will be held': Sir John Humphrey's inquiry was held on Saturday, 20 January. Parcels manager Edward Smith said a man with a moustache, a hat, and dressed as a tradesman, dropped off the box. He gave his name as 'Smith'. The parcel was to go to 'Miss Green, 24 Abbey Road, St Johns Wood' but was returned to the dead letter office when the address proved nonexistent. Police surgeon Dr Yarrow now suspected the girl might have been slowly poisoned. *The Times*, 22 January 1883.

261 'News from Limehouse': *The Times*, 20 January 1883.

262 'Irritation in my gland . . . the fullest pleasure': MSL, Vol. 9, Chapter 12.

262 'Excess of lubrication': MSL, Vol. 4, Chapter 19.

262 'She gave a scream': MSL, Vol. 4, Chapter 15.

262 'Violent pain in my head': MSL, Vol. 9, Chapter 12.

263 'Pain as well as pleasure': MSL, Vol. 10, Chapter 1.

263 'Illness of quite a different class': MSL, Vol. 5, Chapter 9.

263 'Have all men had': MSL, Vol. 1, Second Preface.

263 'Reviewing the memoirs "Victorian Satyriasis"': The entrepreneurs of Grove Press have at last struck real pay dirt, the anti-Comstock lode of lewd literature . . . this first commercial publication of *My Secret Life* makes Fanny Hill look like Mary Poppins. *Time Magazine*, 30 December 1966.

263 'Condition known as hypergraphia': Kaufman, David Myland. *Clinical Neurology for Psychiatrists* (W.B. Saunders, 2001: pp. 215–216). Bear

and Fedio's studies of epileptics suggest those with an epileptic focus of the left side of the brain have an augmented sense of personal destiny and hypergraphia, traits that match Walter's. Maudsley's studies of epilepsy dating to 1874 document homicide accompanied by memory loss. Lader, Malcolm Harold. *Mental Disorders and Somatic Illness* (CUP Archive, 1983: p. 163).

263 'Demon of desire': MSL, Vol. 3, Chapter 4.

263 'Little devil': MSL, Vol. 8, Chapter 6.

264 'I never deliberately': MSL, Vol. 4, Chapter 13.

264 'A gay lady is': MSL, Vol. 7, Chapter 6.

264 'Frontotemporal dementia': the sexual disease, herpes simplex encephalitis, may also cause damage to frontal lobes leading to aggression. Simon, Robert I. and Tardiff, Kenneth. *Textbook of Violence Assessment and Management* (American Psychiatric Publishing, 2008: p. 39).

264 'We struggled': MSL, Vol. 4, Chapter 8.

264 'A man must first': MSL, Vol. 2, Chapter 1.

265 'Unfledged virgin': MSL, Vol. 6, Chapter 6.

265 'Paedophile ring': Walter was into little girls, but he got to know a 'pederast's agent' in Naples who offered sex with boys of thirteen. 'This set me thinking very much, and on reflection, though amusing one's self that way seemed to me most objectionable, yet if men liked it, it was their affair alone.' MSL, Vol. 5, Chapter 1.

265 'Abnormal eccentric tastes': MSL, Vol. 9, Chapter 8.

265 'Anonymous letters': Walter's wife got two letters. 'One said that the writer had seen me going into the cafe with a woman, and named the time. The other that I was seen putting a lady into a cab. Time and place also stated.' Walter realised his reputation was at stake, accused his wife of penning them and destroyed the letters. MSL, Vol. 5, Chapter 13.

Chapter 16 – Who was Walter?

267 'Henry Spencer Ashbee': a description of Ashbee's evenings during the early period of the Ripper murders in 1888 is illuminating. Ashbee had several literary guests at his house in Bedford Square, including Sir Richard Burton. Often they argued the authorship of Shakespeare. 'Ashbee ... was a curiously matter-of-fact, stoutish, stolid, affable man, with a Maupassantian taste for low life, its humours and laxities. He was familiar with it everywhere, from the sordid purlieus of Whitechapel to the bazaars of Tunis and Algiers, and related Haroun Al-Raschid-like adventures with imperturbably, impassive face, and in the language that a businessman uses when recounting the common transactions of a day. This unconcernedness never failed to provoke laughter, even from those who administered rebukes to him. Of art and literature he had absolutely no idea, but he was an enthusiastic bibliophile, and his library, which included a unique collection of rare and curious books, had been built up

at enormous expense. Somebody having described him as "not a bad old chap".' Wright, Thomas. *The Life of Sir Richard Burton* (G.P. Putnam and Sons, 1906: p. 313).

267 'St George Best': Best was an author who wrote for the American literary publishing house, Correll, which printed among other things a highbrow magazine called *John-a-Dreams* in the 1890s. There is a reference to him in the list of archives of the University of Wichita. See http://specialcollections.wichita.edu/collections/ms/89-20/89-20-A.html.

267 'Launched an attack': 'This false and filthy scandal could not but infect the very children with the contagion of vice. The little gutter-girls and street-lasses of East London looked at men passing-by as if assured that their pucelages were or would become vendible at £3 to £5.' Burton, Richard F. *Supplemental Nights*, Vol. 6 (The Burton Club c.1888).

269 'Your names begin': MSL, Vol. 7, Chapter 7.

269 'Gordon Stein': Bullough, Vern L. 'Who Wrote My Secret Life?', *Sexuality & Culture*, 4/1, March 2000: p. 37.

269 'Abroad to look': MSL, Vol. 1, Chapter 2.

271 'Just at that time . . . time of return': MSL, Vol. 2, Chapter 14.

272 'An entirely new candidate': Pattinson put forward his theory in *The Man Who Was Walter, Victorian Literature and Culture* (Cambridge University Press, 2002: pp. 19–40).

273 'Went daily to the W** Office': MSL, Vol. 1, Chapter 10.

273 'A larger house': MSL, Vol. 4, Chapter 7.

273 'Death had done': MSL, Vol. 6, Chapter 9.

274 'Had worked at my house': MSL, Vol. 7, Chapter 2.

274 'I travelled home': MSL, Vol. 6, Chapter 9.

275 'With Winifred terminated . . . give her pain': MSL, Vol. 7, Chapter 6.

275 'The legitimate one': MSL, Vol. 7, Chapter 6.

275 'One woman whom I adore': MSL, Vol. 9. Chapter 2. Walter's year-long affair was with a Jessie C**ts, an upmarket courtesan he met at the Argyle Rooms. The conflict between this relationship, and his ongoing affair with Winifred, brought him to the conclusion he would kill her to save his long-term love. 'I was really loving two women at the same time. I loved Jessie, tho I would have slain her for the other.' Walter saw his contemplation of murder as his 'psychological problem'.

275 'All was I knew': MSL, Vol. 7, Chapter 2.

276 'On my way to': MSL, Vol. 10, Chapter 7.

278 'Titanic . . . last seen holding': Mowbray, Jay Henry. *Sinking of the Titanic: Eyewitness Accounts* (Dover, New York, 1998, reprinted from *The Minter Company*, 1912L: p. 77).

INDEX